MR. & MRS. HOCKEY®

A Tribute to the Sport's Greatest Couple

A Tribute to the Sport's Greatest Couple

KEVIN ALLEN

Foreword by Mike & Marian Ilitch

Immortal Investments Publishing

www.immortalinvestments.com
www.mrandmrshockey.com

All photos were provided by the Howe family, except where noted. Every reasonable attempt was made to give proper credit. If there are any errors, please notify the publisher and corrections will be made in subsequent editions.

Published by Immortal Investments Publishing
35122 W. Michigan Avenue, Wayne, Michigan 48184
1-800-475-2066
www.immortalinvestments.com
www.mrandmrshockey.com

Publisher's Cataloging-in-Publication
(Provided by Quality Books, Inc.)

Allen, Kevin, 1956-
Mr. and Mrs. Hockey : a tribute to the sport's greatest couple : celebrities and others inside and outside of hockey pay homage to the sports legends Colleen and Gordie Howe / by Kevin Allen ; foreword by Mike and Marian Ilitch. -- 1st ed.
p. cm.
LCCN 2003113645
ISBN 0-9723637-1-8

1. Howe, Gordie, 1928- 2. Howe, Colleen. 3. Hockey players--United States--Biography. 4. Athletes' spouses --Biography. I. Title.

GV848.5.H6A55 2004 796.962'092
QBI33-1795

DEDICATION

I dedicate this book to my wife and partner, Colleen who has been my best friend for over 50 years. I also appreciate the love of our children, grandchildren, family and friends. To the hockey fans who have supported us for decades, —thank you and God Bless.

ACKNOWLEDGMENTS

Thank you to all those individuals who shared their story for the book. Also, a special salute to Mike Reddy of Immortal Investments Publishing and author Kevin Allen for ensuring this project became a reality. Colleen and I are honored.

Finally, Colleen and I thank our business associates and close friends Del Reddy & Aaron Howard for their continued dedication and hard work behind the scenes.

Mr. Hockey®
Gordie Howe®

CONTENTS

Foreword ... xi
Preface ... xiii
Introduction ... xv
Scotty Bowman ... 1
Edna Gadsby ... 4
Max McNab ... 8
Rich Margittay ... 11
Paul Stewart ... 14
Mark Messier ... 16
Bob Duff ... 17
Darren Pang ... 19
Ken Holland ... 20
Jacques Demers ... 21
Dave Taylor ... 23
Emile Francis ... 24
Greg Millen ... 28
Steve Charendoff ... 29
Brian Burke ... 32
Dr. James G. Matthews ... 34
Bob Goodenow ... 36
Ron Toigo ... 38
Tommy Ivan ... 40
Jack Adams ... 42
Reed Larson ... 44
John Makar ... 46
Dave Lewis ... 48
Bill Gadsby ... 49
Eddie Johnston ... 51
Rick Dudley ... 53
Dr. Murray Howe ... 55
Colleen Howe ... 57
Meaghan Colleen Howe ... 58
Gordie Howe ... 59
Corey Mark and Sean Murray Howe ... 60

Jim Loria....61
Frank Selke....64
Helen (Howe) Cummine....65
Joe Fallon....67
Lynn Gregg....69
Larry Gach....72
Sue Foster....74
Greg and Sandra Rollheiser....77
Dennis Murphy....78
Ron and Charlotte Grahame....82
Bobby Hull....86
Harry Neale....91
Harley Hotchkiss....96
Hersh Borenstein....97
Greg Wolff....98
Vic Stasiuk....100
Reg and Ronnie Sinclair....102
Tom Webster....104
Chuck Kaiton....107
Aaron Howard....110
Don and Pam Howard....112
Mike Jaszcz....113
Jeanne Gallagher....115
Ralph Mellanby....117
John Stanzik....120
Carl Lindstrom....122
Larry Stockwell....123
Maureen Reddy....124
Ken Daneyko....125
Bob Resch....126
Jimmy Skinner....129
Art Skov....131
Stan Fischler....133
Barbara Armstrong....137
Derik Murray....138
Bert Webbe....139

Robert Puckett....141
Travis Howe....142
Azia Howe....143
Nolan Howe....145
Cathy (Howe) Purnell....146
Bob Purnell....148
Jade Roskam....150
Jaime Greer....151
Ken Kal....152
Rich Delisle....153
Mark Hacala....154
Jim Gray....156
Mel King....158
Nelson "Freckles" Little....160
Bill Dow....163
Felix Gatt....166
Dr. John Finley....168
Genevieve Finley....171
Gerald R. Ford....173
Dave Ponzi....174
Jim Bates....176
Bill Sobel....178
Ron Cantera....180
Andra McLaughlin Kelly....182
Chuck Robertson....183
Nova Lanktree....185
Kevin McCrory....187
Peter Jennings....191
Terry Perrelli....193
Bernie Geoffrion and Marlene Geoffrion....194
Mark Primeau....196
Jay Barrymore....198
Dave Duran....199
Mort Greenberg....201
Delbert McCoy....205
Jim Haskins....207

Dr. Paul Olson.....209
John Littlejohn and Rick Murphy.....212
Del Reddy.....214
Al and Claire Arbour.....223
Christina Lovio-George.....225
Al Sinclair.....227
Bill Swanson.....229
Glenn Davis.....230
Dorothy Ringler.....232
Bob Trimble.....235
Jerry Green.....237
Andre Lacroix.....239
Tom Lennox.....242
Howard Baldwin.....244
Ralph Backstrom.....247
Glenn Hall (Mr. Goalie).....249
Marty Howe.....251
Mark Howe.....254
Vern and Amelia Howe.....259
Vic Howe.....262

FOREWORD

We have had the pleasure of knowing Gordie and Colleen Howe for all of our adult lives. Not only have they touched our lives personally, but the legacy left by this dynamic duo is unmatched in the sport of hockey--perhaps in all of sports.

Gordie's stats speak for themselves. To play the physically intense game of hockey until the age of 52 is remarkable and will remain in the record books forever.

When we retired Gordie's number in 1984, it was a tribute to his talent and the major contributions he had made to the Detroit Red Wings and their success over the years.

However, when we think of Gordie and Colleen, we think of family and the love and commitment they have, not only for their own family, but the families of others as well. Gordie would always show an interest in the youngsters and their accomplishments. He would joke with them and put them at ease. One time our daughter, who was very, very young at the time, asked Gordie for his autograph. In an effort to personalize this signature, Gordie asked Lisa what she would like him to write. Her response was, "your name."

We held special parties at our Little Caesars Pizza Parlors for our amateur hockey teams to celebrate a championship. We would invite Gordie to attend. He never turned us down and never asked for anything in return. He would come and congratulate the teams and would encourage the young players to pursue their dreams.

Gordie once told us that it was better to give than receive. He was referring to his toughness on the ice, but he and Colleen have put those words into action. Over the years, this couple served as outstanding role models, not only by what they said, but by their actions as well. There is no better example of family commitment than when Gordie came out of retirement to play hockey with his sons Mark and Marty who were playing in the WHA.

Gordie and Colleen have enriched the lives of many families outside their own. The mission of their Howe Foundation is to improve the quality of life for children of all ages. Through the foundation and other actions, Gordie and Colleen have helped generate millions of dollars for charities and worthwhile causes, especially those that have had a positive impact on the development of young people. Colleen has left a huge imprint on youth hockey and junior hockey.

Beneath their caring manner, Gordie and Colleen are known as strong individuals as well--Gordie on the ice, and Colleen at the bargaining table. You can be sure her actions strengthened and protected the family core. Both are in the Hockey Hall of Fame--Gordie at the Hockey Hall of Fame in Toronto and Colleen at the U.S. Hockey Hall of Fame in Eveleth, Minnesota. Both have hearts of gold. Their enthusiasm for the game of hockey is unparalleled. The sport of hockey is better for their lifelong commitment to the game, and family values are stronger for those who mirror their actions. They are true friends to us and to the game of hockey we all love so much.

MIKE AND MARIAN ILITCH

Owners, Detroit Red Wings

PREFACE

Mr. and Mrs. Hockey®: A Tribute to the Sport's Greatest Couple honors Colleen and Gordie Howe as the game's foremost ambassadors. In celebration of an unprecedented 50 years of extraordinary accomplishments on and off the ice, the internationally famous duo is extolled by the who's who in their sport. Hockey icons Scotty Bowman, Bobby Hull, Bill Gadsby and other greats share their colorful and personal stories.

They explain why Gordie is the greatest hockey player of all time, and one of, if not the most remarkable athlete in history. They describe how from humble beginnings Colleen became the first female agent- manager in sports and the most influential woman in the history of the game. Colorful anecdotes from hockey legends, business associates, family, friends, fans and other celebrities impart their heartfelt, sometimes humorous, sometimes moving recollections of the powerful duo. Portrayed is how hockey's first couple has unceasingly dedicated their lives to their family, the fans, and their humanitarian endeavors.

Furthermore, their tireless efforts have built and propelled the greatest game in the world to a whole new level. U.S. Hockey Hall of Famer, Mrs. Hockey® is the first woman in the history of the sport to be honored by a major hockey hall of fame. Amazingly, Mr. Hockey® is a member of 15 different halls of fame. He has been tagged the greatest player ever by none other than legends Hull, Beliveau, Orr, Gretzky, Hall, Rayner, and Richard. Recognized as the game's Babe Ruth, his appeal spans the globe.

Accolades aside, the Howes have relentlessly dedicated their lives to building the sport on many levels and in many venues. Their involvement ranges from Detroit, Houston and Hartford to as far away as Russia. Beginning in 1946 with the Detroit Red Wings, Gordie played a world record 32 seasons. His unbelievable talent entertained millions of fans and inspired generations of players. His fame and dominance helped expand hockey from a Canadian game to a North American sport!

While Mr. Hockey® was playing in one of his incomprehensible 29 All-Star games, Colleen was raising their family of four children, running for Congress, co-founding a bank, co-founding a hospital, helping establish the first international hockey alumni association, writing and publishing books, starting a children's foundation and establishing the first Junior A Hockey Club in the U.S. In the 1960's, she mortgaged their middle income home to build the first indoor rink in Michigan. This led to a huge interest in youth hockey. The impact affected thousands of youngsters and families and helped establish Detroit as Hockeytown. Because salaries were much lower years ago, Mrs. Hockey® creatively established many businesses over time to support their family. As a self taught pioneer and trailblazer for women, she negotiated the first multi-player, multi-year contract ever.

This allowed Gordie to fulfill his dream of playing pro hockey together with their two sons Marty and Mark. As great as Gordie was on the ice, he is as famous off the ice for his incredible connection with everyday people. Humble, soft-spoken, good-natured and approachable, he has personally signed millions of autographs for fans of all ages. Admirers seem to never forget their interaction with him; his appeal spans generations. In all likelihood, he has endeared himself to more people than any athlete in history.

Both Colleen and Gordie's willingness to share their time with others is legendary. As hockey's top ambassadors for six decades, they have visited thousands of cities. During each trip, they generate enormous excitement, goodwill, and lifetime memories for all involved.

Over the years and despite a grueling schedule, they have attended thousands of charitable events. Their magical presence has helped generate millions of smiles and millions of dollars for good causes. As a team, they are what is right about sports and about life. They remain mentors, role models, and the greatest couple in the history of the game.

We will never see the likes of Mr. and Mrs. Hockey® ever again and this tribute poignantly captures why this couple is so special.

INTRODUCTION

Whether you believe in fate and soul mates or not, it's hard not to reach the conclusion that the legend of Mr. Hockey would have been far different if he had not enjoyed bowling a game or two in the early 1950's.

By all accounts Gordie Howe was 'wowed' the first time he laid eyes on Colleen at the Lucky Strike Bowling Alley. Although this is a hockey book, it's also a love story. It's about a 51-year marriage between Gordie and Colleen that has dramatically impacted one of the four major sports and the lives of millions of people.

If you listened closely to Gordie through the years, you realize that he believes that Colleen is by far the best line mate he ever had. Gordie has often said that he believes that Colleen has had the greatest influence on his career because "she did everything for me and she never let me down."

The affection they shared has never been more evident than it is now that Colleen is living with Pick's Disease, a rare malady causing a progressive dementia that alters a person's personality and character. There is no cure. At the time this book was completed in early 2004, the disease has progressed to the point that Colleen had limited ability to recognize those close to her. Some of the proceeds from this book are being donated to research that disease.

Now 76, Gordie is helping care for her in his home and it is his intention to continue to do so.

Gordie would have been a hockey mega-star even if Colleen hadn't entered his life, but he is the first to say that Colleen altered the course of his life, particularly with regard to the family's involvement in the sport.

While it wasn't in Gordie's nature to bargain contractual matters, Colleen had superb business acumen. She was trailblazing in "sports marketing" long before people understood the phrase. There is testimony from former NHL players in this book about how Mrs. Hockey's marketing of Gordie paved the way for other players to earn endorsement dollars.

Her most crowning achievement may have been getting the entire family signed by the World Hockey Association.

At one point, NHL president Clarence Campbell was on the phone with Colleen trying to convince her not to allow her boys, Mark and Marty, to sign as under-age players. What he didn't know was that it was actually Colleen who had discovered a loophole that allowed the WHA to draft Mark and Marty.

Colleen's reasoning on the draft issues were rooted in the observation that gifted children in other professions were allowed to enter the work force at a younger age. "Why not hockey?" she asked.

"It was just so unfair," Colleen said in an interview with me years later. "If someone has a good voice, you aren't going to tell them they have to be a certain age to use that voice professionally."

Howe now says that his greatest accomplishment in sports was being able to play professional hockey with Mark and Marty on the Houston Aeros.

This book is not intended to be a critical examination of the Howe's life. Not every rock was turned over to see what was underneath. That should be left to other journalists, some who didn't grow up in Detroit idolizing Gordie Howe. As a seventh grader at St. Mary's School in Wayne, Michigan, I too, was so taken with Gordie Howe that I risked getting in trouble during math class to make a trade for his card. This book is a collection of stories about relationships the Howes had with fans, opponents, teammates, business colleagues, family members and friends.

The objective was to provide unique insight about the Howes based on the accounts of people whose lives they have intersected, and changed. This is a book for those interested in reading stories about a fascinating couple that have been making hockey headlines since Dwight Eisenhower was in his first term as president.

Since this book is heavily dependent upon the memories of people, a diligent effort was made to check the accuracy of the stories. Every attempt was made to guard against exaggeration. A few stories were not used because historical facts didn't support quotes by the interviewees, or because they strained the boundaries of credulity.

As much as we appreciate Bobby Orr, Wayne Gretzky and Mario Lemieux, Mr. Hockey simply had more tools in his box. As a player, he was as ruthless as he was cunning. He was a power forward long before we called them that. And no one can match Howe's durability. Remember this was a man who was playing in the NHL ten years before he qualified for social security.

Detroit News sportswriters Vartan Kupelian and Mike O'Hara, both highly respected by their peers, did fascinating research in 2004 to determine the top scorer in NHL history by comparing the percentage of goals scored by the player to the total goals scored in the league.

To give the analysis more credibility, they judged the modern players only against the top six teams in their league.

The result was that Howe was the top goal scorer based on scoring .0259 of his league's goals during his time in the league and Brett Hull was second at .0244, while Phil Esposito was third and Gretzky was fourth.

Some of the details of Howe's career are well established. He was the fifth of nine children of Albert Clarence and Kathleen (Schultz) Howe and he was born March 31, 1928 in the farming community of Floral, Saskatchewan. Russ McCrory of the New York Rangers was the first NHL scout to show up at Howe's two-storied home on Avenue L North. He had a five-day tryout with the Rangers in Winnipeg. There seems to be some historical debate about what the Rangers thought of the 15 year old. However, it's clear that there was no lasting connection. It was in 1944 that Red Wings scout Fred Pinckney brought Howe to Windsor, Ontario for a tryout with the Red Wings and he was assigned to a team in Galt, Ontario.

By the time Gordie married Colleen, he had won three scoring titles and captured two Hart Trophies. You can't argue that Colleen made Gordie a better player. He was already a near perfect hockey player.

But the theory that resonates through interviews with more than 80 people is that Mr. and Mrs. Hockey seemed to be the perfect team. It was if two people who needed each other found each other in that bowling alley. Gordie needed a wife who could handle his business interests and nurture his family. Colleen needed a devoted, affectionate husband who would allow her to explore her professional interests.

They were bonded by their enjoyment of people, and over the next 50 years their marital harmony would be shared and appreciated by countless others. The Howe marriage evolved into community property--a public trust with benefits received by many.

Colleen's long list of accomplishments -- launching Gordie Howe Hockeyland and the Detroit Junior Red Wings among others -- were impressive. But most of her friends testify to the fact that Colleen's No. 1 objective was to take care of Gordie and her family. She was willing to take bullets for her family and friends, accepting criticism as part of her job description.

Gordie Howe never met a fight that he couldn't win, but he knows he can't win against Pick's Disease. But he won't give in because he loved the woman at the Lucky Strike Bowling alley even more than he loved hockey. Colleen took care of Gordie for the better part of half a century. And he will take care of her.

Hope you enjoy the book.

KEVIN ALLEN

Editor's Note: In the spirit of their role as hockey's foremost ambassadors, Gordie continues to make public appearances and support charitable endeavors. In concert with Gordie, Colleen spent decades helping to build and promote the sport of hockey on many levels. She believed that her life was God's gift to her and her gift to God was how she lived her life. Her legacy is far reaching because she used her God-given abilities to dramatically and positively affect many lives inside and outside the sport.

MR. & MRS. HOCKEY ®

A Tribute to the Sport's Greatest Couple

Scotty Bowman

Nine-Time Stanley Cup Champion
The Most Successful Coach in NHL History

When the *Hockey News* asked Scotty Bowman to cast a vote for the greatest player in hockey history, he didn't need to analyze statistics and ponder differences in eras to make his choice. He just knew that the greatest player of all-time, in his mind, would always be Mr. Hockey, Gordie Howe.

"When I think about players I consider three ingredients: the head, the heart and the feet," Bowman said. "Some players don't have any of those and some players have one or two. But, Gordie had all three in high dimensions." Here is Bowman's breakdown of Howe's attributes:

The head: "He thought a hell of a game. He could play offensively and defensively. That's why he was able to play so long."

The feet: "He was an effortless skater. I used to see him play in his prime in the late 40's and early 50's when I was living in Montreal. That was when Detroit finished in first place for seven consecutive seasons from 1949 to 1955. Howe could have played the whole game. He never got tired. He was like Nick Lindstrom is today."

The heart: "I don't think there was anyone close to him. Some say Bobby Orr, but Bobby only played ten years. Gordie was the ultimate forward, and he could play center. He could play wing. He could even play defense. How many players could actually play both forward and defense? I've only had a couple: Sergie Fedorov and Bob Gainey, who I played back there once when we had injuries."

Bowman coached 30 years in the NHL and witnessed many talented athletes, but he never encountered anyone who could do as much during a hockey game as Howe.

"He was the strongest player in the league for many years and no one was close to him in strength," Bowman said. "In the first year of expansion, he was with a mediocre Detroit team. He got 103 points and he was 40 years of age."

Howe was third in the NHL in scoring that season, behind Boston's Phil Esposito and Chicago's Bobby Hull, but Howe placing among scoring leaders certainly didn't qualify as news around the NHL at the time. At age 21, Howe became one of the NHL's premium scorers, and he remained one until he retired for the first time at age 43. Lost in the marveling over Howe's longevity is the fact that he was a dominant player throughout his tenure in hockey. In essence, he was dominant beyond age 50.

Signing his first NHL contract with the Red Wings before the 1946-1947 season, Mr. Hockey was able to break into the ranks of the leading scorers by 1949-1950 when he finished third behind his production-line line-mates, Ted Lindsay and Sid Abel. That marked the beginning of a 20-season period in which he was in the top five in scoring. He won six league-scoring crowns during that time.

Bowman remembers looking at a list of All-Stars in the Red Wings dressing room and noting that Howe was the first-team or second-team All-Star right wing 21 times in his NHL career. That record may never be surpassed. Howe was a first-team selection 12 times.

"When Gordie Howe was second-team, it wasn't like he was finishing second to ham and eggs," Bowman said. "He was finishing second to Maurice "Rocket" Richard who might be the greatest goal scorer of all-time. Rocket was an outstanding clutch player, but he didn't have the defensive acumen that Howe had."

Another factor that Bowman considered in reaching his conclusion that Howe was the best player of all-time was that Howe was able to recover from a near-catastrophic head injury when he was 21. In the opening game of the 1949-1950 playoffs, Howe suffered a fractured skull when he went sliding into the boards after being smacked in the nose and eye by Toronto Maple Leafs forward Teeder Kennedy's stick. (Howe has said publicly that he believes it was an accident.) Surgeons were forced to drill into his skull to remove swelling and pressure on the brain. He was listed in critical condition for a significant period of time.

After the Red Wings won the Stanley Cup Championship with a dramatic Game 7 double-overtime win, fans began chanting Howe's name. He was forced to come out on the ice in street clothes to quiet them down.

"Not many players could have come back from that level of injury; he was really just starting his career," Bowman says. "He was an amazing athlete and he was on championship teams as well. All of these things add up to be too much for anyone else to overcome. Howe was the best."

Through the years Bowman has also talked to players, such as Jean Beliveau, Dickie Moore and others who faced Howe in his prime. They were in awe of him.

"They thought he was close to Superman," said Bowman.

Editor's Note: In 26 National Hockey League seasons, Gordie Howe played in 23 All-Star games. In 6 seasons, in the World Hockey Association, he played in 6 All-Star games. Amazingly, in 32 professional seasons, he played in a world record 29 All-Star games. In the season, after Mr. Hockey nearly died from his head injury, he led the league in scoring.

Edna Gadsby

Wife of Hall of Famer Bill Gadsby
Close Friend of Colleen Howe

On the night that Bill Gadsby was fired from his job as coach of the Detroit Red Wings in 1969, Gordie and Colleen Howe showed up at the Gadsby house after the game with a six pack of beer and two pizzas. They sat up until 5:30 a.m. discussing Gadsby's future. The Howe-Gadsby story isn't about hockey as much as it is about friendship.

"Gordie and Colleen have stayed true friends through the years," Edna Gadsby says. "When Bill went through his drinking problem and then got help, they couldn't have been more supportive."

Many know that Gadsby and Howe were road roommates and friends in their seasons together on the Red Wings, but what isn't known is that Edna and Colleen were equally close. They are different people with different attributes. Edna likes to explain their differences by recalling that on the day they met Colleen "Colleen was out golfing and I was picking strawberries."

The Gadsbys and Howes became friends when the Gadsbys vacationed in Saskatchewan in 1954. It was the year after Gordie and Colleen were married, and they had gone back to Saskatchewan for the summer.

"We were quite different, but we just hit it off," Edna says. "She took us under her wing and welcomed us to the area. They had many friends and they introduced us to everyone. We had a grand time and kept in touch."

What Edna doesn't say and is obvious to those who know both women, is that their caring nature and their commitment to family bonded them. Edna recognized instantly that underneath Colleen's assertive business demeanor was a woman with a heart overflowing with compassion.

Gadsby was playing for the New York Rangers when their friendship began. However, once he was traded to the Red Wings, the bond between the Gadsbys and Howes reached a higher dimension. They had far too much in common, starting with hockey and ending with each couple having four children around the same age. Even today, Gadsby's children, some in their 40's, refer to the Howes as Uncle Gordie and Auntie Colleen and vice versa.

"Colleen always included us in family gatherings," Edna says. "We never spent Christmas and Thanksgiving alone. We always spent it with them. She was very good to me. She treated me like an older sister."

With the exception of family, few people knew, understood and appreciated Colleen more than Edna Gadsby.

"She was often misunderstood," Edna says. "She was the wife of the superstar, but she never acted that way. She acted more like a hostess. When someone was traded to Detroit, she would like to help them meet people. That's how she was. Really, she just wanted to be one of the gals."

Edna was always perplexed about why some folks questioned Colleen's motivation for wanting to assist people.

"It was hurtful for her sometimes because she couldn't understand why she would be criticized for being nice to people," Edna said. "But, that's really the kind of person she was. She loved to surprise people."

Edna's birthday was on Halloween. One year Colleen invited her over to her house a few days before her birthday. When Edna arrived, there were lots of her friends and a birthday cake.

"She loved doing that," Edna said, "not just for me, but many people. She always did a lot of little things for people that no one will ever know."

Remember that this was an era when NHL players weren't receiving lucrative salaries, and the Gadsbys know that Colleen purchased groceries for a player's family on more than one occasion.

The Howes considered Michigan their permanent home in the 1960's, and the Gadsbys returned to their permanent home in Edmonton every summer. They rented a home in Michigan during the season, and they didn't always have all the household items that Edna would have liked to have there.

One season Edna's parents were about to make their first visit to the Detroit area and Edna recalls, "I was complaining to Colleen that my parents are coming and I didn't have enough dishes and I didn't even have a cream and sugar bowl."

Edna also had been concerned because they were going to have to rent a car because they only had one car in Detroit.

The next day two floral arrangements were delivered to the Gadsby home. One arrangement was in a creamer and the other was in a sugar bowl.

Edna didn't have to read the card to know who had been so thoughtful. Included was a note saying that Colleen wanted Edna to use one of the Howe's cars while her parents were there.

When Bill Gadsby accepted the job coaching the Red Wings in 1968-1969, the family was already permanently moved to Edmonton. Colleen immediately phoned Edna and told her how thrilled she was that the Gadsbys were coming back to Detroit. She also informed Edna that she had lined up a real estate agent to help them find a house, and that the Gadsbys should stay in their home and use their car when they flew in to Michigan to begin their search for a home.

In 1977 when Gordie and Colleen's son, Marty, was getting married in Houston, Colleen invited Bill and Edna to vacation with them after the ceremony. The idea was that Gordie and Colleen would help Bill and Edna celebrate their 25th wedding anniversary. What Colleen didn't say was that the trip was to Hawaii. She didn't say she invited the Gadsby's children. She didn't say that when they had their anniversary dinner there would be cards and telegrams from all of their friends. Colleen had arranged it all.

"That's just the way Colleen was," Edna said. "She just loved doing things for people."

Colleen enjoyed a multi-layered lifestyle that would have surprised many who didn't know her well.

"She liked the business end of hockey. Really, she loved it," Edna said. "She would get into these projects and tell me, 'you would really love to do this.' I would be honest with her and say I have no interest in doing that. But we always did the things that we liked to do together."

One day, Mrs. Hockey was a mover and shaker in the business world, ably representing her family's interests. On another day, she would be taking crafting classes with Edna.

"She was a wonderful seamstress," Edna said. "She also did decoupage, which was all the rage in the 1960's. She made a mosaic coffee table with a Red Wing's emblem. She enjoyed all of that."

In the midst of their busy schedule, Colleen and Gordie found countless hours for charity. "They did a lot of things that people didn't know about," Edna said. "Colleen would get very attached to the people they helped."

When Colleen moved out of Michigan, Edna new she would get regular updates on how the family was doing. Colleen would make sure Edna had all the addresses and phone numbers every time a family member moved.

"What we had in common is that we put Gordie, Bill and the kids first. It's still that way," Edna said.

If the true test of a person's caring side comes in his or her treatment of the in-laws, Colleen again receives an exceptional passing grade. "She loved Gordie's mother and treated her like a queen," Edna recalled.

Thinking back to the night Bill Gadsby was fired, Edna recalls that by coincidence she had been with Colleen at the rink. Colleen wanted Edna to see Gordie's new insurance office before the game. Before the game, Colleen took Edna into the main office where the owner Bruce Norris' cronies were all hanging out.

After some introductions, Edna left the room to meet some other friends. Not long after Edna left, Norris' friends told Colleen that Norris was upstairs firing Gadsby.

Being the true friend that she was, Colleen rushed out of the office to find Edna. "Colleen was beside herself and found me at the wash room. Of course, I was beside myself," Edna said.

All the Howes cared about that night was that good friends were hurting. "What I love about Gord and Colleen is that you could always be yourself around them," Edna said.

Even when she lived out of state, Colleen would call Edna and talk for a long time. "I would tell her we've been on the phone for a while, and she would say 'that's okay, you're worth it,'" Edna said, chuckling.

Their closeness endures even though Colleen is suffering from Pick's Disease, a progressive form of dementia that alters a person's personality and character. There is no cure and its progression cannot be slowed.

Every Sunday, after church, Bill and Edna visit the Howes. Bill and Gordie sit in the kitchen chatting over coffee, and Edna sits and talks with Colleen, even though no one is sure if Colleen recognizes her.

"Gord has lost his wife, and I have lost my friend," said Edna.

Editor's Note: Mr. and Mrs. Hockey provided the foreword to the Gadsby's book *The Grateful Gadsby*.

In 1993, Colleen Howe co-authored a book with Gordie titled *After the Applause*. The book chronicled the unique stories of 10 famous hockey legends and their wives. She arranged for the wives to autograph the books along with their famous husbands when book-signing appearances were scheduled. It was a bestseller in Canada.

Max McNab

Detroit Red Wings Teammate
From 1947-1948 and 1950-1951

In addition to all of Mr. Hockey's pro accolades, he may have the distinction of being the only intimidating stick boy in hockey history.

When McNab was playing junior hockey for the Saskatoon Quakers in the Saskatchewan Junior Hockey League before World War II, Howe was the team's stick boy. The Quaker's players were all 16 and 17 years old; and Howe was 13 at the time, but he was allowed to practice with the team.

"Bob Dawes was our captain, and I remember he went to our coach and said, 'We don't think the stick boy should work out with us anymore because he's going to hurt someone,'" McNab said, laughing at the recollection.

McNab, from Watson, Saskatchewan, was aware of Howe's stature as a schoolboy legend before he played junior hockey. Word spread quickly about Howe being a hockey prodigy.

"When Gordie was going to public school in Saskatoon, they had a Howe rule," McNab says. "All the coaches voted on it, and put into place that Gordie had to play goal in their games. Otherwise, the other team wouldn't play because when Gordie was on the ice it was a man against boys." McNab calls Howe "nature's biggest mistake. Every part of his body was made for the game," McNab said. "Wayne Gretzky beat his record for points, but it was a different era then. The Original Six was pretty tough hockey, and once Gordie got to the top on points and goals there was no carrot for him."

McNab's contention is that Mr. Hockey might have generated even gaudier offensive numbers if someone would have set the bar higher from a previous era or from his own era. He passed Elmer Lach to become the NHL's all-time assist leader in 1957-1958. He passed by Maurice "Rocket" Richard to be the point's leader on January 16, 1960. On November 10, 1963, he scored his 545th goal to pass Richard again to be the NHL's all-time leading goal scorer. The only yardsticks Howe had to measure himself by in the last 17 years of his career were his own accomplishments.

"There were a lot of nights when Gordie could have piled it on and he didn't," McNab said.

In those days dressing room stalls were organized by player numbers, and since Howe wore number 9 and McNab wore number 10 they sat next to each other. He got to know Howe quite well.

"Gordie was Mr. Relaxed," McNab said. "Between periods he was so relaxed it almost seemed like he was meditating."

McNab had to clear out of the way quickly after a game because the reporters in every NHL city would rush to Howe's dressing area first.

"In most games he was the deciding factor," McNab said. "If it was a rough game, he was doing the fighting. If it was a high scoring game, Gordie was doing the scoring."

McNab said Howe's reputation for being a rough player was deserved, although Howe never went out of his way to look for trouble. "They used to call him *Power*," McNab said, "He accepted the responsibility of breaking up every fight. He could move in and stop things pretty abruptly."

"Players would only get too close to Gordie once," McNab said, chuckling. "He wanted a little room out there and he got it. He wasn't an instigator, but he had a long memory."

McNab was on the bench the night that Howe suffered a severe head injury during a 1949-1950 playoff series against the Maple Leafs. "He went into the boards face first and it was scary," McNab said. "From what I saw, I don't think Kennedy did anything illegal."

In those days, the Red Wings brass would sequester the players at a hotel in Toledo, Ohio, during the playoffs. It was clear to Detroit players that Howe had suffered a life threatening injury. "We were sick with worry," McNab said. "There were half-hour radio updates about his condition. We stayed up all night listening to news bulletins because the station had someone down at the hospital. At six o'clock in the morning all of us came down for coffee because we hadn't slept."

Given that Howe seemed to be an extraordinary human specimen, McNab was not shocked that Howe enjoyed a longer-than-expected career. However, he certainly did not anticipate that Howe would play 32 seasons, including 26 in the NHL and 6 more in the WHA totaling 2,421 games! It's more remarkable when it's considered that he played every game for his NHL team 17 times in 26 seasons, and he missed more than a handful of games only twice in his NHL career. He missed 20 games in 1948-1949 and 13 games in 1970-1971.

"In the bad old days, guys would do almost anything not to reach the age of 30 because that seemed like the kiss of death," McNab said. "Teams wanted to trade you."

He laughs, "Sid Abel, former Detroit Red Wings player, was 25 when he went overseas during World War II. He was over there three years and the program said he was 26 when he came back. They wanted him to stay young."

Howe's decision to sign with the Aeros at age 45 to play with Mark and Marty did not surprise McNab "because he was a family man, and those kids were his whole life." That's why Max and his wife June had taken an instant liking to Colleen and Gordie.

"Colleen was a great family person. Her children were always number one. And to my wife June and me, our boys were always number one," McNab said. "Colleen and June compared notes and got along very well."

He said Colleen's approach to business was rooted in a single thought. "She was protecting the herd," McNab said. "She looked after her boys. If you knew her, you knew she was doing it for them and not for herself."

According to McNab, Mr. and Mrs. Hockey were both such warm and friendly people that they were naturals for promotional work. They also had an uncanny knack of delivering in a big way. Such was the case when he brought them both out to promote the San Diego Gulls minor league team when McNab was general manager. McNab remembered that Howe met with journalists and sportscasters and told enough hockey yarns to keep everyone entertained.

"The next day we went to La Costa Country Club, and I'll be a son of a gun if Gordie didn't get a hole in one. There is really nothing he couldn't do in sports," McNab said, laughing. "His name was all over the paper the next day and we got our money's worth out of the Howes." He laughs again. "The Howe story is an amazing story."

Editor's Note: In 1979-1980, at the age of 52, Mr. Hockey played all 80 games of the regular season and led the Hartford Whalers into the playoffs.

Rich Margittay

Retired Police Officer and Freelance Photographer

Many Gordie Howe admirers have put together collections of Howe memorabilia, but Rich Margittay's collection contains a rare kind of film footage and photographs that are the envy of hardcore collectors.

Growing up in the Queens borough of New York, Margittay didn't originally develop an affinity for hockey. "Mickey Mantle was my hero," Margittay says. However, after moving to the Detroit area in the late 1950's, Margittay became curious about an athlete whose name was synonymous with his sport. His interest in Mr. Hockey turned into a fascination after he watched Howe live for the first time at a 1970 Red Wings playoff game against Chicago. By the time Margittay was able to play on a line with Howe during a 1973 charity game, between the Gordie Howe All-Stars and the Dick Purtan All-Stars, he had already decided Howe was the most remarkable athlete he had ever witnessed.

"What I remember was him standing there after that game in a white trench coat signing autographs until everyone had one," Margittay said. "I had seen him do that before. He just kept signing. That's why Gordie became my hero and why he is a hero for many people."

Margittay was such a fan that he began to film and take still photographs of Howe at games and public events. His earliest film, taken with a 1940's triple lens Kodak 8mm camera inherited from his father, is from Howe's charity golf tournament at Plum Hollow Country Club in 1970. "Everyone is wearing plaid pants," Margittay says with a chuckle. However, the Margittay films that are the envy of Howe collectors, include the 8mm silent film he shot when Howe played a pre-season game with the WHA's Houston Aeros against the Los Angeles Sharks at Detroit's Cobo Arena on October 8, 1974. Howe scored a pair of goals in the Aeros victory. Considering the Sharks didn't last long, this is indeed a rare film. Howe never played a regular season game in Detroit wearing an Aeros uniform. The Aeros game in Detroit had been scheduled for February.

"I bought a ticket to get into that game," Margittay said. "Today they wouldn't let you bring in a camera, but back then they wanted you to film the game." Not long after Margittay upgraded his equipment to a Super 8 sound camera, which allowed him to create some more special keepsakes. He has video of the last game ever played at the revered Olympia Arena, an alumni game that featured many former Red Wing greats against the Red Wings team. When Gordie Howe was introduced, the alumni all bowed to him as if he were the King. Margittay has that on his tape.

"Greg Joly scored the final goal at Olympia in a regulation game, but Gordie Howe got the final goal in the alumni game," Margittay says. "People wondered if Rutherford let that go in, but I've watched the film and Gordie scored that goal."

A year later, when the Red Wings moved to Joe Louis Arena, Margittay filmed, with sound, the Hartford Whalers game against the Red Wings. It featured Howe playing on a line with sons Marty and Mark. Stationed at ice level, Margittay also has footage of Howe conversing on the bench with fellow Whalers, Dave Keon and Bobby Hull.

Another treasure in Margittay's collection is his personal film of the 1980 All-Star Game when Howe received a standing ovation. "He is such a humble man that he looks almost embarrassed by it," Margittay recalled.

Margittay said Howe was his inspiration to take up playing hockey in his early 20's. The first game he ever played was at a charity game involving the Dearborn Police force. Ironically, Mr. and Mrs. Hockey were in attendance to drop the puck.

Two decades after Gordie played his last game Margittay still finds himself chronicling Howe's life. His photography has appeared in a variety of publications, including *Sports Illustrated.* He also works for some newspapers in the Detroit area, and it was in that capacity that took him to the Ford Senior Players Championship at TPC of Michigan in Dearborn, July 9, 2003.

When Gordie Howe showed up to observe Pro-Am day, Margittay went to tell his editor Scott Salowich of the *Dearborn Press & Guide* that the photo they needed was The Golden Bear posed with Mr. Hockey, hockey's greatest player, standing shoulder to shoulder with golf's greatest champion. Ultimately, Howe came together with Jack Nicklaus near the practice range. Together the two taped an interview with broadcaster Fred Heuman at the invitation of tournament director Tom Clark. While media swarmed around the two legends, Margittay approached Howe's agents Del Reddy and Aaron Howard about photographing Howe and Nicklaus together. Reddy and Howard told Margittay that the timing was perfect because they came to the event with Gordie to talk to Nicklaus about doing a special memorabilia project called "The Kings of Their Sport" involving the two greats.

Reddy spoke with Jack Nicklaus. He agreed to have his picture taken with Mr. Hockey, but it had to be quick because he was due to tee off shortly. Margittay positioned his camera and captured the two icons in a photo that both of them prize. Margittay also came to realize that even superstars from other sports revere Howe. Margittay dropped off the photos at Nicklaus's locker and asked him to sign the picture for Gordie. The inscription that Nicklaus wrote said, "I've been a fan of yours forever, kindest regards, Jack."

Margittay senses there was a bond between these two athletic greats, even though they did not know each other well. Nicklaus noted that Howe's elbow was swollen, and Howe told him that he was now paying a price because he had used that elbow to break his fall too many times during his 32-season career.

Margittay understood everyone's fascination with Howe. Not only was Howe a superstar, but he was also very approachable. He was like the Clark Kent/Superman dual identity. Off the ice, Howe seemed like the perfect next-door neighbor. On the ice, he seemed superhuman.

"He was such a personable guy, down to earth and with a good sense of humor," Margittay recalled. "He talked to everyone and signed autographs for everyone. He is like a cat. He's always playful and always pawing at you. He sure made me feel special."

Editor's Note: In his prime, Gordie Howe was a scratch golfer. Many times, he drove golf balls 300 yards. This happened at a time when this feat was considered a rarity.

Paul Stewart

Former WHA Player and NHL Referee

Although loquacious Paul Stewart has never been short on words, he didn't know quite what to say when he lined up opposite one of his idols, Gordie Howe, during a World Hockey Association game.

"What I said was 'I named my dog after you,'" Stewart recalled. "Gordie sort of blinked a little bit, but didn't say anything." Howe made his reply once play began.

"I was back checking on him on that shift," Stewart said. "He was still pretty quick and pretty strong for a 48-year old guy, and he hit me with a roundhouse elbow that left me flat as a mackerel."

Stewart woke up in the dressing room staring up at the light. He asked what had happened to him, and he was told, "Gordie got you."

In the next period, Stewart was back on the ice opposite Howe and as they waited for the face-off, he turned to Howe and said, "Nice elbow." Expecting to be attacked, Howe raised his stick ever so slightly.

"Hey, no problem, Gordie," Stewart told him. "But you remember that dog? I'm going to go home and choke the bastard."

Stewart has told that story often to his friends, and he included that tale when he was a roaster at a dinner honoring Mr. and Mrs. Hockey in 1996. As much as Stewart admired Howe when they played against each other in the WHA, Stewart's respect grew as he became more acquainted with both Gordie and Colleen.

"Colleen was probably the best sport agent I ever met," Stewart said. "She not only had to be savvy to get the Howe family the best deal, but she also had the best interest in the game at heart. She was cognizant of Gordie's public relations ability, and also of her boys, Mark and Marty."

Stewart was among the WHA players who understood the Howe family importance to the WHA. Those who know Colleen closely said she tried to promote the league as much as her family.

Paul was the grandson of the late Bill Stewart, a former NHL coach and referee. Stewart grew up with an appreciation of the Howe impact—even though Bill Stewart had already left the NHL by that time.

Howe played his first game with the Red Wings in 1946-1947. However, Bill Stewart, a Boston Bruins season ticket holder, had regaled his grandson about Howe's unique talents. "He would say the guy has power and how strong he was, how he controlled the puck along the boards and how no one bothers him," Paul Stewart remembers.

He had trouble separating the respect he had for Mr. Hockey with the reality that Howe was an adversary. He remembers that when he was going hard after Howe and his back was turned, he would yell that he was coming. The irony of that was that Gordie Howe was also known for giving that same kind of warning to a few select players he respected in the NHL.

One night Howe carved up Robbie Ftorek during a WHA game, and Stewart remembers teammates "looking at me like, okay that's your job, get him." I looked at Peter Marsh, a teammate at the time, and said, "Are you kidding me, that's Gordie Howe."

Howe at times played with a ruthless edge, but Stewart was impressed that Howe played by a code of honor. One night Stewart knocked Mark Howe wacky with one of his checks, and Stewart's teammates began preparing eulogies for Stewart in anticipation of what Gordie Howe was probably going to do to him. Stewart skated by Howe, expecting the worst, but Gordie said to him "don't worry about it." It had been a clean hit, and Howe would not seek retribution for a clean hit.

Stewart wasn't the only player or fan who had difficulty viewing Howe as an adversary. "When he touched the puck, you would be on the bench hoping he would do well," Stewart said. "Everywhere people pulled for Gordie. Even in the opposition's buildings, people would cheer if he got a point. I thought it was pretty cool."

He says he has never forgotten the graciousness of the Howe family. Although he was an adversary for many years, Colleen in particular has always made Stewart feel as if he had been a teammate.

When he was diagnosed with colon cancer, he received a supportive letter from Colleen that touched him. "She has always had a class about her," Stewart said. "After games Gordie would go outside and sign autographs for everyone, and she would retire off to the side until he was done. Even though I was on the other team, I would go over and talk to her. I remember thinking, '"This is one elegant woman.'"

Editor's Note: Colleen Howe is the first female agent-manager ever in sports. As a positive person, she approached business with a win-win mindset for all involved.

Mark Messier

New York Rangers Captain

Mark Messier's NHL career spans nearly 25 seasons and during that time he established some outstanding records and benchmarks.

Messier inherited immense respect for Mr. Hockey from his father Doug. He was a former minor league player who attended a Red Wings training camp, and played some pre-season games with Howe.

"Gordie Howe was a big name in our house," Messier said. "My dad had tremendous respect for him, not only as a player, but as a person."

Clearly, it isn't merely coincidence that Mark Messier ended up playing with the same high-octane blend of grace and grit that also defined Howe's career. Each was known as much for the sharpness of his elbows as he was for the magnificence of his talent. The many points Messier garnered may not be as impressive as the number of scores he had to settle, the number of teammates he had to defend, and the sum total of elbows he threw to get in Mr. Hockey's league. When you review Messier's growth as a player, he appeared to be patterning himself after Howe, right down to insisting upon retribution for sins against him.

"The Gordie Howe stories were told many, many times in our house," Messier said.

But maybe Messier's true apprenticeship began when he signed with the WHA's Indianapolis Racers as a 17-year old in 1978-1979. It can be said that Howe, then 50 and playing for the Houston Aeros, mentored Messier in a unique fashion.

"I was the recipient of one of Gordie's elbows," Messier said. "I think he did it more so that I can talk about it for the rest of my career rather than of bad intentions. It was a way of welcoming me to the league."

Clearly, Howe had an impact on Messier in many different ways.

Bob Duff

Windsor Star Columnist and Hockey Historian

Duff is one of a small number of people in North America who could intelligently debate whether Howie Morenz or Steve Yzerman was a better all-around player. He can argue the merits of Eddie Shore vs. Ray Bourque. Some people collect coins, stamps or hockey cards. Duff collects hockey's historical facts. He keeps them in files, and more importantly, in his mind. In addition to being a skilled writer, he is also one of the more gifted hockey historians.

After years of study and contemplation, he has reached many different conclusions, not the least of which is that Gordie Howe is the best hockey player of all-time. "He was the most complete player," Duff said. "He could be a tough guy. If you needed someone to fight, he could do that. If you needed a scorer, he could do that. If you needed a checker, he could do that. Howe could also play any style of game and fill any role necessary, whether it be a tough guy, playmaker, goal scorer, checker or grinder. And he did this over the span of five decades."

Duff is steadfast in his conviction. "Wayne Gretzky was the most creative guy, Bobby Orr was the most exciting and Howe was the best player," Duff said. "Gordie could be intimidating by scoring or by his physical toughness."

A Toronto native, Duff is old enough to have viewed Howe playing in the NHL and the WHA. "He slowed the game down by controlling the pace," Duff said. "Everyone remembered Bobby Hull for his speed and shot, but Howe took charge of the game. He would dictate how it would be played. If it was going to be rough, he set the tone. If it was going to be a scoring game, he set that tone as well. This is why I think Howe is the game's greatest player."

According to Duff, Hull's signing gave the WHA credibility, but it was Mr. Hockey's decision to come out of retirement at age 45 that gave the fledgling league visibility. "He gave the WHA a storyline that transcended the game," Duff said. "Hull got the hockey world's attention when he went to the WHA, but what Howe actually did was bring the sports world to the WHA. Even people who weren't staunch hockey fans could be fascinated by a father playing with his sons because it hadn't been done before."

Howe's longevity also played a role in helping Duff reach his conclusion. He considers Howe's achievement of scoring 16 goals for the Hartford Whalers at age 52 to be sports greatest age-defiance accomplishment, superior even to George Blanda playing in the NFL at age 48.

"Getting 16 goals is astonishing when you consider how many guys today in their prime aren't going to even score 15," Duff said. "He wasn't a place-kicker like Blanda was late in his career. He played all 80 games that season. He didn't take back-to-back games off like older players do today."

A journalist for more than two decades, Duff has grown to know Howe and found that the man's charisma is no myth. He spent some time with Mr. Hockey in Howe's native Saskatchewan. Howe told him that the football stadium in Saskatoon is on what was once farmer's field land. Howe's first job was hunting down and killing gophers in that field.

By the way, the football stadium on that field is called *Gordie Howe Bowl*. "When they name a football stadium after a hockey player, it tells you how significant he is," Duff said.

Darren Pang

Former NHL Goaltender
Current ESPN Analyst

In Darren Pang's way of thinking, Colleen Howe was to Gordie Howe what Bryan Trottier was to Mike Bossy. As individuals, Trottier and Bossy were All-Stars. Together they were unstoppable.

"The saying 'behind every good man there is a terrific lady' comes through with the Gordie Howe story," Pang says. "He was an unbelievable athlete with a great personality and she had a good business mind. That combination was perfect."

Pang says most athletes will admit that they can't handle the business aspect of their profession.

"Their focus is on the game and on becoming better players," Pang said. "They don't have the mindset or attention to detail that is needed to take care of things. That's why they get agents."

Colleen was serving as an agent long before agents operated in the mainstream in the NHL. "She was involved in everything her family did," Pang said, "I think she is a brilliant lady."

Ken Holland

Detroit Red Wings General Manager

Ken Holland has known the Howe family for almost 20 years. But truthfully, Holland felt as if he had known the Howes forever the instant he met Mr. Hockey. Holland was a minor league goaltender playing with Marty Howe in Binghamton, New York, when he was introduced to Gordie Howe. But he remembers Gordie treated him as if he were Glenn Hall. "He just has a way of making everyone feel important," Holland said. "I was just a minor league goaltender, but he just had this way of making everyone feel comfortable around him."

Howe had already retired by then, and held every conceivable record, but Holland remembers that it was clear that Gordie Howe didn't want to be treated like an icon. "He was cracking jokes and just being one of the guys," Holland said. "That may be his greatest quality. He is one of the all-time greatest athletes in professional sports; but no matter who he is with, he wants to be just one of the guys. He loves being around the game."

Holland said Gordie's son, Mark, who works for Holland as the Red Wings professional scout, "is exactly the same way and I don't think there is a harder working scout anywhere," Holland said. "He wants to be around the game. He goes to American League games and NHL games. He will hop in his car and drive two or three hours to a game one night, and he's right back at it the next night."

Holland figures Mrs. Hockey also had a big role in Mark's work ethic. In addition to knowing how hard Gordie worked on the ice, Mark knew how hard his mother worked behind the scenes. "She had a big, big, big role in that family," Holland said. "She and Gordie deserve a lot of credit for who their boys are today. They're good people."

Holland still sees Mr. Hockey around Joe Louis Arena, and he is struck that time hasn't altered Howe's approach to life. "He has never changed," Holland said. "He treats players, coaches and fans with respect and he just wants to be treated like a regular guy."

Jacques Demers

Former NHL and WHA Coach
Current Broadcaster

Coach Jacques Demers didn't just witness Gordie Howe's defiance on the aging process, he was victimized by it.

Howe was 45 when he joined the Houston Aeros of the World Hockey Association and he still managed to score 174 goals and register 334 points for 508 points in 419 games before the NHL annexed the league. That's a scoring average of 1.21 points per game. Demers was coaching in the WHA during Howe's tenure.

"I don't see anyone else playing at 50, let alone make it to 52," Demers said. "Igor Larionov is the oldest player in the league today at 42, and he would still have to play 10 more years."

Even with the attention modern athletes pay to conditioning and nutrition, Demers is convinced it won't happen.

"With all the money players make today, I don't see it happening," Demers said. "But I don't think Gordie did it for the money. He loved the game. And he wanted to play with his sons. I think he wanted to show people he could still do things that no other athlete could."

He certainly did that. Remember Mr. Hockey helped the Aeros win back-to-back WHA Championships in 1974 and 1975. Howe won the Most Valuable Player award in 1973-1974 when he produced 100 points (31 goals and 69 assists). He led the WHA with 14 playoff assists in 1973-1974, and he was even better the following season when he led the Aero's march to the Avco Cup Championships. He totaled 8 goals and 13 assists in just 13 games.

Howe's first Avco title came in the form of a four-game sweep against the Chicago Cougars. Pat Stapleton was officially the playing general manager/coach of that team, but Demers was the bench coach. He remembers Howe being the primary figure in the Finals. Howe registered eight assists in those four games.

"He dominated us," Demers said. "But what I really remember is that Larry Maverty gave Howe a shot in the corner and Gordie came back and busted his nose."

Demers considered Howe one of the true athletic marvels in sports history.

"He was 50 years old and still dominant," Demers said. "And the hockey was still pretty good back then."

According to Demers, one of the highlights of his coaching career was being able to put Wayne Gretzky on a line with Gordie and Mark Howe in the WHA All-Star series against a Soviet squad in 1979.

Gretzky has always appreciated Demers' decision to put Howe on his line. Howe has often told this story about playing with Gretzky in that series. He said, "There was a Russian hacking away at Wayne all night and he was getting really frustrated. So I told him, the next time you get the puck, bring it up right wing. When you hear heavy breathing, get out of the way." Howe leveled the Russian with a devastating check and went to the bench as the Russian trainer tried to revive the fallen player.

Howe continued, "We were sitting on the bench, and I said, 'damn!'"

Wayne asked, "What's wrong, Gord?"

I said, "He's getting up."

What Demers has always admired about Mr. Hockey is that he was a warrior on the ice and a gentleman in street clothes. Although Howe and Jean Beliveau played vastly different styles on the ice, Demers said they are very similar as people because of the way they treated others.

"They are both classy, classy gentleman," Demers said. "When Rocket Richard died, Gordie Howe was there at the funeral. He was there paying his respects to another great player. That's the way Gordie Howe is."

Through the years, Demers also got to know Colleen and he thought they were a matched set in terms of the classy way they dealt with others. Interestingly enough, his fondest memory of the Howes isn't associated with any moment that occurred on the ice. It came at one of the worst times in his professional life.

"When I got fired from the Detroit Red Wings, Gordie and Colleen called me," Demers said. "They told me I had done a good job, wished me the best and told me to keep my head up. That's the kind of people they are. I'm never going to forget that."

Dave Taylor

Former NHL Player
Current Los Angeles Kings General Manager

If you ask Dave Taylor about the magnitude of Gordie Howe scoring 16 goals at age 52, he offers that there is a greater statistic about Howe that is often overlooked. "When he was 50 years old he scored 34 goals," Taylor said. "That's pretty impressive."

One of the other remarkable aspects of Howe's career is that he played in the NHL in five different decades. He made a one-shift appearance for the International Hockey League's Detroit Vipers to add a sixth decade to his resume. However, what many fans don't realize is that Howe played against NHL players from nine different decades. When Mr. Hockey joined the Detroit Red Wings in 1946-1947, there were players remaining from the 1930's and even Dit Clapper from the 1920's. Mark Messier is still active in the NHL today, and he played against Howe in the WHA and NHL.

What that means is that there are plenty of eyewitnesses available to testify to the impact he had on the ice.

Taylor only played a season against Howe in the NHL, and yet he has vivid memories of how fascinated players and fans were with this legendary figure.

In one game in Los Angeles, Howe was checked rudely into boards by scrappy Kings rookie J.P. Kelly. As was Howe's custom, he made a mental note of Kelly's number for future reference. Later in the game, Howe decided to seek his retribution. He spotted his target and hit him. Howe's stick came up high and opened a nice gash on his face.

The problem was that Howe hadn't properly identified who had ripped him along the boards. He had high-sticked Bert Wilson instead of Kelly.

Nobody did anything to Mr. Hockey, but a couple of teammates and Kings players told Howe he had nailed the wrong guy.

"Later on he skated by the bench and said, 'Tell Bert Wilson that I said I'm sorry,'" Taylor said, chuckling.

Emile Francis

Hall of Fame NHL Player, Coach and General Manager

In 1946-1947, Emile Francis was a 19-year old rookie goaltender playing his fourth game for the Chicago Blackhawks when he spied a hulking forward with the puck on his stick roaring down the right wing like a freight train. Instinctively, Francis moved to the left corner of the crease to cut down the angle.

"I remember thinking, I have you right where I want you," Francis recalled, with a chuckle. "Then all the sudden he switched hands on me and put the puck into the far corner." Francis had never before seen a right-handed player switch the stick in his hands and fire a puck left-handed.

"Who the hell is that guy?" Francis said to his captain John Mariucci.

Mariucci just shrugged. "Just some kid they brought up from Omaha." Mariucci said.

The 18-year old kid from Omaha was Gordon Howe of Floral, Saskatchewan, and it wouldn't take long for Francis to be convinced that Mr. Hockey would be the closest he would ever see to a perfect hockey player.

"In my book, the best player of all time is Gordie Howe and no one will ever convince me differently," Francis said.

According to Francis, Howe was probably the first true power forward the NHL had ever experienced. "He could play any way you wanted to play," Francis said. "And he had many ways to get rid of checkers." And, many of Howe's methods for shedding checkers were painful to those checkers.

In addition to possessing unprecedented skill, Howe was an intimidating presence. Players worried about what Howe would do to them if they wronged him. The fear of Howe had an impact in every game he played.

Francis remembers that his Blackhawks squad, and presumably all teams, would scheme aggressively to shut down Howe and it didn't matter. "He had two guys on him all the time," Francis said. "You put your toughest defenseman on the left side to deal with him and you put your toughest winger playing the left side, and they were just plain lucky if they weren't crippled by the end of the game.

As an athlete, Francis insists, Howe had no peers. He became more convinced of that when he saw Howe play baseball for the Saskatoon team in the summer in a Western Canada semi-pro baseball league. This wasn't a recreation league. Some players would come up to Canada to play because they could earn $500-$600 per month compared to the $300-$400 they would earn playing Double-A or Triple-A baseball in the states.

Francis, who managed a team in North Battleford, said one summer 26 players signed bonus contracts. Jerry Adair received $75,000 to step out of the league and play for the Baltimore Orioles. Former Los Angeles Dodgers outfielder Ron Fairly launched his career in that league and got a $125,000 signing bonus. Former major leaguers Tom Alston, Don Buford and Ron Perranoski were signed out of this league. There was no major league draft in those days and scouts would flock to this league to find talent.

"It was at least a Double A league," Francis recalled.

Francis said Howe "hit like hell" in that league that was dripping with pro baseball talent. According to Francis, one summer Howe was batting .340 when a Detroit Red Wings scout spotted him playing shortstop one night.

"He got on the phone to the Detroit general manager, Jack Adams, right away," said Francis, who was wired into the baseball community back then. "Adams called Gordie and said, 'You are through, don't you play another game of baseball as long as you are in Saskatoon.'"

Francis believed that Howe was talented enough to play pro baseball, and "he probably could have played football, too."

Long after Howe had quit playing baseball, Francis was driving by Cairns Field in Saskatoon and noticed the lights were on and the parking lot was full. He knew no baseball game was scheduled that night so curiosity prompted him to enter the stadium just in time to hear the announcer deliver: "Now batting for the Saskatoon team, Detroit Red Wings player Gordie Howe."

More than 6,000 fans had jammed into Cairns Field to watch an exhibition game with local celebrities and fastball legend Eddie Feigner as the star of The King and his Court. Feigner is considered the greatest softball pitcher of all-time, once being clocked at 104 mph. His four-man softball team would barnstorm around North America and put on exhibitions. Feigner was known for being able to pitch from second base blindfolded. Launching their act in 1946, The King and His Court were considered to be like the Harlem Globetrotters. They combined superb athleticism with major league theatrics. Although Feigner does not pitch as often anymore, The King and His Court are still barnstorming today and Feigner pitches an inning or two and provides commentary from the sideline.

When Howe faced Feigner, he was considered virtually unhittable. In a two-inning exhibition in 1967, Feigner fanned major league legends Willie Mays, Willie McCovey, Brooks Robinson, Maury Wills, Harmon Killebrew and Roberto Clemente. Mays' third strike came on a behind-the-back pitch from The King.

"The right-field fence at Cairns was 298 feet, just like Yankee Stadium," Francis said. "It was on Feigner's second pitch that Gordie hit that ball over that fence so far that it is probably still rolling. He was an incredible athlete."

Even after Howe retired from the NHL, he was still an athletic marvel. In the early 1980's, Francis set up an oldtimers tour in the Connecticut area with proceeds going to the youth hockey groups. The only stipulation he had was that teams had to be made up of over-30 year old players because the former National Hockey Leaguers thought there might be some potential for trouble if they had to play some young hot shots looking to make a name for themselves. "We didn't want to play any young teams because we weren't out to prove anything," Francis said.

The tour went smoothly until near the end when one hockey group decided to use players in their early 20's. "We hadn't lost a game until that point and we knew they were going to try to whip our ass," Francis said. Sure enough, a youngster crosschecked Howe from behind and knocked him to the ice. He then made the ghastly mistake of saying to Mr. Hockey, "You had better be careful old man."

"I'm on the bench thinking, Uh, oh!" Francis recalled, laughing.

Three shifts later, Howe hit the youngster with the force of a charging bull. "That guy thought he was in hell," Francis said, laughing. "And Gordie said, '"Don't you ever call me an old man.' When he was chasing him down, I thought he would kill him."

Francis believes Howe could have played in the NHL beyond the age of 52 when he finally retired. "He didn't retire on his own," Francis said. "He wanted to keep playing. At the All-Star game at Joe Louis Arena, he was really the first star of the game at age 52. He played a great game. I just think people thought it was time for him to retire because of his age. But he wasn't ready then."

What Francis is sure of is that one of the most special moments in Howe's life came when he met and married Colleen.

"Gordie was lucky she came along when she did because he was such a nice guy he would have done everything for nothing," Francis said. "He needed someone who could be a little tough to represent him and to negotiate for him. He was just too nice of a guy to do that."

Francis became one of Colleen's friends when he became general manager of the Hartford Whalers. At the time, Howe was under contract with the Whalers to do community service. He found Colleen to be firm, but fair.

On the first day he arrived in Hartford for his new job, he received a call from the Boston Bruins saying they were exercising their option to return the Howe's son Marty to Hartford. The Bruins had acquired him a year earlier, but the two teams had agreed that Boston would have return privileges.

As soon as Colleen received word that Marty would be returned to Hartford, she was on the phone to Francis asking for a meeting to discuss Marty's future.

"She came in with a big folder," Francis recalled.

She said, "Where does Marty stand now that he's coming back to Hartford?"

Francis gave this answer: "There are a lot of players here that I've seen play, but I don't know them well enough yet. Marty will be treated like the rest of them. He will come to training camp, and he will have the same opportunity to make the team as everyone else. If he doesn't, then he will have a choice. He can go to the farm team in Binghamton or we can negotiate a buyout. But until he competes, we really don't have anything to talk about."

At that moment, Francis was sure Colleen would react. But she smiled and said, "I'll tell you something, Gordie said you are the most honest man he knows and what you just told me is fine with the Howes."

Marty did earn a Whalers roster spot that following season, but more importantly, Francis and Mrs. Hockey developed a lasting friendship.

He believes that Colleen often did not receive a fair assessment of her work because she was a woman operating in a man's world.

"She was a very good business person," Francis said. "She was well organized, and she had every bit of information at the tips of her fingers. She looked after her family. I respect her for that."

Greg Millen

Retired NHL Goaltender
Current Television Analyst

Goalkeeper Greg Millen is convinced that some of Howe's exploits after his retirement were as impressive as his accomplishments as the game's greatest player.

Upon retiring from the NHL the second time as a player at age 52, Gordie continued to do community relations with the Whalers. But he couldn't resist getting on the ice during Hartford's practices.

"The amazing thing was that he would come on the ice with no equipment on," Millen said, shaking his head at the memory. "All of a sudden, he would jump into a penalty kill situation and he would be knocking pucks out of the air and throwing them down the ice."

Millen was playing for the Pittsburgh Penguins when Howe was playing his final season in 1979-1980, and he remembers the hockey world "being in awe of Gordie playing."

"He certainly held his own obviously," Millen said, laughing. "And boy did he get a lot of room on the ice. He could hurt you, and he could especially hurt you if you touched one of his sons and everyone knew that."

According to Millen, even when Mr. Hockey was in his 50's his hand-eye coordination "was unbelievable." He had this long reach," Millen recalled. "He would push the puck over to one side, and yell, 'The puck has eyes.' He would giggle at you and he would put it right off the far post and into the net. You couldn't stop him. He drove me nuts."

Even after the Howes retired, Mr. and Mrs. Hockey were central figures in the Hartford community. "I found Colleen to be a gracious, caring person," Millen said. "She always made everyone feel welcome. That was her way. She protected the Howe's interest. But let's separate the business from the person because Colleen was a very caring person."

Editor's Note: While living in Hartford, both Colleen and Gordie were extensively involved in charitable events. In fact, they both were honored a number of times for their tireless commitment to a variety of charities and philanthropic endeavors.

On March 31, 1928 Gordon Howe was born in this home in Floral, Saskatchewan.

Colleen as a young lady. In the ensuing years she would become the most influential woman in the history of hockey.

Hockey's greatest player ever entered the NHL in 1946 at age 18. He scored a goal in his very first game against Toronto Hall of Famer Turk Broda.

Mr. & Mrs. Hockey® were married on April 15, 1953.

Gordie and Colleen enjoy their honeymoon in Fort Lauderdale, Florida.

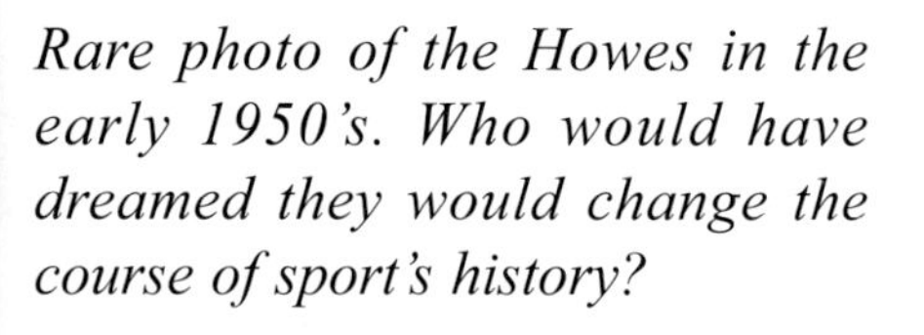

Rare photo of the Howes in the early 1950's. Who would have dreamed they would change the course of sport's history?

Many pro golfers attest to the incredible skill Gordie displayed on the links.

Mrs. Hockey® was the founder of the Detroit Junior Red Wings, the first Junior A team in the United States.

Mr. Hockey® as a young Red Wing in the 1950's when the Wings won 8 out of 10 league championships.

Many experts rank Gordie as the toughest player of all-time. If he had pursued it, he may have been heavyweight champion of the world.

Colleen signs autographs for young fans at Olympia Stadium. In 1993, she established the Howe Foundation to benefit children.

Colleen attended over 200 hockey games a season for her sons Marty, Mark, Murray, and her husband Gordie.

Colleen and Mark at Olympia Stadium in 1962. In 1972, Mark at age 16, earned a silver medal in the Olympics.

Colleen and Gordie have dedicated their lives to their children Marty, Mark, Cathy and, Murray. Today, they also dedicate their time to their nine grandchildren.

The Howe Family with the Geoffrions at the 1972 Hockey Hall for Fame induction of Gordie and "Boom-Boom". In the same year Mr. Hockey® earned the Order of Canada.

Gordie appearing in Saskatoon during a tour with Eaton's. He poses with his parents Ab and Katherine and his sisters Edna, Joan, Gladys, Vi and Helen. Not pictured are brothers Vern, Norm, and Vic.

Colleen with best friend Edna Gadsby.

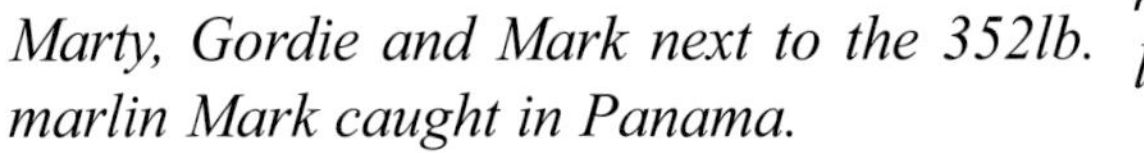

Marty, Gordie and Mark next to the 352lb. marlin Mark caught in Panama.

Gordie could have been a major league ball player. The homeruns he hit out of Tiger Stadium are legendary.

Mr. & Mrs. Hockey® once owned a herd of Hereford cattle near Jackson, Michigan.

Hall of Famers Bill Gadsby and Mr. Hockey® pose with a fan at a Red Wing Alumni game.

Colleen surprised the Gadsbys with a 25th wedding anniversary trip to Hawaii.

Mr. Hockey® drops the puck at Gordie Howe® Hockeyland. This was the first private indoor hockey rink in the state of Michigan. Colleen convinced Gordie to mortgage their home to build the arena.

Gordie, Mark Howe and special friend Chuck Robertson.

Amazingly, Mr. Hockey® played 25 consecutive years with the Detroit Red Wings. He also played 7 more seasons with Houston, New England and Hartford. In his career, he amassed more records than any athlete in history.

Gordie, Marty and Mark are the first father and sons combination in sport's history. A father's dream came true!

A great couple, Mary and Marty Howe.

Marty, the assistant coach of the AHL's team Chicago Wolves, with his parents after the Wolves won the championship.

Gordie, Mary, Marty and Colleen in Glastonbury, Connecticut.

In 1999, at the NHL Heroes game in Tampa, Mark, Gordie and Marty re-create the 20th anniversary photo of their last pro season together. They starred with the Hartford Whalers of the NHL in 1979-80.

Photo by Eric Chenoweth

U.S. Hockey Hall of Famer Colleen and Hall of Fame son Mark enjoy the enshrinement ceremony.

Photo by Lynn Gregg

Grandchildren Azia, Travis, and Nolan Howe.

"Honey" and Azia. Azia has many of the fine qualities of her grandmother.

Photo by Jim Gray

Mark Howe and son Nolan, with Gordie, riding in the Detroit Red Wing's Stanley Cup parade in 1998.

Photo by Helen Cottrell

Travis Howe, Brian Burley, Gordie, Lynnette Shady, Steve Ludzik, and Colleen. Steve was Mr. Hockey's® last coach.

Photo by Lynn Gregg

2000—Granddaughter Jade Roskam holds the trophy presented to Colleen, Gordie, Marty and Mark for their enshrinement into the U.S. Hockey Hall of Fame. Colleen was the first woman ever inducted. Also pictured are Cathy and Bob Purnell and Mary Howe.

Photo by Lynn Gregg

Colleen and Gordie with their daughter Cathy and her husband Bob Purnell at the Hockey Hall of Fame in Toronto.

Gordie, Cathy and Jaime in Augusta, Georgia at the National Barrel Race Championsips.

The Howe genes are evident in their granddaughter Jade Roskam. She is a tremendous volleyball player.

Granddaughters Jade Roskam and Jaime Greer pose with their mom Cathy and her husband Bob Purnell.

Jade, Cathy and "Honey" at Cathy's home in Montana.

Colleen Howe poses with her namesake--daughter-in-law Colleen.

Gordie and Colleen with son Dr. Murray Howe. Murray is a prominent radiologist in Ohio.

"Honey" with grandkids Gordie, Meaghan, Corey and Sean, when they appeared in a Ford television commercial filmed in 2001.

"Pee Paw" and "Honey" with Murray, Colleen and their children Meaghan, Gordie, Sean, and Corey during the filming of the Canadian documentary "Snow How!"

"Honey" and "Pee Paw" surprised their Granddaughter Meaghan with a visit to her classroom.

Grandkids Sean and Corey Howe with "Pee Paw" and the Howe's dog Rocket.

Grandson Gordie Howe with Grandpa Gordie. Both were pictured together in a card by Upper Deck® in 2003.

Photo by Aaron Howard

Ameilia Howe, Colleen, Vic and Vern Howe, and Gordie at the Howe's home in Michigan.(2003)

Photo by Jim Gray

Colleen excitedly greets her only uncle, the late Jay Ford, at her surprise 65th birthday party.

Family and friends celebrate Mr. & Mrs. Hockey's® 50th wedding anniversary, Gordie's 75th birthday and Colleen's 70th in 2003.

Steve Charendoff

Owner of Rittenhouse Archives

Although in his youth, Connecticut-bred Steve Charendoff had watched Gordie Howe rule the World Hockey Association, he didn't ponder the magnitude of Howe's greatness until his hand was consumed by Mr. Hockey's paw in their first handshake years later.

"It was a powerful handshake," Charendoff recalled. "One of the most memorable handshakes I've ever had. It was as if I was shaking the hand of someone who held *the sword*."

Charendoff has a unique perspective on Mr. and Mrs. Hockey because their paths intersected in unique settings over the past quarter century. Growing up as a Hartford Whalers watcher, Charendoff knew Gordie Howe first simply as a fan.

"What stands out most in my mind is that he commanded so much respect from the other players," Charendoff says.

When the NHL annexed four WHA teams before the 1979-1980 season, NHL players didn't know what to expect from Mr. Hockey. Remember that Howe hadn't played in the NHL since the 1970-1971 season. Many of the Howe's contemporaries had retired while Howe was ringing up points in the WHA. He was playing against a new generation of competitors and most of them knew him only by reputation. A few of them hadn't even been born when Howe had retired from the NHL the first time.

"The other players were a little cautious," Charendoff remembers, "because you never knew when the elbows would come out and work their magic. He was such a crafty player that guys still had to fear him. That was still Gordie Howe, and he still might pull out a trick or two at any time."

Charendoff knew the players better than an average fan because he was a friend to Marge Kravitz. She and her husband, Mark, owned motels and restaurants. Hence, players always knew the Kravitz family. Some stayed at the Kravitz home and some stayed at the "Kravitz motel," but all the players knew them. The Kravitz house was also a favorite player gathering spot. Charendoff remembers one Thanksgiving morning arriving at the Kravitz home and seeing many of the Whalers players and their wives, including Gordie and Colleen Howe.

"Gordie was always easy going and Colleen was always nice," said Charendoff.

Charendoff recalls that one night he went to the game with Marge Kravitz and the Howe's son Marty and his wife, Mary. After the game, the foursome was heading down to the Whalers dressing room when they realized that Charendoff was the only one in the group that didn't have the proper credential to enter the dressing room area.

The plan was hatched that guards would be told that Charendoff was Marty Howe's cousin visiting from out of town. "For about ten minutes I was a member of the Howe family," Charendoff says, laughing.

Several years later, Charendoff worked for the NHL public relations office and ran into Gordie Howe again and they swapped Hartford stories. Years later, Charendoff was employed by a memorabilia company, and was assigned to work with the Howes on a signing. He was stunned when Colleen remembered him from Hartford.

"Colleen Howe was shrewd and on top of things and she wasn't going to take any guff," Charendoff said. "She was a sweet, sweet lady, too."

Through his work, Charendoff got to know many superstar athletes from all sports. He developed a fondness for gentlemanly Sandy Koufax, and remembers Willie Mays taking time to discuss the art and strategy of playing centerfield. But Charendoff says the Howes were "at the top of the list" in terms of the professionalism they brought to their business relationships.

In any deal with the Howe family, first you had to negotiate with Colleen, who seemed to have no difficulty being a woman in a man's world. With more than 30 years logged as a player representative, Mrs. Hockey is viewed as a pioneer for women in the agent business.

Although Colleen was known as a shrewd negotiator, Charendoff said he always looked forward to working with her because she was as professional as anyone he has come across in the sports representation world.

"She approached business in a fair manner and it was what's fair for both sides," Charendoff said. "Unlike other agents, many of whom you wouldn't trust, she was interested in working with people. So many agents want to destroy the other side. That's not how she approached it. She was always easy to talk to, easy to work with."

Likewise, Howe brought the same professionalism to his business dealings as he brought to the ice as a hockey legend. He never gave less than his best effort to every business partnership he had. Charendoff said that wasn't always the case with other athletes.

"He was never put off by doing what needed to be done," Charendoff said. "He always seemed interested in being there, saying hello and being cooperative."

In an autograph world where athlete signatures have become more scrawl than cursive, Mr. Hockey is a Hall of Famer once again. "Coming from Timbuktu, Saskatchewan, you wouldn't think he would have great penmanship," Charendoff jokes, "but his signature is one of the nicest and most consistent in the industry."

Charendoff hasn't come across an athlete who shares Howe's blend of professionalism, courteousness and good humor. The only other celebrity he has met in Howe's league is Stan Lee, who gained national fame as an artist for Marvel Comics.

"They are always engaging, never seem to be in a bad mood and always happy to be where they are," Charendoff said. "Both Stan and Gordie never made a ton of money, but they both made their money doing something they love. Both consider it a privilege to live the life they have. Whether they made money or not, Stan would have enjoyed making comic books and Gordie would have enjoyed playing hockey."

Charendoff seems to accept the argument that Colleen was Gordie's all-time best line-mate.

"They balanced each other," Charendoff said. "She took care of him in ways he couldn't take care of himself, and I think he took care of her as well. It seemed like they were very good for each other."

Brian Burke

Vancouver Canucks General Manager

Shortly after Brian Burke was named president and general manager of the Hartford Whalers, his father Bill was reading names in the team directory section of the media guide when he came across the name Gordie Howe under community relations.

Bill Burke had never been an avid follower of the sport, but he certainly knew that Gordie Howe was a magical name in sports. Bill asked his son, "Do you think he's related to *the* Gordie Howe?" When Brian revealed that the man who worked for the Whalers was the same Gordie Howe who had dominated hockey for more than four decades, his dad acted as if he had never been prouder of his son.

Brian played college hockey at Providence and enjoyed a short stint in the American Hockey League. He had graduated from Harvard Law School and gone on to establish credentials as one of hockey's most respected agents. His hockey and financial expertise was impressive enough that the Vancouver Canucks hired him as an assistant general manager, and then after paying his dues, he was hired to manage the Whalers.

However, as impressive as Brian's resume was, it hadn't wowed his father until he had developed a connection to Mr. Hockey. Bill Burke said, "Gordie Howe works for my son,'" Burke said, with a hearty laugh. "I was just named president and GM of a NHL team, but that wasn't good enough. To him, Gordie working for his son was the crowning achievement."

Brian enjoyed a friendship with both Mr. and Mrs. Hockey. He spent time with them socially through the years. "What I say is that walking with Gordie is like walking with the Pope," Burke said.

"We were walking along the beach in Florida once and joggers would stop in their tracks to shake his hand. And another time Gordie and Colleen met my wife, Jennifer and me, for dinner in Vancouver. When he walked through the restaurant it was really like the Pope had arrived. He had to stop at every table. He is so gracious. He signs every autograph and poses for everyone with a camera."

Burke calls Colleen "a neat, neat lady." What he really appreciated, was the chemistry that the Howes enjoyed as a couple. It was clear to him that they both believe they found the perfect mate. They seemed to complete each other, and they shared a terrific sense of humor about their relationship.

Dr. James G. Matthews

Obstetrician

In his 50 years of practicing medicine, from 1942 to 1992, Dr. James Matthews helped 14,000 babies enter the world. Some years he assisted more than 300 deliveries at Detroit Osteopathic Hospital. But he didn't need to consult medical records to know that he registered a medical hat trick when it came to the children of Gordie and Colleen Howe.

"They had four children and I delivered three of them," Matthews said. "Colleen went into labor a little earlier than I thought on the fourth child and my associate had to deliver."

Matthews, now retired in Texas, has always had affection for Colleen because she made it a point to keep in contact with him years after she needed his medical care.

At one point, Detroit Osteopathic Hospital owned what Matthews called "a world record" for the number of consecutive births without experiencing a maternal fatality.

When a symposium and dinner was held to honor Matthews' contributions to the hospital's success, it was Mrs. Hockey who flew in to address the assembly about the care she had received under Matthews' supervision.

"I don't remember where the Howes were then, but I know she wasn't right handy," Matthews said. "She came in and talked of her experiences and going through her pregnancies with me. She was very generous with the way she expressed herself about the care she had received."

Matthews and the Howes always joked that it was right and proper that he should be their doctor because the middle initial "G" in his name stood for "Gordon."

According to Matthews, many people don't know that Gordie Howe was the first father to be allowed in the delivery room for a birth at Detroit Osteopathic Hospital. When the decision was made to open the doors to dads, Mr. Hockey seemed like a natural choice to be first.

"I'm not sure whether Colleen had to talk Gordie into doing it, probably not," Matthews recalled. "I know he didn't have any problem coming in there to see it. He was very calm."

Howe's composure was noteworthy to Matthews because some of the first group of fathers who entered the delivery room clearly had some misgivings about the program.

"One of the problems we had was that husbands would faint," Matthews recalled, chuckling. "We had two or three other hockey players who came in for their wife's delivery. I won't say who it was, but I will tell you that one of them fainted. He was supposed to be a tough guy. Gordie came in and got a big kick out of it."

Clearly Matthews admired the way Colleen Howe handled herself as a patient and as a person. As Gordie Howe's wife, Colleen's pregnancies became part of the public domain. She had less privacy than most expectant mothers are allowed. However, Matthews said Colleen was always able to find a balance to the events of her life.

"She was always stable under any circumstances," Matthews said. "There was always a lot going on with the team or with her life. There was always a lot written in the paper. She always remained steady. Whatever problems she had she was always able to work through them. This is a woman who always had her feet on the ground. All and all, she is one remarkable lady."

Bob Goodenow

Executive Director of the NHL Players Association

Bob Goodenow is a Harvard graduate and yet he believes the education he received by watching Gordie and Colleen Howe when he was a youngster has probably served him as well as the lessons he received in the Ivy League classroom.

Goodenow played on teams with the Howe's sons and spent time at the Howe home. He traveled in their company and ate at their table when he was an impressionable youngster.

"Watching them and how they acted had a major impact on me," Goodenow said. "How you need to behave was all imparted to all of us young players by the Howes. Obviously, we studied every thing they did; how they walked, talked, dressed and greeted people. We got an inside view on how a superstar lived. It's not what he said, but what he did. To be around them was a life experience for us. Either directly or sublimely, we carry benefits of having those experiences."

When Mark and Marty were playing, Mr. and Mrs. Hockey would go to the rinks, sit, and watch. There was no pretentiousness, no ivory tower attitude. "Even in Canada they would go and sit in the stands," Goodenow recalled. "I think it was so special that they were able to function as a family in and around Detroit. They showed a lot of class in handling that. Their presence was immense."

Goodenow said the Howes made a comfortable living in that era, but hockey hadn't made them wealthy. "I remember Gordie saying, in our family, hockey pays the bills," Goodenow said.

One of Goodenow's fondest memories came when he played with the Dearborn Fabrication Midget team. The team advanced to the state playoffs in Muskegon, Michigan, and Gordie made the trip to watch.

On the first night, some of the players stayed out past curfew, and when they straggled back to the hotel the word spread that Gordie Howe had called a team meeting.

"There were 17 guys crammed into this room, and Gordie started talking," Goodenow said. "He was smiling, but there was a little edge in his voice. He probably wanted to be asleep, but he obviously felt a point had to be made. He said he had done some traveling, and there is nothing wrong with going out; but you ought to be able to go out, get in all the trouble you need to get into and get off it and still be in bed before midnight."

To have Mr. Hockey lecture them on the need for some self-discipline probably influenced their thinking more than 100 chalk talks and 500 practices. "The end to that story is we won the tournament," Goodenow said. "Those words coming from him meant a lot to us."

Goodenow has unshakable admiration for Mrs. Hockey's ability to create change in the hockey world. "She was the kind of person that would listen to people say how things should be. Then, she would go about and make it happen," Goodenow said.

It was clear to Goodenow that Colleen's objective was the growth of youth hockey. "She had visions, and she was an organizer and a doer," Goodenow said. "There was a tremendous shortage of facilities and she helped in those areas and she helped with the Detroit Junior Red Wings. She cared about the sport and she had access to people from all areas of the sport. She cared about issues like practice time and coaching."

Colleen pushed for the development of Gordie Howe's Hockeyland in St. Clair Shores.

"I know all the guys I played with should have gratitude to Colleen for what she did," Goodenow said. "She helped pave the way for things to happen, and she deserves great credit for the progress that was realized at that time."

According to Goodenow, Colleen's assertiveness was crucial to her success as a dealmaker. "She knew how to push and make things happen," Goodenow said. "And there weren't women at that point and time that would get involved at that level. I know at times, because she was a woman, she ruffled some feathers because some guys saw her as a threat; but she got things done and she got people to move on some issues."

Editor's Note: In the 1960's, Colleen encouraged Gordie to mortgage their home to build the first private indoor rink in the State of Michigan. This led to a youth hockey revolution. She is also the founder of the Detroit Junior Red Wings, the first Junior A Hockey team ever in the United States.

Ron Toigo

Owner of the Vancouver Giants Junior Hockey Team

When Ron Toigo was trying to sell the idea to Mr. and Mrs. Hockey about becoming part owners of a Vancouver major junior team before the 2001-2002 season, he knew he was preaching to the choir. "They embraced the idea in a hurry," Toigo recalled. "Colleen called me and talked about her involvement in starting the Detroit Junior Red Wings years ago. Anything to help youth hockey, and the Howes would want to be involved."

Toigo previously owned the Tri-City Americans in the Western Hockey League. He had negotiated a few deals with the Howes to make promotional appearances for that team. What he learned was that when you enter into a deal with the Howes you got a relationship, not people looking to earn a dollar on the run. Toigo and the Howes became friends as well as business associates. Gordie and Toigo occasionally took fishing trips together.

Toigo was amused to find out that Howe is as legendary as an angler as he was a hockey player. "I really didn't believe there was an art to fishing. All I know is for every one I was catching, he was catching four," Toigo said. "I guess the fish know he's Gordie Howe, too." The fishing guides certainly knew he was Gordie Howe on one particular ocean excursion. Toigo recalls that both he and Mr. Hockey hooked a fish at the same precise moment and the guide went immediately to Howe.

"I said my fish is ready to come in and he said, "I'm working with Mr. Howe," Toigo said, laughing. "So a seal comes and takes my fish and Gordie lands his." What Toigo really enjoyed is the time spent with Howe because Howe's personality helps take the tension out of life.

"The Howes always had time for people," Toigo says, laughing. "They would be signing autographs, and the lines would move slowly because Colleen and Gordie would both take time with each person and make them feel special. Even when Gordie comes out to sign now, he will be there until one o'clock in the morning or until everyone is taken care of. Someone would say 'I remember you signed in Saskatoon at Eaton's in 1968 and Gordie would start talking about Saskatoon.'"

Toigo says Colleen Howe was "one of the biggest masterminds in the development of sports memorabilia," Toigo says. "She would come up with ideas like plates, bobbleheads, pictures and book signings. She developed a whole industry for Gordie that wouldn't be there if she hadn't been involved." Over the years, Colleen probably tallied as many deals as Gordie scored goals. In addition, her experience always showed and she understood promotional value and Gordie's worth. "I always found her extremely sincere and she was willing to listen if you disagreed with her," Toigo said.

He laughs, "But that didn't mean she would change her mind."

About a year after the Howes became a minority partner in the Vancouver Giants, Colleen was diagnosed with Frontal Temporal Dementia. That also came around the time the community of Abbotsford, B.C., was honoring Gordie and Colleen Howe by naming a new 600-student middle school after them. The objective was to name the new school after a person or persons who would be good role models and the Howes certainly fit that description.

In making the announcement, Board Chair John Smith and school Principal Stan Peterson noted, "The Howe name is synonymous with many of the values our school district wishes to promote in Abbotsford, values that form the basis for middle school education. The Howe name stands for a strong sense of family, the importance of positive adult role models, a commitment to community and most importantly, a positive development of children."

Toigo and the Howe's associate Aaron Howard attended the school's dedication. He recalls that it was one of the first business trips Gordie made without the woman he had been married to since 1953. "The kids treated Gordie like a rock star," Toigo said. "Part of his speech at the dedication was that this was the first time he had done this kind of thing without Colleen. He was choked up. He had a hard time getting through it, but he refocused and carried on. It was quite emotional."

In 1993, Colleen Howe founded the Howe Foundation, whose mission is to improve the quality of life for children of all ages. The Howes have nine grandchildren, and she was always interested in youth projects. She had been particularly proud to have a school bearing her name. "Colleen would have wanted to be there;" said Toigo, "because that's what she is about, doing things for kids."

Editor's Note: It is believed that Mr. and Mrs. Hockey are the only sports couple in North America to have a school named in their honor.

Tommy Ivan

Detroit Red Wings Coach
From 1947-1948 until 1953-1954

Before Tommy Ivan died in 1999, he mailed a letter to the Howes in which he spelled out that coaching Gordie had been among the highlights of his Hall of Fame career.

"So the years have passed," Ivan wrote to Mr. Hockey, "thousands of miles we have traveled together and the record books overflow with your goals and assists. Too bad they don't reflect what you meant to your teammates and tens of thousands of youngsters for whom you always had a minute to chat and to sign an autograph."

Legendary Jack Adams was Howe's first NHL coach in 1946-1947, but the following season he decided to concentrate solely on his managerial duties and named Ivan to go behind the bench. Over the next six seasons, Ivan guided the Red Wings to three Stanley Cup Championships. Ivan's reward for a great coaching job was to be named general manager with the Chicago Blackhawks in 1954. Although he held that position for 25 years, Ivan clearly never forgot the enjoyment he had coaching Mr. Hockey.

"My entire life has been spent in this great game of hockey, and above all I've had the rare distinction of being able to say I had the best and you made that possible," Ivan wrote to Howe. "I thank you, Gord, from the bottom of my heart for giving me the great privilege to say that I had the greatest all-around hockey player who ever laced on a pair of skates and boots."

"The years have passed much too quickly," Ivan continued. "One by one the great voices of hockey that would have wanted to be heard have been silenced forever—Red Wing scout, Fred Pinckney, who was responsible for bringing you to the Red Wing camp at Windsor, Ontario, and the likes of Carson Cooper who always believed in you as long as he lived. But above all, there is one voice that I would like to take liberty of paraphrasing, and I'm certain he would be pushing up on his nose with his thumb and casually hook the other thumb in his belt. That's right, I'm talking about the late great Jack Adams who would have said, 'Give the big guy my best. I thank you again Gord for making my life in hockey so rewarding. You were the greatest part of that reward.'"

Ivan was in command of the Blackhawks when Bobby Hull, Stan Mikita and Glenn Hall came to the team. He was elected to the Hall of Fame in 1974, and won the Lester Patrick Award for service to hockey in the United States in 1975. In 1994, he won the King Clancy Award for continued service to hockey.

Jack Adams

Detroit Red Wings General Manager
Signed Gordie Howe

Gordie Howe's moniker of "Mr. Hockey" is one of the most recognized nicknames in the history of professional sports; but some of his teammates and adversaries, particularly in the 1950's, knew Howe by the nickname of *Power.*

That was the name his Hall of Fame NHL coach Jack Adams pinned on Howe and everyone in the NHL understood its meaning.

Adams, who died more than 35 years ago, was a hard-nosed, old school NHL manager. He preferred rugged hockey and he admired tough competitors. He spent more than a half-century in pro hockey, starting out as a player with the Toronto Arenas in 1917-1918. He didn't dispense glowing praise and high compliments like they were penny candy. That's why Adam's words about Howe in a *Michigan Sportscene* article in December 1967 would be significant from a historian's perspective.

"He is to hockey what Babe Ruth was to baseball, only more so," Adams told writer Mike Sarri.

At that point, Adams was five years removed from being the Red Wings boss. After leaving the Red Wings in 1962, he became president of the Central Hockey League. The magazine clearly figured Adams to be in position to compare Howe with other hockey superstars.

"Impossible," was Adams' reply. "There's Gordie Howe and there are several other hockey players who are merely great. The big guy is in a league by himself."

Adams did agree to contrast Howe's specific skill set with the attributes exhibited by other players. For example, Adams believed that Howe and Maurice "Rocket" Richard used their powerful wrists on shots more than most players. "They were both smart players and knew what to do with the puck," Adams stated in the article. "But I've got to add that I feel the Canadians set up Rocket a lot more than the Wings did Howe."

Although Adams was known to be a Jean Beliveau admirer, Adams seemed to suggest that Howe had an advantage over Beliveau in durability. Adams pointed out that Beliveau's career was undermined by injuries. "So he's had a lot of in and out seasons," Adams said. "Howe has been more consistent."

Adams did believe that Milt Schmidt's ability to play through pain put him in Howe's league; he clearly concluded that Howe was the best at overcoming injuries.

"Look at Howe. He had both knees operated on, plus he had several other serious injuries and he's still managed to be the best in the league and longer than anyone else," Adams insisted.

Howe was never listed among the NHL's swiftest skaters, but Adams believed Howe's speed "was deceptive."

"He's an easy skater," Adams told *Michigan Sportscene*. "He takes long strides. But just watch him when he gets a little jump on a defenseman. He really turns it on."

Adams suggested that Howe's stickhandling knack placed him among the top puck wizards ever to grace NHL ice.

"Howe's an artist with a hockey stick," Adams offered. "His secret is that he handles the puck close to his feet and he has so many different passes. He has a soft pass, a hard pass and medium speed pass. Another thing he's got going for him is the fact that he's ambidextrous. He can pass from either side of the ice, and dig the puck out from the corners and get it out in front of the net."

In comparing Howe to proficient stick-handler, Stan Mikita, Adams said, "No contest here."

The tone of the article was that Adams felt it was no contest to compare Howe against anyone who had played in the first 50 years of NHL existence.

"Howe is the greatest player that ever put on a pair of skates," Adams said. "He's one of those athletes that come along once every fifty or one-hundred years. He's got everything going for him; size, disposition, reflexes and strength."

Remember Mr. Hockey was 39 when Adams gave this interview, and presumably, Adams would have been thinking that Howe was in the twilight of his career.

Adams died about six months after that article was published, never knowing that Howe would not hang up his skates permanently for 13 more years. Adams probably would not have been shocked that Howe was able to play beyond age 50.

Reed Larson

Former NHL Superstar

When Reed Larson stood near Mr. Hockey during the pre-game introductions at the 1980 NHL All-Star game, at the newly christened Joe Louis Arena in Detroit, he knew he was witnessing one of the most memorable moments in hockey history.

As the Red Wings lone representative, Larson received a thunderous ovation; but when Hartford Whalers standout, Howe was introduced, the applause was deafening and almost never-ending.

"I don't remember seeing a longer standing ovation," Larson said. "Five minutes is forever for a standing ovation, and this one was at least ten minutes. Sometimes it's difficult to judge but this one was that long."

The game, played on February 5, was also the first All-Star game for Wayne Gretzky, but what everyone remembers is how Detroit welcomed home Howe for his 29th All-Star appearance.

"What I remember was that he was making jokes about himself, calling himself an old man and saying he wouldn't be able to keep up with us," Larson said, laughing.

Howe would turn 52 in a couple of months, but he set up Real Cloutier for the Wales Conference's final goal in a 6-3 triumph against the Campbell Conference.

"He played very well in that game, and that's pretty wild when you think how old he was," Larson said. "I'm 47 and I know how I feel today. How did his body feel?"

Larson recalls marveling at the mastery Gordie had over the basic elements of skating, stick handling and shooting. Even at an All-Star game where the league's best players were gathered, Howe seemed like a master artisan in a crowd of laborers.

"He was really smooth and graceful," Larson recalled. "Some guys look like they are going 90 mph, and they really are. And some guys like Gordie Howe are going a lot faster than they look. What I remember is that he never bobbled the puck, he always made the right play at the right time. At his age he was playing like Jean Beliveau, never making a mistake. He was very strong and his elbows were up. I don't care who you are, you begin to shrink as you get older, but he still seemed like a big man."

Larson's other observation about Howe was that his intentions were written into his expression. "You could read him in his eyes," Larson said. "When he was mad, one eyebrow would go up."

Larson also remembers that Howe treated him as if he had been his teammate for 20 years, and still to this day he greets Larson like a long-time former teammate.

"He took me under his wing," Larson said. "First I thought maybe he was doing that because I played for his former team, the Red Wings, and then I realized that he does that for everyone."

Larson says even Howe's gaudy offensive stats don't provide the proper insight into Mr. Hockey's greatness as an athlete.

"He was the prince of our sport, and thank God for him," Larson said. "He set a precedent for how you should behave and act as an athlete, and how you treat the fans and treat your teammates. He was a role model for a lot of players for a lot of years, always positive and calm."

John Makar

Historian and Volunteer for The Michigan Sports Hall of Fame

With a degree in history, John Makar knows that finding the truth about legendary figures involves the excavation of what's below the surface. Some men putter in the garden, in the yard, or under the hood of their Chevy. However, Makar putters around with statistical comparisons and anecdotal evaluations. He has long been fascinated about sports figures as historical figures. Particularly intrigued by Mr. and Mrs. Hockey, Makar has spent time reviewing their accomplishments and contemplating their place in sports history. He has reached a couple of interesting conclusions.

First, he believes Gordie Howe is without question the top player in NHL history and believes he might be the greatest professional athlete of all time. Second, his assessment is that Colleen Howe has been overlooked for her contributions to the growth of hockey, particularly at the youth level. "When you look closely at the statistics, you start to see things," Makar says about his review of the goal scoring accomplishments of the top players in NHL history. Makar reviewed a variety of statistical categories in reaching his conclusion about Howe, but the two factors that seemed to influence his thinking the most were quality of goaltenders and penalty minutes.

In a goal-by-goal analysis of Howe's goal numbers, Makar discovered that 508 of his 801 NHL regular-season goals came against 13 goaltenders. He notes that six of those goalies were Hall of Famers. He looked at other goaltending challenges faced by other scorers, Wayne Gretzky in particular, and concluded that Howe faced a higher quality of goaltending than most of his scoring rivals faced in subsequent years.

Makar also argued that Howe's whopping penalty minute total (1,685 minutes in the NHL and 399 in the WHA) would also suggest that he was more involved at all levels of the game. A review of the NHL's all-time leading scorers shows only Mark Messier in Howe's neighborhood with more than 1,900 penalty minutes in the NHL and 58 more in his one season in the WHA. By comparison, Marcel Dionne had only 600 penalty minutes and Gretzky retired with 577 penalty minutes in the NHL, plus 19 for his one season in the WHA. "The more you look at the numbers, the more you realize Gordie Howe is one hell of an athlete," Makar said. "If he didn't take all of those penalties, he might have scored 1,000 goals in the NHL."

In addition to statistics, Makar also has been influenced by anecdotal evidence, such as the fact that a player who boasts a goal, an assist and a fight during a game is said to have achieved "a Gordie Howe hat trick." To Makar, the linking of Howe's name to that distinction would suggest a respect for the overall impact Howe had on games as a physical force and an offensive contributor. The fact that the phrase is still used almost 25 years after his retirement from the NHL is added evidence to place Howe in hockey history. "Without a doubt, he is the greatest scorer of all-time," Makar said.

Makar says, "I think Colleen's been overlooked for the work she did with minor hockey. I don't see why she shouldn't be elected to the Michigan Sports Hall of Fame. She just needs to be nominated and that's something I've considered doing. Someday she should be elected to the Hockey Hall of Fame in Toronto for her work in promoting minor hockey and getting the whole hockey system under way. What particularly impressed me was when I discovered that Colleen decided to mortgage their house to get that first hockey rink opened."

In his search about Mr. and Mrs. Hockey's place in sports history, Makar was left with his own questions. "Listening to him talk, he's such a knowledgeable person about hockey. It surprises me that no one used him as a coach or general manager," Makar said. "He knows hockey history because he lived hockey history. This is a guy who can say my buddy Terry Sawchuk…"

Makar was struck by how comfortable he was meeting Howe for the first time. "He's engaging," Makar says. "He's not full of himself. He's easy to get along with, even though he is the greatest athlete in Michigan sports history and maybe in all of pro sports history."

Makar ponders before speaking, "I've talked to other athletes whose accomplishments were significant, but they were nowhere near what Gordie's accomplishments were to his sport. And when you talk to them, they act as if they walk on water or that they could raise the dead. They act like they are doing you a favor by talking to you. I've never gotten that impression from Gordie."

Editor's Note: Mr. Hockey scored 1,071 career goals and garnered 2,589 points with 2,421 penalty minutes. He is the all-time leader for game-winning goals. In 2004, Mrs. Hockey was nominated for induction into the Michigan Woman's Hall of Fame.

Dave Lewis

Detroit Red Wings Coach
Former NHL Player

When 75-year old Gordie Howe visited the Red Wings dressing room during the 2003-2004 season, Detroit Coach Dave Lewis joked that he was going to combat a rash of player injuries by calling up Mr. Hockey to play. The media, and maybe even Lewis himself, could only be about 96 percent sure he was kidding.

Lewis was keenly aware that at age 69 he had played a shift for the Detroit Vipers against the Kansas City Blades in an International Hockey League contest. Lewis also was playing in the NHL in the 1979-1980 season when Howe established the record of being the oldest player in NHL history at 52 plus years.

"It was a thrill for me to play against him," recalled Lewis. "I think that's how we all felt. We had the Al Arbour rule when we played Gordie. You could check him, but you couldn't go out of your way to hit him."

Arbour, then coaching the Islanders, was Gordie's former teammate and good friend. He had advised his players to approach Gordie with both respect and caution. "The main reason we didn't want to touch him is that we were pretty sure we would get a stick in the face if we did," Lewis said, laughing. "Everyone was simply in awe of him."

Years later, Lewis was invited to participate in a celebrity cruise that included Mr. and Mrs. Hockey on the guest list. It was somewhere in the Caribbean that Lewis discovered Howe was a polished practical joker.

Lewis was snorkeling in shallow waters off the beach when he suddenly realized that there was a swarm of fish swimming straight at him at top speed. It seemed as if there were hundreds of them. Somewhat alarmed, Lewis stuck his head out of the water to see Gordie Howe standing over him with a bag of potato chips he had been crumbling and sprinkling into the water to attract the fish.

"My wife was crying she was laughing so hard," Lewis said. "And there was Gordie standing there with a big smile on his face. He and Colleen are just wonderful people."

Bill Gadsby

Hockey Hall of Famer
Co-Author of "The Grateful Gadsby"
Close Friend of Mr. Hockey

When Hall of Fame defenseman Bill Gadsby used to prepare to lay a heavy hit on Gordie Howe along the boards, he was never sure who was going to suffer the most from the experience. "When you hit Gordie, it was like running into a stone wall," Gadsby insists. "I hit guys who were bigger than me and never felt a thing; but when you hit Gordie or Maurice "Rocket" Richard you felt it. You could feel their body strength."

Few people have as much perspective on Howe's career as Gadsby possesses. They both broke into the NHL at the same time in 1946-1947 when Howe was with Detroit and Gadsby with the Chicago Blackhawks. Gadsby knew Howe as an adversary for 15 seasons and then as a teammate for five more. He coached him for one full season and part of another and they have been friends for more than half of a century.

"He was the best player I ever saw because he could do everything," Gadsby said. "To me, the game comes down to being able to do five or six things on the ice, like setting up goals, scoring goals, playing defensively, playing physical, and killing penalties. Gordie could do them all and do everything exceptionally well."

According to Gadsby, the major difference between Howe and other premium players through the years was the physical dominance he could utilize at all times. "He was meaner than heck," Gadsby said. "We played each team 14 times back then. If you did something Gordie didn't like, he would pick the right time to get you back and he would get you back good. It may not be this game or the next, but he was going to get you. He was intimidating."

While Gadsby acknowledges the offensive prowess possessed by Wayne Gretzky and Mario Lemieux, he believes Howe's offensive skill was at their level. Again, Gadsby believes Howe's physical presence gave him an advantage that neither Gretzky nor Lemieux commanded. "I can tell by watching a guy on one shift whether he liked to go into the corners," Gadsby said, chuckling. "And I would have loved to go into the corners with Lemieux and Gretzky. Nobody liked going into the corners with Gord."

Gadsby insists that Howe's skating ability was often underrated or misjudged by those trying to defend against him. "He was deceptive," Gadsby said. "You just didn't think a big guy could get going the way Gordie could get going. Sometimes he didn't look like he was moving as fast as he was. I watched a lot of good skaters try to catch him from behind and never make it."

Before the days of radar guns, Howe's wrist shot was judged to travel at more than 100 mph by some physics experts, but Gadsby said the real terror of Howe's shot was the quickness of his release. "I don't think I ever saw him take a full wind up for a slap shot," Gadsby said. "He could get the puck away quickly, especially if it was in close to his body. He was like Brett Hull is today. He had a little snapper. He would bring the stick back about six, eight or ten inches and *whack*! The puck was in the net. He was so strong in his arms."

Although adversaries for years, Gadsby and Howe had a mutual respect based on how they played the game. Howe admired Gadsby's blend of toughness and skill and had lobbied the Red Wings for years to trade for him. The Red Wings brass also liked Gadsby, but no deal was struck until 1961-1962. After that, the Howe and Gadsby families became inseparable. Gadsby and Howe were roommates on the road, and the families often took vacations together. "We miss Colleen's friendship," said Gadsby about how Pick's Disease has robbed Colleen Howe of her memory. "She was so good to my family through the years."

Gadsby views Howe as a Hall of Fame friend as well as a Hall of Fame player. "What a lot of people didn't know about Gordie is that he would often sit down with players who were down in the dumps and talk to them," Gadsby said. "Gordie was a good listener. If you had a problem, on and off the ice, he would talk to you about it. I saw him do it with a lot of the guys. And he and I had a lot of talks."

Like Gadsby, Mr. Hockey seemed to have a code that he lived and played by. On the ice, each man believed in a justice system that was clearly defined. Off the ice, both Gadsby and Howe believed family was the most important aspect of their lives. They were both proud of their work ethic.

"In all the years I watched Gordie play I never saw him play a bad game," Gadsby said. "I've always said he is not only the greatest hockey player of all time, but the greatest athlete."

Eddie Johnston

Former NHL Goalkeeper

Although the phrasing hadn't yet become mainstream, Gordie Howe clearly was among the first NHL players to be identified as a power forward. Other than Maurice "Rocket" Richard, no other player in Howe's era came close to matching Howe's ability to use his strength and snarl to enhance his scoring touch. That is certainly what goalie Eddie Johnston recalls about Howe.

"Defensemen never liked playing against him because he always had his elbows in their kisser," Johnston said. "And the messages Howe sent out early in his career with that fight against Lou Fontinato had an effect. Everyone said, 'Let's not wake him up.' Nobody wanted to go near him."

The Howe vs. Fontinato battle on February 1, 1959, established Howe as the toughest man in hockey. Johnston was still playing for the Edmonton Flyers in the Western Hockey League, but this fight was considered a clash of titans and details of the Howe triumph over steel-fisted Fontinato stampeded across the hockey world at a furious pace. Defenders had always given Mr. Hockey plenty of room, but after that heavyweight scrap, Howe seemed to have license to use his strength even more. Howe didn't have to fight much after that bout. By the time Johnston had arrived in the league in 1962-1963 with the Boston Bruins, Howe had essentially franchised the art of driving to the net with purpose. In Johnston's rookie season, Gordie was 35 and led the NHL in goals and points. He was also the league's MVP.

"He was a bull," Johnston said. "If there was no room to shoot the puck, he would try to jam on you and drive you and the puck into the net."

What impressed Johnston even more is that such a rough competitor could also play a finesse game. He was fascinated that Howe could shoot the puck right-handed or left-handed. He had never seen a hockey player shift the stick in his hands while a play was evolving. Goalies became mesmerized, or at the very least frozen, by Howe's switch of hands. It was like watching a huckster beat you with a pea and shell game. You become so intent on trying to watch the pea that you forgot to notice that you are getting stripped clean.

"He probably got 50 or 60 goals like that in his career. A puck would be in his skates and he would kick it to the other side," Johnston said. "Then he would shoot it left-handed and it would catch you by surprise."

Johnston was also amused that this monstrous force on the ice was such a gentleman when the game was over. Said Johnston, "He's one of the classiest men I ever met and what an ambassador he's been for the game."

Rick Dudley

Florida Panthers General Manager and Coach

What Rick Dudley remembers most about the night that 69-year old Gordie Howe played a 46 second shift for the Detroit Vipers in an International Hockey League game on October 3, 1997, is that Howe came close to scoring.

Starting on right wing, Howe headed straight to the Kansas City Blades net after the puck was dropped and Vipers defenseman Brad Shaw's long shot deflected off Howe's leg and toward the net. Blades netminder Jon Casey was forced to make a save.

"Can you imagine what the reaction would have been if that puck had gone in?" said Dudley who had given Howe the opportunity to play in his sixth decade. Howe began his professional hockey career in 1946-1947, and closed out his career with Hartford in 1979-1980.

Dudley was the Vipers general manager that season, and he had known the family since playing against Mr. Hockey in the World Hockey Association. When it became clear that Howe was interested in achieving one more milestone, Dudley was happy to oblige. "Gordie Howe has meant so much to the game," Dudley said. "He was such a classy guy. Why shouldn't we have given him this opportunity?"

Colleen Howe negotiated the deal with Dudley for Mr. Hockey's appearance. "She was very organized, very business-like," Dudley said. "She knew exactly what she wanted from the Gordie Howe Viper Night. I found her easy to deal with. She had her ideas, and if it was something you didn't agree with, you had to really convince her."

What Dudley remembered most about Mrs. Hockey's participation in Howe's IHL appearance is that she invited a child suffering from an incurable illness to be part of the day's festivities. The boy was alongside Colleen constantly during the day. "I found her to be a very compassionate person. The time she spent with the child was impressive," Dudley said. "In seeing her compassion, I realized that her business side was completely different than her personal side. I grew to admire her a great deal."

The capacity crowd of 20,182 that viewed the game included ageless Minnie Minoso who played in six different decades as a major league baseball player. The crowd chanted "Gordie, Gordie, Gordie" as he was introduced to play in a professional game for the first time since April 11, 1980, when he retired as the games all-time superstar.

Probably another record was established that evening; longest period between appearing in a minor league game and in a professional hockey game. Before playing for the Vipers, Howe's last minor league appearance was in 1945-1946 when he played for the Omaha Knights in the United States Hockey League.

When Howe was asked what the night meant to him, he joked, "Survival. I am suffering from arthritis and maybe this will be a little pat on the back to people suffering from arthritis." Dudley said it was a special night for him because he had always been a Howe fan.

Like most Howe opponents, one of Dudley's favorite memories involved a physical confrontation when they played against each other in the WHA. Dudley was playing for the Cincinnati Stingers when he and Howe traded assaults during a game in the 1970's. As Dudley recalls it, Mr. Hockey high sticked him and he countered by running Howe along the boards.They glared at each other, and some unpleasantness was exchanged, but it didn't escalate into combat.

After the game, the media came to Dudley for an explanation because he was not a player who shied away from a tussle.

"But really it was simple," Dudley said, laughing. "I couldn't win no matter what I did. I didn't want to be the player who beat up Gordie Howe and worse I didn't want to be the player who got pounded by a 48-year old player. Gordie was still a strong player then and he could still throw me. If he respected you, he left you alone. If he didn't, he could be cheap with you. I didn't want to get on Gordie's bad side."

Dudley paused, "But I know I will always cherish the fact that I played against Gordie Howe."

Editor's Note: The original idea for Gordie Howe to play in 6 decades was actually Wayne Gretzky's. When Wayne played with the Los Angeles Kings, he thought it would be great for Gordie to play in a game with him. The idea was abandoned because another NHL team held Mr. Hockey's rights.

During the intermission of the record setting Viper game, Colleen arranged for their family to be at center ice to enjoy the historic festivities.

Dr. Murray Howe

Son of Gordie and Colleen

Whenever Dr. Murray Howe is asked what it was like to grow up as the child of Gordie and Colleen Howe, his one word response is always, "awesome."

"I lived an idyllic childhood," says Howe, a physician in Sylvania, Ohio. "Off the ice my dad was laid-back, loving, gentle, encouraging, helpful and humble."

Sometimes he offered advice, like when he said, "Murray, never read your own press clippings; you might start to believe them."

This was a hockey family, but Colleen and Gordie wanted their children to explore their own interests and talents. They didn't expect every member of the family to make their living in hockey. When Murray Howe was cut from the University of Michigan hockey team, he remembers his father's reaction was "Well, I guess you will have lots of time to study now."

"No pressure, no worries. He was just always a great dad," Murray says.

Gordie Howe probably taught his four children more about being a spouse and a parent than he did about hockey.

"He always set a good example by helping out around the house like doing dishes, vacuuming, making beds, or doing yard work," Murray said. "He loved doing chores, whether they were for his kids, his wife, his neighbors or a stranger. He might clean the windshield of the next car while pumping gas or shovel your driveway."

Murray always believed his father was happiest when he had a chore to accomplish. "When you grow up in Saskatoon, Saskatchewan, you learn that it is more important to be generous and helpful than to drive a fancy car," Murray says. "He has never forgotten that and that's why I admire him."

Even with all the attention that hockey received in the Howe house, hockey was still second to family.

"Mom was always our biggest fan," Murray said. She was 100 percent devoted to her children and her husband, supporting our dreams and applauding our achievements. She taught us to stand up for what was right, to defend those who couldn't defend themselves and to never give up. We learned to have faith in God, and rely on His power to make things right."

Murray says his mom "always had a million ideas floating around in her head, as well as a great sense of humor."

He always looked forward to telling his mother about his day because he knew she would respond with compliments, insights and observations that would always keep him entertained.

"Even today, her personality seems to overpower her dementia," Murray Howe says. "Though it is difficult for her to speak, she listens intently, laughs easily and greets us with the same enthusiasm as when we were kids. Somehow, she rises above herself to give us what she has always given us, which is absolutely everything she has."

Colleen Howe

Wife of Murray Howe
Daughter-in-Law of Gordie and Colleen

Colleen Howe had vision to see things the way they could be as opposed to the way they were. Her family says that applied as much to household chores and decorating as it did to the hockey and business world.

Whether you were looking to remodel your home or restructure minor hockey, Colleen Howe was the right woman for the job.

"I will never forget the year we bought our place on Bear Lake in Kalkaska, Michigan," says her daughter-in-law Colleen. "It was January 1994 and it was cold! I had big plans to renovate the place, seeing that the shag carpet and 1970's décor didn't quite fit my style. After learning that our pipes, well and septic system were frozen and could not be thawed until April, I knew it was time to call in an expert."

The call went to her mother-in-law, not a plumber. "Colleen, would you have time to come over to Bear Lake and help me?" she asked, already knowing the answer.

Over the next three months, Colleen would make the trip from Traverse City on Saturday mornings to pitch in as both a laborer and advisor.

"We would plan, dream and work the day away," Colleen remembers. "After spending the night, we would do it all over again. We had an elaborate bathroom system set up with plastic bags or three-foot mounds of snow."

What seemed like work back then is now a cherished memory for Murray's wife who clearly enjoyed her mother-in-law's company.

"We had jugs of water for drinking and washing with, and well-timed trips into town," said the daughter-in-law. "And we had each other."

Meaghan Colleen Howe

Daughter of Murray and Colleen Howe
Grandaughter of Gordie and Colleen

One of the most fascinating aspects of Colleen Howe's personality is that she was as equally comfortable playing with her grandchildren as she was negotiating six-figure promotional contracts. Most know Colleen's reputation as a negotiator, but Meaghan Colleen Howe's (16 years old) words about her grandmother show the other side of Colleen that many did not know.

"If there is one thing I have acquired from my grandma ("Honey"), besides her spontaneous ideas and love of life, it is her generosity and care for others. There has never been a time that I have seen my grandma put anybody down if it was not for the protection and good of others around her.

"Going shopping with my favorite partner, Grandma and I would not necessarily hit every store in the mall, but enjoy and make the best of our time together. Once I said I liked a pair of shoes and they remain in my closet to this day. Every time I put them on, my grandma's bright laugh and smile race through my mind.

At night, I sometimes think about how I am not able to spend as much time with "Honey" anymore as I desire to.

"As Honey has taught me, though, worrying won't get me anywhere; I am so fortunate to still have a person like her in my life. It is amazing that despite her illness, my grandma still has her spunk! *I love you, 'Honey!'*"

Gordie Howe

Son of Murray and Colleen Howe
Grandson of Gordie and Colleen

Several interview subjects for this book have suggested that Gordie Howe is a man everyone wants to have as his or her grandfather. Words from his namesake suggest that the reality of Mr. Hockey is the same as the perception.

"What is there to say about the great Gordie Howe? He is the one I was named after, who has accomplished so much, yet asks for nothing in return of his great deeds. His legacy goes far beyond the hockey arena. While I have only lived to see the aftermath of his awesome career in hockey, I have seen greater things done by him.

"It isn't uncommon to see him playfully tweak the ear of one of the young kids, and then when he is caught, he laughs and acts innocent." He also takes many hours out of his life to make appearances, give speeches and sign autographs," says Gordie (14 years old). "His ability to continually stand by my grandma throughout the time of her disease and still be able to hold himself up is another thing that I aspire to. My grandpa is a great man. "This is why I am proud, when someone asks my name, to say, 'Gordie Howe.'"

Corey Mark and Sean Murray Howe

Sons of Murray and Colleen Howe
Grandsons of Gordie and Colleen

"Our grandpa is a great person! He is funny, hardworking and loving. It's so easy having a grandpa like him, because his life is great material for school reports (until the teacher catches on). We love you Grandpa!" Corey Mark is 11 years old and Sean Murray is 6 years old.

Jim Loria

President and Part Owner of Sioux Falls Stampede

Before Sioux Falls hosted the 2002 United States Hockey League All-Star game, event organizers decided to survey local folks about who should be chosen as the honorary host and ambassador for the game.

Flash cards were made and the images and names of Bobby Orr, Bobby Hull, Neil Broten and others got varying reaction from survey takers. However, when Gordie Howe's name came up, the reaction was instant and overwhelming."

"Everyone reacted to Gordie Howe's name whether they knew hockey or not," Loria said.

Today, Loria is so thankful they decided to survey fans because the decision to bring Howe as the centerpiece for the All-Star festivities created one of the more memorable events in the city's sports history.

"When we brought in Gordie it electrified the whole city," said Loria. "The whole city was abuzz. For this type of market, it was like bringing in Babe Ruth."

Loria has a long history in junior and professional hockey, and he says Howe's goodwill visit to the city "was some of the most touching moments I have witnessed in this business."

"There was a love affair between the people of the city and Gordie," Loria said. "A lot of athletes take the support of the fans for granted. But Gordie doesn't forget he's there for the people."

Loria recalls that he called Power Play's office and spoke to Del Reddy, the Howe's agent and business manager, inquiring if Gordie could sign some special items for 20 local sponsors of the event. He could not believe it when Reddy called back and said, "Mr. Hockey wanted to inscribe what you needed on every item."

"Every note was handwritten and that blew everyone away," Loria said. "The fact that this man would take the time to do this is why he is truly regarded as Babe Ruth here."

The USHL is the premium league for America's teen-age players, with many of their players expected to earn college scholarships. Howe wanted time with the players.

"He was busy, but he wanted to be at the early morning practice and he went up and introduced himself to each of the players, like he really needed an introduction," Loria said. "They wanted to know how he did things, and he showed them. It was like he was giving them the tricks of the trade."

Having worked with many athletes, Loria expected Howe to want to stick to a strict itinerary. Instead, he found Mr. Hockey wanted more time at his stops, not less.

"If he walked down an aisle, you had to budget an hour because you knew if he saw a child he was going to stop and talk to that child," Loria said.

Loria recalls a humorous story about the event that sheds some insight on Howe's attitude about handling all matters with the right touch of etiquette, which is clearly something that Colleen always stressed. An older man had stood in line to have a photograph signed and he asked Howe to inscribe it to him and his wife.

Gordie said he wouldn't sign it because the man said he wanted his name first on the inscription.

The autograph seeker seemed crestfallen because Gordie wouldn't sign his item, and Gordie finally made his intent more clear.

"What I said was I wouldn't sign it if your name is first," Gordie said, laughing. "I'll be happy to sign it if I can write your wife's name first. I always believe in writing the wife's name first."

Everybody laughed, but the moment was perhaps a window into the amount of respect that Gordie believes a man should have for his wife.

Although Gordie ruled the NHL with an iron fist, he has always had a mild-mannered demeanor. Mr. Hockey didn't always like how General Manager Jack Adams managed the Red Wings, but he only confronted him one day. That's when Adams made some disparaging remarks about Colleen and the wives of teammates, Ted Lindsay and Marty Pavelich.

What Gordie told Adams was that while Colleen didn't score goals and have assists, she served the Red Wings interests by making Gordie's life easier. He pointed out that not only did Colleen take care of the children and run the house, but she also would often get everyone out of the house just so Gordie could have a nap before the game. He ended the conversation by saying if Adams didn't want to respect Colleen's role, he was "sure some other organization would want me."

Although Loria spent just a couple of full days with Howe, he came away feeling he had known him forever.

“I think everyone would love to have Gordie Howe as their grandfather,” Loria says. “You could just see him sitting by the fire telling stories.”

Even today, Loria says, the event is still talked about in the city. About 900 people showed up to hear him speak at the banquet. Howe’s luggage was lost en route to his destination and all he had for the first night’s activities were the clothes on his back. That may have overwhelmed others, but not Mr. Hockey. He pulled on a USHL All-Star jersey and went to the banquet. He seemed touched by a 20-foot action photo that a local company had turned into a banner.

When Howe started his speech, he talked about how his wife had been ill and he had considered not making the trip.

“But when you make a commitment,” he said, “you should live up to that commitment. And I’m so glad I came because you have all made me feel so welcome.”

Two years later when Loria read a *Sports Illustrated* article detailing the impact of Colleen’s diagnosis of Pick’s disease, he put together a timeline in his head and realized that Howe was dealing with the shock of Colleen’s illness at the time he came to Sioux Falls.

“All of this was coming down on him and yet he came here and did all that he could for us,” Loria said. “It just makes you want to cry.”

Frank Selke

Former Managing Director of the Montreal Canadiens

The late Frank Selke was such a respected figure in the NHL that it was considered a major news story when he said in 1960-1961 that Gordie Howe was the best player in NHL history. Selke made this declaration after witnessing Howe play about 45 minutes for the Detroit Red Wings in a 6-4 loss to the Canadiens.

"I've been watching the game as a fan and club official for more than 50 years. I've never seen anyone combine as many faculties," the *Associated Press* quoted Selke as saying. "He is simply the greatest."

Howe played on a line with Alex Delvecchio and Vic Stasiuk. Detroit had just acquired Stasiuk from Boston. Howe even played defense on penalty killing. He was also on the ice for every minute of every Detroit power play. He seemed to be everywhere at once. "His big assets are his almost superhuman strength, powerful wrists, passing, playmaking, shooting and stickhandling," Selke was quoted by the *Associated Press* as saying. "There doesn't seem to be anything that Gordie can't do, except sit on the bench."

The *Associated Press* considered Selke's opinions about Mr. Hockey significant enough that an entire story was dedicated to his words. Remember this story was datelined Montreal where Maurice "Rocket" Richard had retired the season before and Jean Beliveau and Bernie Geoffrion were competing for the scoring championship. It required fortitude to exalt Howe above all Montreal Canadiens' legends.

"Howe is a composite of some mighty fine stars, including Maurice Richard, Jean Beliveau, Milt Schmidt and many others," Selke said.

In the loss to the Canadiens, Howe had drawn three assists and according to the *Associated Press*, "narrowly missed" several goals. The Red Wings were a fourth-place team that season. Selke said, "He didn't know what the Wings would do without him and there isn't another club in hockey that depends on one so much," Selke continued. "He's an inspiring leader."

In the story, Selke said it was the best game Howe had ever played at the Montreal Forum. "He doesn't play a bad one often," Selke was quoted. "But this time, he seemed to dominate the entire rink."

Helen (Howe) Cummine

Gordie's Sister

Gordie Howe always enjoyed a reputation as a prankster and jokester in the NHL and that skill was developed back in Saskatchewan right along with his hockey talent.

His sister, Helen, remembers that Gordie and her other brother, Vic, who also ended up playing in the NHL, used to have fun at the expense of his sisters when they were youngsters. Helen and her sister, Joan, were frequently the targets of their boyish humor.

"They would tie us up to the banister leading upstairs and then get out a brick of ice cream," Helen recalled. "They would cut it in two, and sit and eat it in front of us, saying when we got loose we could have what was left."

Of course, there was never any ice cream left by the time the girls had worked through the knots.

When Helen and Joan were older and started to work, they packed their lunches the night before. Gordie was still coming home for the summer at that time, and he hadn't gotten over his love for a good prank. When they bit into their sandwiches the next day, they realized that Gordie had removed the meat from between the bread.

"He got a big laugh out of that," Helen says.

Helen recalls going to see Gordie play and sitting with his then girlfriend Colleen.

"I remember when I saw her I was very nervous as there was this beautiful blonde with a nice outfit and fur coat," Helen said. "I felt like a bumpkin and I wasn't sure how to act during the game."

Helen wasn't sure how she should act around such a seemingly sophisticated woman. She was thinking maybe she should just sit quietly, rather than be herself. Maybe Colleen sensed Helen was feeling inhibited because when Gordie was rudely body-checked Colleen quickly made Helen feel more comfortable.

"Colleen stood up hollering and offered a few choice words," Helen said, obviously amused at the memory. "Then I knew it was going to be easy going after that."

After Gordie and Colleen were married, they would return to Saskatchewan for the summer and Helen remembers spending time with her sister-in-law. One time the two women were visiting the Saskatoon Golf and Country Club when Colleen asked Helen if she wanted to drive Gordie's new automobile.

"Of course I said yes even though I had no driver's license," Helen said. "I did well until I was crossing the narrow bridge and hit a taxi. I was *sooooo* scared to face Gord and explain what happened to his car"

But Gordie didn't get mad. He just shook his head, and said, "You two are crazy buggers."

Helen says her sisters Vi and Gladys were older and had left home much earlier, but Gladys remembered that Gordie would come over and help on their farm with the pigs, chickens, hay and cows. When the chores were completed, Gordie liked to play horseshoes every night.

What the Howes remember most is that it was always fun when Gordie and Colleen were around.

"It's just such a sad way that they have to spend their remaining years with such tragedy," Helen says. "He takes good care of her with some help."

That commitment to his wife may say more about Gordie Howe than any of these stories do.

Joe Fallon

Upper Deck's Group Manager for Product Development

On a Saturday morning, Joe Fallon was at work putting together a 30-card Mr. Hockey insert series for Upper Deck's next hockey card offering when the phone rang. The Howe's agent and business manager, Del Reddy, was double checking with Fallon about some images that were needed for the set. After talking with Reddy, and much to Fallon's surprise, Gordie was on the line. He said he had been looking through his photo albums; he believed he had some unique photos that might make it a better set.

"You always get a very personal touch from Gordie and you don't get that from a lot of athletes today," Fallon says.

Wrapped around that story is the explanation of why Upper Deck decided to sign Howe to an exclusive deal as a spokesman for their trading cards.

"If you look at our roster of players, we sign up the best athletes and Gordie is the best," Fallon said. "We have Michael Jordan and we have Tiger Woods and Gordie certainly fits into this category."

As much as Upper Deck was interested in landing professional hockey's all-time top goal scorer (1,071 regular-season and playoff goals in NHL and WHA), company officials were probably more interested in partnering with Howe's image. Few retired athletes generate as much goodwill as Mr. Hockey.

"Today's athletes are rushed and they seem to have a lot on their minds," Fallon said. "Gordie takes time with everyone. He tells stories, asks questions and interacts. He gets to know the person even if it's just a 30-second meeting. It's always a genuine meeting."

The other attraction to Howe is that his popularity might be even stronger today than it was when he played. "Interest in him never wanes," Fallon said.

Fallon said he has asked Mr. Hockey that when he meets modern athletes would he please "point them in the right direction" when it comes to signing autographs.

"He makes sure everyone loves that signature and recognizes his signature," Fallon said. "He has a trademark on his name, but he could really have one on his signature. It's so distinct and legible. It's really a sharp contrast from the younger guys."

Fallon laughs when he remembers his first meeting with Howe. "My first thought was what huge mitts he has," Fallon said. "Then you talk to him for a minute and you realize that he's not like other athletes. We see superstars in sports, not so much hockey but in other sports, and that's how they act, like superstars. "Gordie is not like that at all. I was left with a very positive feeling after meeting Gordie. It made my week."

Lynn Gregg

John Glenn High School Administrator, Photographer and Friend

Although Mr. and Mrs. Hockey's name transcends the sport of hockey, it's necessary to witness a public appearance to appreciate the drawing power of the famous couple.

Lynn Gregg can testify to that fact. Lynn was a new assistant principal at a Westland, Michigan, high school in 1995 when he was approached by one of his former students about possibly using the sale of Gordie and Colleen's book *and...HOWE!* for a fundraiser. The former student was Del Reddy, who also happened to be the agent for the Howes.

Gregg had taught Reddy at Stevenson Junior High School, and their mutual enjoyment of photography had helped them form a strong teacher-pupil bond. However, that didn't mean that Gregg eagerly embraced the idea of the fundraiser.

"With a new leadership team at the helm of the school, we tended to tread cautiously when approached by vendors and individuals who stopped by the school to promote fundraising ideas and products," Gregg said. "It's all too easy to get 'burned' by someone who doesn't necessarily have your school's best interests in mind."

In addition, Gregg also knew that a school could have just so many candy bar drives, Christmas wrap sales, etc., before everyone becomes weary of the sales pitches that promise to raise funds for various clubs and teams. Reddy's enthusiastic and unique plan was at least novel enough to pique his interest.

As far as Gregg was concerned, the chief selling points were that the Howes would appear at the school and sign every book that was sold, and the school would receive half the proceeds.

"The only requirement was that it was necessary to pre-sell 500 books," Gregg said. "I took Del's proposal to Neil Thomas, the principal. He was skeptical at first. Five-hundred books could be a difficult sell, even in a community like Westland that loved hockey."

Thomas weighed the pros and cons, and finally decided that the lure of having Mr. and Mrs.Hockey in the school, coupled with the possibility of raising plenty of money, was too good.

"But privately he wondered if the Howes would really show up for a signing at his school," Gregg said. "What would happen if they were no-shows on the signing day?"

After meeting with Thomas, Gregg, Reddy, and his Deputy School Superintendent Greg Baracy, Superintendent Duane Moore gave approval. Administrators designated it as a school fundraising effort. The school had two months to sell 500 books. Sales teams were organized. The local media was notified. "Everyone was excited at the prospect of John Glenn High School hosting hockey's greatest couple at the school for a fundraiser," Gregg said.

The school sold numbered tickets that entitled the bearer to a book and to meet the Howes on signing day. Soon the momentum of the project carried the school well beyond their 500-book goal. By the time the Howes were scheduled to arrive, John Glenn had sold more than 1,000 books. Their profit would be over $16,000.

The signing was scheduled for 1:00 in the afternoon on a December afternoon, and school officials took great care in planning for the event. Welcome signs were made, the local media was invited and a line formation set-up had been designed to minimize confusion.

"Principal Neil Thomas was still worried about what would happen if the Howes didn't show up," Gregg recalled. "Even though Del had assured everyone that the Howes would be appearing as planned, there was always some skepticism. After all, none of us really knew the Howes. We hadn't even met with them face-to-face."

The Howes and Reddy arrived at noon, an hour before the signing began.

Principal Thomas' nervousness was evident as he greeted Gordie, "Hi, Gordie, I'm Neil Howe, the principal."

The Howes quickly put everyone at ease with their congenial and relaxed manner. According to Gregg, Gordie and Colleen Howe seemed genuinely excited to be at John Glenn High School.

"The book signing was an incredible event," Gregg said. "Lines of people snaked through the halls of John Glenn. Mr. and Mrs. Hockey personalized each book they signed. They posed for pictures when anyone asked, and they chatted with each person as they individually signed each book."

It took about five hours for the Howes to autograph 1,000 books.

"When the last person had gone through the line, the Howes were obviously tired," Gregg said. "They had signed their names over 1,000 times and had written numerous personalized greetings as well. We expected that they would be on their way home, but that isn't what happened."

Administrators were shocked and thrilled when the Howes and Reddy accepted the administrator's offer of a dinner in the school library.

"The Howes stayed another two hours with our school staff, posing for pictures, telling stories about their careers in hockey, and genuinely joining in with our celebration for the exciting day that we had," Gregg said. "We were just so amazed that the Gordie and Colleen would spend so much time with us and that they were so willing to give so much of themselves. Also, we were very thankful that Del Reddy helped us bring the Howes to the school for a memorable day for the community."

Editor's Note: Colleen Howe established Power Play Publications in 1995 and self-published *and...HOWE!* Mr. and Mrs. Hockey, with associates Del Reddy and Aaron Howard, traveled to over 400 book-signing appearances throughout North America. Over 125,000 books were sold. These sales helped generate nearly a million dollars for various charities. Because the book is the best selling self-publicized sports autobiography of all-time, the Howes, Reddy and Howard were inducted into the Self-Publishing Hall of Fame.

Larry Gach

E Series Marketing Manager
Ford Division Commercial Truck

Mr. Hockey's ability and insistence on playing through pain is a given in his promotional work as much as it was in his playing days.

Ford Motor Company executive, Larry Gach, came to realize that one morning in 1999 when Howe was scheduled to be the celebrity at a golf outing on a mountainous course in Colorado. This was a major event for Ford because guests included the top 12 dealers from that region of the country.

When 71-year old Howe awakened that morning, he discovered his chronic knee problem was flaring up again. "His knee was locked up pretty severely," Gach recalled.

The Howe's agent Del Reddy, who traveled with Howe to the appearance, expressed his concerns to Gach about Gordie's condition. Gach said, "Gordie you need to go see a doctor, get some therapy or get some medicine. The guy just refused treatment as he probably did his whole life. He just wanted to play through the pain."

Howe couldn't drive the ball without almost toppling over. Instead of going home, Howe opted for the plan of dropping his ball around the green to allow him to chip and putt with his group.

"He just wouldn't walk away from his commitment, which was such an unbelievable thing," Gach said. "The dealers are never going to forget that day."

That weekend also provides evidence to the name recognition Howe has even in non-traditional hockey areas. The guest dealers had generated about 40 percent of the region volume, and Gach wanted to throw them a party they would never forget. He decided a theme of "legends."

He surveyed the 12 dealers about who they considered legendary figures in history, sports, stage and screen. Their top responses were General George Patton, Marilyn Monroe and Gordie Howe. "Fortunately, Gordie was still around and we were able to bring him in," Gach said.

What makes Gach's survey interesting is that the dealers were from Phoenix, Las Vegas, Denver, New Mexico and other areas in the West. That isn't exactly hockey country, and yet five of the 12 listed Howe on their ballot.

To appreciate how big this party was, consider that the entertainer hired was legendary comedian Carl Reiner.

Among the memorabilia given out to dealers in drawings were Michael Jordan autographed shoes, an oil painting signed by Marilyn Monroe, a painting signed by Princess Diana and a sweet 1955 Thunderbird.

"Gordie was fantastic," Gach said. "That's because Gordie will hang out and talk to everybody and he won't move on until he has to. He will continue to keep talking to people as long as there are people there."

Howe understood how important this event was to Ford, which is why he insisted the morning after the party that he was going to play golf whether his knee would cooperate or not.

Since that weekend, Gach has worked with the Howe's business manager's Reddy and Aaron Howard to have Mr. Hockey appear at some other special events. One of his favorite stories is that Gordie was a guest at his home in Utah. Says Gach, "What a thrill it is to drive up to my house with Gordie Howe and to have my then four-year old take out his net and have Gordie show him how to score."

Sue Foster

Life Partner of the Late Carl Brewer

Former NHL players, Carl Brewer and Gordie Howe, two men with vastly differently personalities and philosophies of life, formed a friendship late in life based on their common belief that unfairness always needed to be remedied.

Brewer made no secret of how surprised and pleased he was that Mr. Hockey stood beside him and five other players in a pension legal fight against the NHL league president John Ziegler and the NHL Pension Society that yielded a $40 million verdict in favor of the retired players.

"Gordie's endorsement sent the message to one and all that the matter was serious and that there was strength and commitment behind it," said Foster who had been Brewer's life partner since the late 1970's.

Before he died in 2000 at age 62, Brewer had a letter delivered to Howe. Actually, it was more of a story or an interpretive writing exercise that he entitled, "The Greatest Story Ever Told."

In that story he depicted how the congenial, trusting Gordie Howe had been taken advantage of by General Manager Jack Adams and the Detroit Red Wings during his tenure with the club.

Then he talked about how more than 100 retired players, including Hall of Famers and stars, gathered at the Ramada Inn in Toronto to discuss whether to sue the NHL for pension money they believed belonged to them.

"Out of that gathering of the clan emerged a very different Gordie Howe," Brewer wrote.

"When it was roll-call time, Gordie walked to the front of the room and signed up to serve on the organizing committee."

Later, Howe would attach his name to the lawsuit that was filed in 1991. Brewer noted that Colleen had been surprised at how strong Gordie felt about this issue, although both Colleen and Gordie had long been outraged that his pension after 26 NHL seasons was $14,000.

"In my estimation, Gordie played a pivotal role in the eventual outcome of the court case," Brewer wrote. "Gordie's presence and commitment were highly profiled."

Mr. Hockey and Brewer had been Red Wings teammates in 1969-1970, but they had been rivals for most of their careers. Brewer had been an eccentric boat-rocking, anti-establishment athlete during his career and Howe had opted to be far more politically correct. Nevertheless, they did share a common outrage for how former NHL players had been treated.

"For me personally, it was a joy to watch Gordie and Carl, as middle-aged men, distanced by decades from their hockey rivalries and experiences, simply become friends who enjoyed one another's company as they were kibitzing, while sharing laughs and memories together," Foster said.

Brewer, Foster and the Howes spent much together, in the courtroom and away from it. They became close friends.

"Colleen and Gordie were a real inspiration. Their genuine warmth, generosity, caring, and sincere interest and concern for others touched us both deeply," Foster said.

Foster and Colleen Howe had commonality because both were intelligent, cause-oriented women who were comfortable navigating in a man's world.

"Hockey needed more brave and feisty ladies like Colleen Howe," Foster said.

She admired Colleen because she had "personally observed Colleen being rudely and unfairly criticized and chastised" for playing the role she did in the relationship.

"Colleen was often forced to be the 'heavy' to confront people and situations to protect her husband and her family," Foster said. "In the male dominated world of hockey, her critics seemed unable to understand or appreciate her courage in standing up for her family when necessary."

Foster said she came to understand what Gordie Howe stood for when they had lunch together in a courthouse cafeteria during the Court of Appeal process.

A passerby came along and asked Gordie how he liked being on the road again. Howe shyly answered, "It's not so bad. I'm used to it."

Then, after a moment's pause, his face lit up and his eyes glistened and he said, "And we're together, that's what's important."

Foster had known Brewer since 1963, and she was heavily invested in the pension fight. She said both she and Carl believed it was "monumental" when the Howes threw the weight of their name into the fight.

As expected, the NHL appealed the players' victory, and when the case reached the Ontario Court of Appeals on September 21 through September 24, 1994, the Mr. and Mrs. Hockey probably had their greatest impact.

Brewer wrote that he believed that the appellate judges "were not judging, but rather being judged by the greatest of them all. And they knew it!"

He opined that with Mr. Hockey in the courtroom, the three judges "did not want to come up short. They were fans."

"Gordie and Colleen sat in the courtroom throughout the entire proceedings," Foster recalled. "Carl and I both believed that their presence was pivotal and placed a heavy burden on the three judges to do the right thing."

Based on the Appeals Court upholding the $40 million verdict, Brewer wrote, "About 1,400 hockey players owe a debt of gratitude to Gordie Howe, the greatest of them all."

Upon Brewer's death, Hall of Famer Frank Mahovlich said Brewer should be in the Hall of Fame as a builder because he did more for the game than some owners and managers.

No present day players attended Brewer's funeral, and Brewer's friend Gordie Howe said that current players should erect a plaque in his honor because Brewer had done more for them then they will ever know.

Editor's Note: Both Colleen and Gordie, along with Sue Foster and Carl Brewer, dedicated an enormous amount of time toward the pension case. Colleen was very instrumental in securing archived documents that helped swing the case in favor of the players.

Throughout his incredible 32 season career, Mr. Hockey® dominated the game both offensively and defensively. He scored 1,071 goals, earned 2,589 points and appeared in a world record 29 all-star games.

Photo by Frank Lennon

At age 46, Gordie amazed the Russians with his dominance in the 1976 Team Canada Series.

Gordie and Mark race up the ice. Along with Marty, they led the Houston Aeros to consecutive world championships.

Mr. & Mrs. Hockey® received the March of Dimes National Lifetime Achievement Award in 1997.

The Howes enjoy a break at their Northern Michigan cottage in Bear Lake.

Mrs. Hockey® has always been her family's biggest supporter.

Remarkably, Gordie skated with the NHL's Hartford Whalers at the age of 52! He played all 80 games and led the team into the playoffs.

Colleen, THE POWER MAKER, in a 1981 congressional run. (Hartford, Connecticut.)

Mr. & Mrs. Hockey® helped create a hockey stronghold in Hartford, Connecticut.

Mr. & Mrs. Hockey® have attended hundreds of charitable events raising millions of dollars for good causes.

The Howes and Gadsbys. They have been great friends for almost 50 years. Colleen was the first to encourage them to author their own book "The Grateful Gadsby."

Rich Devos, legendary Amway® co-founder, with Colleen and Gordie at an Amway® business meeting in Grand Rapids. Mr. and Mrs. Hockey® rate Rich as the finest speaker they have ever witnessed.

Dr. Jack Finley with his wife, Genevieve, their daughters and the Howes at a Detroit Red Wing's game.

Mr. Hockey®, Mark Howe, Coach Bill Dineen, Colleen and Marty Howe. Gordie received the MVP award at age 45. Subsequently, the trophy was named after him.

President Gerald Ford offers words of encouragement to Colleen during her 1980 Congressional run.

Houston Aero's goalie Ron Grahame embraces Gordie after the Aeros clinched the Avco Cup Championship. Mr. Hockey® was MVP that year at age 45.

Colleen surprised Joe Dimaggio with this special painting by Curt Flood that she purchased at a charity dinner. It brought a tear to his eye.

Mr. Hockey® and the extraordinary Bobby Orr. Bobby has said many times that Gordie is the all-time greatest player.

Colleen and Gordie with WHA and New England hockey pioneer Howard Baldwin. Today, with partner Karen, Howard heads, a leading film company in California. Baldwin is endeavoring to make a major motion picture about the Howe's remarkable lives.

Mr. & Mrs. Hockey® with friends Donna Martyn and her husband Bruce. Bruce was the legendary Hall of Fame broadcaster for the Detroit Red Wings.

Always devoted to their family, Colleen and Gordie are terrifiic grandparents. They once drove 400 miles just to see their grandson play in a soccer game!

The "King of Talk Television," Larry King, with hockey's greatest duo at the WHA reunion in Windsor, Canada. The special event was organized by WHA co-founder Dennis Murphy.

Photo by Clifford Cook

Photo by Jim Gray

Fox 2's Jennifer Hammond interviews Mr. Hockey® during a break at a Red Wing Alumni game.

Photo by Aaron Howard

Mrs. Hockey® self- published their autobiography "and...HOWE!" The book sold over 125,000 copies and raised nearly a million dollars for hundreds of charities.

Photo by Alex Cabildo

Neil Thomas, Mr & Mrs. Hockey®, Lynn Gregg and Duane Moore at John Glenn High School. Colleen presents them with a proceeds check for $16,000.

Self- Publishing Hall of Famers Del Reddy, Colleen and Gordie Howe® at John Glenn High School in December, 1995. Mr. & Mrs. Hockey® autographed 1,000 "and...HOWE!" books at the incredibly successful fundraiser. Colleen and Gordie, along with Del and Aaron, travelled to over 300 events and elevated "and...HOWE!" to become the best selling, self-published sport's biography of all time.

Photo by Lynn Gregg

Photo by Del Reddy

Colleen & Gordie with Hockey Hall of Fame executive Ron Ellis. They appeared with Walter Gretzky at his 1996 charity golf outing in Brantford, Ontario.

Dave & Fil Ponzi, power seller Jerry D'Adamo along with the Howe's pose for a newsletter photo for the Italian American Club of Livonia. The Ponzis hosted an "and...HOWE!" book fundraiser.

Photo by Clifford Cook

Vinnie Johnson, Mark Howe, Colleen, Gordie and George Blaha at the Michigan Jewish Sports Hall of Fame dinner. Mr. & Mrs. Hockey® received the Alvin Foon Award for Lifetime Achievement in Sports. Colleen was the first woman ever honored.

Photo by Clifford Cook

Colleen, Lorraine Mahoney, Carl Brewer and Sue Foster in Toronto. This group changed hockey history with their tireless efforts battling the NHL pension suit.

Photo by Del Reddy

Colleen & Gordie with the late Sarah Geng. The Howes toured Canada raising awareness about the crippling effects of arthritis.

Photo by Aaron Howard

Gordie with "Slapshot King" Reed Larson at the Heroe's All-Star game in San Jose.

Mr. Hockey® with "Mr. Goalie" Glenn Hall. Many historians rank these superstars as the all-time greatest at their positions.

Photo by Del Reddy

Photo by Douglas Tanglewood

Mr. & Mrs. Hockey® with good friends the Hanson Brothers. Dave Hanson, Steve and Jeff Carlson.

Photo by Eric Chenoweth

Both Mr. & Mrs. Hockey's® extraordinary efforts helped launch a youth hockey revolution.

Photo by Jim Gray

Colleen congratulates Gordie on playing in his sixth decade with the Detroit Vipers. Six decade baseball star, Minnie Minoso, attended the historic occasion.

Dr. James Marion Gray

The "Babe Ruth of Hockey" with Babe Ruth look-alike, "Buster the Babe."

Mr. Hockey® becomes "Dr. Hockey" after receiving an honorary doctorate at the University of Regina.

Photo by Del Reddy

Many believe that Colleen should be inducted into the Hockey Hall of Fame in Toronto for her pioneering contributions as a builder of the sport.

Photo by Del Reddy

Mr. Hockey® with Commissioner Gary Bettman on hand for the banner raising cermony to commemorate the 1997 Detroit Red Wing's Stanley Cup Championship.

Photo by Jim Gray

Mr. Hockey® pictured as a Detroit Viper in 1997--at age 69!

Pam Howard, Dr. Jim Gray, Colleen and Ebony discuss the Howe's move from Traverse City to metro Detroit.

Photo by Helen Cottrell

Mr. & Mrs. Hockey® receive a standing ovation while preparing to drop the ceremonial puck at an Ottawa Senator's game.

CBC Sports Journal producer Terry Walker with Mrs. Hockey® and Del Reddy. After consulting with Power Play's Reddy, Mr. Hockey® and Aaron Howard, Terry created an outstanding profile for Canadian national television that highlighted Colleen's impact on the game of hockey.

Photo by Helen Cottrell

Gerard Hisala

The greatest hockey player with the greatest basketball player, Michael Jordan, at the ESPY award's show in Las Vegas.

Photo by Helen Cottrell

WG Authentics, Mike Brown, with Mr. Hockey® at Power Play's office. Mike is a true leader in the memorabilia industry.

Photo by Helen Cottrell

Mrs. Hockey® and Mike Ilitch, Jr. face-off at the Red Wing's Alumni game while Mr. Hockey® drops the puck.

Youth hockey sponsors extraordinaire Chuck and Jean Robertson of Paddock Pools. The Robertsons attended a dinner where the Howes were honored for their non-smoking advocacy.

Superstar stylist and friend Sherri Van Antwerp poses with Mrs. Hockey® .

Detroit Junior A Red Wing's coach, Carl Lindstrom, with team founder Colleen.

Greg and Sandra Rollheiser

Worldly Fans from Saskatoon

Greg Rollheiser's employment as a construction equipment distributor for CAT has allowed his wife Sandra and him to become world travelers. Furthermore, they understand that Gordie Howe's name translates into greatness in any language.

Starting from a CAT dealership in Saskatoon, Greg was asked to manage a dealership in Kyrgyzstan, which had gained its independence after the disintegration of the Soviet Union. With modernization on the rise in that region of the world, there is heavy demand for CAT heavy equipment. A German company hired Greg to set up a Cat dealership in Turkmenistan, another country that gained independence after the Soviets embraced democracy. This is a country of 5-million inhabitants, located north of Iran, with access to the Caspian Sea. This is a desert country, and hockey should be the farthest sport from anyone's mind.

One day Greg and Sandra Rollheiser were strolling through a small bazaar in Ashgabat, Turkmenistan, when a native shopkeeper asked if the they were Americans. It was a difficult conversation because the Rollheisers didn't speak the native Turkman language. They communicated through broken English and the bits of Russian that the Rollheisers had learned during their travels. They finally made the shopkeeper realize that they were Canadians, not Americans.

"He asked what city, and we were sure he would not know Saskatoon," Sandra said. "But as soon as we said Saskatoon, he became very excited and began to shout 'Gordie Howe, Gordie Howe.'" The Rollheisers were stunned because even the Americans they had run into didn't know where Saskatoon was.

Still to this day, the Rollheisers don't know the man's name. "And we probably couldn't pronounce it even if we did," Sandra said. He calls the Rollheisers "Mr. and Mrs. Saskatoon, and they call him Mr. Gordie Howe."

Whatever his name is, he's probably the only man in Turkmenistan with an autographed picture of Mr. and Mrs. Hockey. The Howes sent it to him after hearing the story.

Dennis Murphy

Founder of More Pro Leagues than Anyone in History

As the former WHA co-founder and commissioner, Dennis Murphy witnessed many instances of Mr. Hockey bailing out his team with enormous goals and awesome passes. However, his favorite Howe story involves the night Howe came to his rescue with a perfect speech.

In 1975, the Howe-led Houston Aeros captured their second consecutive WHA Championship with a four-game sweep against the Quebec Nordiques. At the age of 47, Howe had played magnificently in the post-season, posting 20 points in 13 games, including 5 goals and 3 assists in the Quebec rout.

"Gordie had absolute charisma and the fans loved him, even in Quebec City," Murphy remembered.

Howe's popularity turned out to be a blessing to Murphy when he went to award the Avco Cup to the Aeros at center ice. It's customary, maybe even demanded, in Quebec that all public addresses, even in the sports arena, start with some words in French, which is the principal language of the region. Murphy was certainly aware of that, and one of his French-speaking employees had penned some French phrases for him to use in a pre-game speech. It had been well received, and Murphy felt as if he had followed protocol.

But protocol wasn't on his mind during the wild post-game scene on the ice, especially when television producers informed him that he had only two minutes to present the Avco Cup to the Aeros before the network switched to regular programming.

"I got to the microphone and started to make the presentation to Gordie and the fans started to boo like hell," Murphy recalled.

Startled, Murphy turned to his friend Howe and asked why everyone was booing him.

"Because you are supposed to say something in French before you say something in English," Howe reminded him.

Realizing his error, but having no prepared statement, Murphy again turned to his friend for help. "What do I say?" Murphy asked.

Howe quipped that he should say, "Parlez-vous francais?" not realizing that Murphy would do exactly that. The crowd booed even louder when Murphy asked fans if they spoke French.

Howe realized it was time for action, and he grabbed the microphone and addressed the crowd in his friendliest of tones. "It was one of his most eloquent speeches," Murphy recalled.

"He said my friend Murph is an American, and he's a nice guy, but he doesn't know our customs. When he was through, they gave him a standing ovation."

When Howe was on the ice, he liked to shovel up some ice shavings with his stick and flick them on his friends. Murphy remembers as they walked across the ice, Howe gave him another flick, "bailed you out again Murph."

"Besides being the greatest hockey player ever, he is just such a great human being," Murphy said. "He relates so well with people. I can't say enough good things about the man."

It's not difficult for Murphy to remember his emotions when it became clear that the Howe family was coming to the WHA. "We were ecstatic," he said.

"Bobby Hull was electricity for the WHA," Murphy said. "He brought 61 guys over from the NHL with him. When Gordie came with his two sons and Colleen, he gave us a second shot. Then when Wayne came along it was a third shot."

Murphy recalls that around the WHA office Houston Coach Bill Dineen was "known as 'foxy Dineen' because he pulled a few fast ones."

But Murphy said Dineen had plenty of help because Colleen was doing the preliminary work.

"Colleen was the power behind the scenes," Murphy said. "She was a great business lady. Gordie played hockey and she kept everything else in order."

Murphy said WHA officials knew that NHL officials were trying to woo Howe with a lucrative offer of a job as a league goodwill ambassador. Murphy believed Howe was offered $500,000 and there were rumors about that, but Howe says the discussions never reached the point where a dollar amount was revealed. Regardless of how much Howe would have been paid, Murphy was convinced that Howe would have come to the WHA because his only objective was to play with his two sons.

"How many people can say they played a pro sport with their children?" Murphy said. "Maybe you could believe there was a chance someone might do it in baseball, but hockey is a rough game. It's amazing what he was able to do. The other thing that is often forgotten is that Mark and Marty were good players in their own right.'

Murphy points out that both Mark and Marty would have been significant contributors, with or without their dad on the team. Anecdotal and statistical evidence supports that contention.

At 18, Mark scored 38 goals in 76 games to win the Lou Kaplan Award as the WHA Rookie of the Year and was named a second-team All-Star. This wasn't shocking because at 16 Mark had been talented and poised enough to earn a spot on the U.S. Olympic team for the 1972 Games in Sapporo, Japan.

He was a teenager during the Aeros' back-to-back championships, and yet he posted 19 goals and 22 assists for 41 points in the 27-playoff games needed to secure those championships. He led all WHA playoff scorers with 10 goals and 22 points in 1974-1975. In 426 WHA games, he produced 208 goals and 296 assists for 504 points.

After the NHL annexed the WHA, Mark enjoyed a stellar career that will draw him consideration for the Hall of Fame. In fact, many of those who played with and against him wonder why he hasn't already been honored.

He played wing in the early days of the WHA, but he had settled into defense by the time he arrived in the NHL. He was named a first team NHL All-Star three times, including in 1985-1986 when he led the NHL in plus minus with an astonishing $^{+}$86. Over a six-year period from 1982-1983 to 1987-1988 he had a combined plus minus of $^{+}$293. Mark Howe is generally regarded as one of the best American-born players in hockey history.

Marty is 13 months older than Mark and spent his entire career on defense. Although overshadowed by his father and brother, Marty was actually one of the most accomplished defenseman in the WHA. He was named a second-team WHA All-Star in 1976-1977 and over a five-year period from 1975-1979 Marty totaled 63 goals, a noteworthy total for a defenseman. In 1976-1977, Marty had 17 goals and 28 assists. His penalty minute totals were always similar to Gordie's numbers, suggesting that Marty inherited much of Gordie's grit.

It always bothered the Howes that Marty didn't get more recognition. Anyone who ever asked Mrs. Hockey about the Howe family hockey successes would receive as much information about Marty as they would about Mark.

"Marty was probably one of the most underrated players in the league." Gordie has often said, "Marty played with a special inner strength that gave him the ability to analyze the game."

Gordie also likes to point out that in races down and back up the ice, Marty would beat him and Mark.

"Marty was a steady player," he said. "There was nothing too flashy about him, but he was a fast and smooth skater."

Today, Marty is coaching for the Chicago Wolves in the American Hockey League.

Murphy argues that the WHA was like Marty in that it never got enough credit for its talent level. "We had Hull, we had Gordie and we had Wayne Gretzky. We hit the trifecta."

In the 62 exhibition games that were played between the WHA and NHL from 1974 to 1978, the WHA won 33, lost 27 and tied 7. The Howe-led Aeros beat St. Louis in the first NHL-WHA exhibition on September 26, 1974.

"Gordie was such a physical marvel," Murphy said. "Maybe other people can give you an argument, but I think Gordie was the greatest player. If you ask Bobby Hull, he would say the same thing."

Editor's Note: Colleen Howe dramatically changed hockey history when she realized that the fledgling World Hockey Association did not have the same age restrictions as the National Hockey League. Previously, underage players were precluded from playing in the NHL. The historic discovery allowed her teenage sons to join their father with the Houston Aeros. This opened the doors for other underage stars to get their early professional start. Those who benefited included Wayne Gretzky, Mark Messier, Mike Gartner and others. Mrs. Hockey also engineered the first ever multi-player, multi-year family deal in pro sports history.

Ron and Charlotte Grahame

Former WHA and NHL Goaltender and Wife, An Executive with the Colorodo Avalance

---

The only vintage hockey photo in Charlotte Grahame's office shows her husband Ron being hugged by Mr. Hockey after Ron captured the Gordie Howe Trophy as the World Hockey Association playoff's Most Valuable Player in 1975. To her it is the perfect reminder of what she considers the best days of her husband's professional career. "It makes me want to cry when I talk about how good the Howe family was to us back then," Charlotte said. "They treated us like we were members of their family."

Ron was a 23-year-old rookie out of the University of Denver and Charlotte was his girlfriend, and not yet his wife, when he joined the Houston Aeros in 1973-1974. By their own admission, they were starry-eyed and perhaps a bit nervous in this new hockey environment. "The first time I met Gordie I kind of stood in front of him in awe," Ron Grahame recalls. "He came over to me and said, 'Hi, I'm Gordie Howe.' I was so speechless and dumbfounded. *I'm thinking of course you're Gordie Howe*. I didn't know what to say or do, but Gordie always has this way of making you feel welcome."

The Aeros trained in a suburban rink with no seating, and there were no special amenities for players. Nevertheless, to Grahame, from Victoria, British Columbia, it seemed like a shrine as he dressed every day with legends such as Gordie Howe, GM/Coach Bill Dineen, Assistant Coach Doug Harvey and goalie Wayne Rutledge. "With Doug Harvey being the forerunner of the great defensemen and Gordie telling stories every day, it was hard to believe where I was," Grahame remembered. "These guys were pretty good rivals in their day, and here they are swapping stories about the good old days."

Grahame was up and down between Houston and their Macon Whoopies farm team, but the inconvenience of that lifestyle was reduced dramatically by the Howe's hospitality. "Colleen used to pick me up at the airport when I would come in," Charlotte said. "And she welcomed me into her home if Ron was sent down. They are special people."

By all accounts, the Aeros family atmosphere may have played a role in their success. Mr. and Mrs. Hockey always had players over at their house, especially on the holidays. "The stature that Gordie and Colleen had was that they were celebrities, but you never had that sense," Ron Grahame said. "You never had to watch what you said around them. They showed everyone what to do and how to act, especially the younger people."

Gordie looked after the younger players on the ice as well. One of Ron's favorite videos of his playing days shows a game between Houston and Winnipeg during which Ron lost his cool with officials after giving up a goal in a five-on-three situation. "I got very upset with the referee and I went after him," Ron says. "I have me chasing after the referee on tape. I went ballistic. I didn't know it at the time, but the tape shows Gordie trying to corral me and pull me away from the referee. Gordie had his share of altercations and misunderstandings with officials, but there he was trying to be a peacemaker."

Grahame said everyone on the Aeros squad, and in the league, looked up to Gordie Howe. Even though Bobby Hull's defection from the NHL had given the WHA instant credibility, Graham believes it was Howe's decision to sign that firmly established the WHA's legitimacy. "With Gordie coming over, the hockey world really started to watch the WHA," Grahame said. "For young players, it started to look like a viable place to play. Gordie carried the league for three or four years. I wish he was a little bit younger because I think the WHA would have lasted longer, or at least more WHA teams would have been absorbed into the NHL."

While Grahame was soaking up the Aeros family atmosphere and learning how to be a pro from Mr. Hockey, he was developing into one of the WHA's premium netminders. He won the Ben Hatskin Trophy as the league's top goalie in 1975 and 1977. In 1975, he posted a 12-1 playoff record, with 3 shutouts and 2.00 goals, against average to earn the post-season MVP honors. The league had commissioned the Gordie Howe Trophy that is essentially a sculptured bust of Howe. "It's so life-like that it's scary," Grahame said. "There aren't many of these and it should go to the Hall of Fame, but I'm a little reluctant to give it up," Grahame said. The trophy is too meaningful to Grahame. The picture of Grahame and Howe hugging after the award presentation is among his most prized possessions.

"It is pretty special to win an award named after a man who has meant so much to the game," Grahame said. "To be playing with someone who has a trophy named after him is a unique experience."

Grahame said Howe always viewed himself as a teammate, not a superstar. He gave guidance and certainly protection to those around him. If there was mayhem on the ice, Howe was never a bystander. He has a sense of honor and fairness in him that wouldn't allow him to make any concession to age.

"He was loyal to his guys, but he was most loyal to his sons," Ron said. "He expected them to stick up for themselves and they really could. But there are guys out there who could tell you a story or two about an elbow to the side of the head, or a stick to the ribs they received from Gordie because they had gone after one of his sons." Grahame recalls that Gordie probably got into more tussles over Marty than Mark, because Marty played a more physical game than Mark. "Mark was more of a finesse player and he had the skill and speed to get out of trouble," Ron said. "But Marty played defense and he was in more physical battles, and he liked to stick his nose in there a little more." Grahame used to marvel at the physical and mental tools that Howe commanded.

"I have never experienced any player who had the power, the strength and the understanding of the game that Gordie had," Ron Grahame said. "He could make things happen. I marvel at the players with the great motors that never get tired. There are a few defensemen in the NHL like that today, and Gordie was like that."

Remember that Grahame was a teammate when Howe was 45 to 48 years old. "But even at that age, he was an athlete who was single-minded when he stepped on the ice," Ron said. "He knew what his job was, and he was going to do it one way, and it didn't matter what you thought of it."

When Dineen would make an effort to rest Mr. Hockey, it would make Howe mad. "He didn't want to rest. He wanted to play," Grahame said. "Resting wasn't in his mindset. He expected to be out there every second or third shift, kill penalties and to be on the power play."

When the announcement was made that Howe was going to play in Houston, there were many skeptics about his ability to play against players who were half his age. Howe answered the critics by finishing third in the league-scoring race with 100 points in his first WHA season, and placing second with 69 assists.

A quarter of a century after the WHA was folded into the NHL it has been forgotten how much talent the WHA possessed. Ron Grahame went on to play in the NHL for four seasons after the WHA's annexation, and he was convinced that the top players in the WHA would have had the same impact in the NHL. "The big difference was depth," Grahame said.

"The NHL had more talent, but there were players on every WHA team that could play in the NHL, maybe five or six forwards and three defensemen."

Gordie Howe was always matched up against the top line on the other team, and never faced inferior competition. Even in his mid-40's, Howe never found any situations where he was over-matched. "You wouldn't rate Gordie as a fast skater," Grahame said. "But he was powerful and he could get to where he needed to be and create issues when he got there. He could take over somebody and he was great at controlling the puck along the boards. And with his meanness..."

Years later, though, it's the camaraderie and not the competition that the Grahames most remember. They remained friends through the years. When the Howes ran hockey camps in spots around North America, Ron was asked to help as an instructor. The Grahames also visited the Howes at their former home in Traverse City, Michigan.

In 2001, Charlotte, who works with Colorado Avalanche organization, invited Howe to be the guest speaker at a 1,000-person fundraiser in Denver. His appearance reminded her of how thankful she is that Mr. and Mrs. Hockey entered their life 30 years ago. The message of Howe's speech that night was how athletes should give back to the community. After the speech, hundreds of people lined up to receive Howe's autograph and he signed every photo, card, program or arm that was put before him, personalizing those who wanted it that way. It was well after midnight when the 73-year old Howe was finished signing. "He has arthritic hands now, but he made sure every person was taken care," Charlotte said. "It was impressive. It was remarkable, really. People talked about it afterward."

Ron and Charlotte today are the proud parents of John Grahame who plays goal for Tampa Bay Lightning. They have had many great moments in their life, but she considers her husband's days with the Houston Aeros to be among her favorite. Ron and Charlotte say Gordie and Colleen were their mentors. "It was all about family with the Houston Aeros," Charlotte said. "It was an exceptional group of people that came together back then and Gordie and Colleen were at the heart of it. They took care of everybody and literally taught us how to be professionals. I took that with us and as I got older, I tried to take care of the young people that wanted some help. We try to do that to this day because the Howes were the people who helped us."

Bobby Hull

Superstar of the NHL and the WHA

When Bobby Hull's dad was in the mood to liven up a dull evening, he used to tell his wife that their son Bobby "couldn't play in the same league with Gordie Howe."

"My mother didn't think I could do anything wrong," Bobby says, laughing. "So that would start a family row. Howe was always my dad's favorite."

Hull's connection with Howe pre-dates The Golden Jet's debut in the NHL in 1957-1958. Hull met Howe for the first time in 1949 when the 10-year old Hull attended his first game at Maple Leaf Gardens. His encounter with Mr. Hockey that night would help shape his thinking on how professional athletes should treat fans.

It was 120 miles from Hull's hometown of Belleville to Toronto, and the Hulls didn't have advance tickets. They bought standing room for $1.25 (as Hull recalls), and Hull's father stationed young Bobby at the door with instructions that when the doors were opened, he was to race through the turnstile and up the stairs and turn right when he reached the green level. He obeyed every command, and when he reached his destination, he found himself in heaven. He was standing above the south end blue line, where the Maple Leafs defended twice. His hands were outstretched to save a spot for his mom and dad. For a minute or two, it seemed as if he and the well-dressed ushers were the only people in the building. If he had lived a better moment at that point in his life, he didn't know when it had been.

"If there had been sun coming down from the top of the building I would have had sunburn at the top of mouth I was in such awe," Hull recalled "Everything was pristine. The ice was so smooth and the blue lines were so blue." It was a perfect evening because his dad's favorite player scored right in front of them. Hull says he has a vivid memory of Howe coming over the blue line "and snapping his big arms and goaltender, Al Rollins, picking the puck out the net behind him."

"My dad turned to me and said, 'and Robert when you shoot the puck like that you can play in that league,'" Hull recalled.

With time to kill before the next train to Belleville, the Hulls hung around in the lobby until the players started exiting the dressing room. When Howe came out, Hull's father, tore a top off a cigarette package, gave Bobby a stub of a pencil and told him to go ask Howe for an autograph.

Young Bobby Hull was too shy. He hid behind his father's pant leg. "I watched the goings on, saw that kids were getting autographs and coming back from a visit with Gordie with their heads still on their shoulders," Hull recalled, laughing. "Pretty soon I ventured over and said, 'Excuse me, Mr. Howe, but can I have your autograph.'"

Howe rubbed Hull's head, and signed with great patience and care, Hull remembered. The moment had a lasting impact on Hull's attitude about being a professional athlete.

When Hull became a star, he always remembered that moment when fans would ask him for autographs. "My mother used to say don't forget these fans are the most important people in the business," Hull said.

When Howe and Hull played in the NHL and WHA at the same time, it was no coincidence that there were many photographs snapped of the two chatting together before hockey games. They genuinely liked each other, and perhaps more importantly, respected each other's skills and talents.

"It was mutual admiration for one another," said Hull who entered the NHL in 1957-1958 when Howe was a 12-year veteran. "He knew that I was out there to play as hard as I can within the rules and Gordie was the most competitive guy I ever played against."

After The Golden Jet had spent some time in the league, the Blackhawks started to use him matched up against Howe's line. As a left wing, Hull was always matched up opposite Mr. Hockey.

"Whenever we would line up for face-offs, he would always have something positive to say or something not about hockey," Hull recalled. "But once the game started, he knew he didn't have to watch his back and I knew he would let me play my game." Clearly, both men enjoyed the challenge of playing against each other.

"Some of the greatest games I played were in that old Olympia playing head-to-head against Gordie," Hull said. "They were fabulous games because we were just trying to out-skate, out-think, out-pass, out-position and out-shoot each other. It was quite a spectacle."

Hull and Howe became such good friends that Hull was able to get to know the Howe family as well. He knew when he came to Olympia the Howe's son Mark would be at the door of the visitor's dressing room waiting for him. Remember, Gordie was a right-handed shooter and Mark shot left-handed so Gordie's sticks were no good to Mark, but Bobby's were perfect. "I used a short stick and Mark really loved the way I had them hooked," Bobby said, laughing. "I always made sure I fixed up a good one for Mark. He was always a good kid."

Hull also respected Colleen. "She was a powerhouse with that family," Hull said. "She was the force behind the scenes. All Gordie ever wanted to do was play hockey. He just wanted a jacket with a winged wheel on it and the chance to go fishing every summer. Colleen helped Gordie realize it was big business."

Hull knew Howe well enough that he began to believe that Gordie would want to play in the WHA even before the Houston Aeros plan was revealed. He knew Howe would be intrigued by the idea of playing with his sons. He knew that the Howe boys, even as teenagers, would probably be able to handle the competitiveness of the WHA. Mark Howe was a star with the Toronto Marlies, and Marty was projected to be a solid pro defensemen.

Before the WHA, Hull actually had urged the Winnipeg Jets to draft the Howes, figuring as Colleen had, that you couldn't really stop the drafting of 18-year old players, even though the NHL was drafting 20-year olds. "When I brought it up, they said, we aren't drafting a 45-year old guy," Hull remembered. Hull couldn't convince them and as the Howe boys were drafted and it became clear that Gordie planned to play with them, it was Hull who got the last laugh. "When they had all the Howes, what I said was well now the only one left you can draft is Colleen," Hull said.

Hull had no doubt about Howe's ability to play at 45. He wasn't surprised that Howe finished third in the point race that season with 100 points, and was second among assists with 69. Hull finished fourth that season with 96 points. It's forgotten sometimes that Mark Howe had 38 goals his first season as an 18-year old, and Marty was a 19-year old regular defenseman on a team that won the WHA Championship that season. Mr. Hockey had eight assists in the four-game sweep over Chicago in the finals.

They played together, along with all the other premium WHA players, in the 1974 Team Canada vs. Soviet Union series. They didn't play together on the same line. Hull played with John McKenzie and Andre Lacroix and Gordie played with Mark and Ralph Backstrom. The Soviets won that series 4-1-3, even though Team Canada gained a tie and a win in the first 2 games.

Thirty years later Bobby Hull still believes that tactical blunders, two of which involved the use of Mr. Hockey, prevented the WHA players from either winning or at least producing a much better showing.

Bobby Hull had netted a pair of goals in a 3-3 tie in Game 1 in Quebec City, and Team Canada won 4-1 in Game 2 in Toronto. That's why Hull is still mad to this day that management and coaches decided to rest several players in Game 3, including Gordie Howe, Frank Mahovlich and goalkeeper Gerry Cheevers.

The Soviets won Game 3 by an 8-5 count in Winnipeg. "I'm convinced that it would have been different if they hadn't decided to rest Gordon and the others in Game 3," Hull insists.

Although the Soviets were from a closed society, they all understood Howe's aura and reputation. He was 46 years old at the time, but the Soviets were still intimidated for good reason.

"He was still tougher than a night in jail," Hull recalled. "One of those big Russians hit Mark one time, and the next shift he wished to hell that he hadn't. Gordon went all the way across the rink and gave him everything he had, stick, elbows, fist and shoulders."

After Game 1, the Soviets were constantly double-teaming Hull, and he wondered why Team Canada coach Billy Harris didn't put him on a line with Howe in Moscow. The Soviets wouldn't have been able to double-team either one of them then. When the series was over, Hull and Howe were the top two scorers with nine and seven points respectively. Before the series, some members of the media had wondered whether Howe, at 46, would be able to handle the Soviet's speed. By the end, it was clear to all that he had been one of the best players in the series. He was used in every key situation, including penalty killing.

"Gordon played very well in Moscow," Hull remembered.

He actually left after one period of Game 2 because of an injury. He really had his seven points in just six full games, plus a period.

Hull has always said Howe was the best player he has ever seen.

"Over the years I've always insisted that consistency is the mark of true professionals and year after decade after decade Gordon Howe was there and didn't disappoint anyone," Hull said. "He's still the strongest guy I ever played against and he could play 35 to 45 minutes and play in every situation. Furthermore, Gordon Howe never did anything detrimental to the game."

When Colleen Howe was diagnosed with a dementia that was robbing her of her ability to recognize even her own family, Hull expected that Gordie would insist upon being heavily involved in her care.

"He's the kind of guy who will look after her," Hull said. "That's the character in him," Hull said. "When everything is gone by the wayside, the only thing that remains is character and Gordon Howe has character."

Harry Neale

Former WHA and NHL Coach

As the countdown for Gordie Howe's 1000th professional goal was winding down in early December of 1977, New England Whalers coach Harry Neale looked down the bench during a game and noticed Howe had both gloves off and his right hand submerged in a bucket of ice.

"He had an arthritic wrist and quite often during games he would have a pail of hot water on the bench so he could reach back and put his hand into it to keep his wrist feeling good," Neale recalled.

Knowing this wasn't Howe's usual treatment, Neale inquired about the extent of the injury. Howe pulled his hand out of the water to reveal a grotesquely purplish, swollen mass of flesh that had only a slight resemblance to a human hand. "You could hardly even see the knuckles it was so swollen," Neale recalled. Alarmed, Neale asked Howe when he had been injured and was told it had been a couple of games before.

"Gordie," Neale said, "you had better get that looked at because there might be a fracture there."

"There might be," Howe said. "But I will be all right."

Two games later, Howe beat goalkeeper John Garrett of the Birmingham Bulls for the 1000th goal of his professional career not really knowing or caring whether his hand was fractured or not. Having played through so many injuries throughout his career, it was quite appropriate that he would be fighting through another for such a monumental goal.

Howe's milestone goal against Birmingham on December 7, 1977, made him the first major league player to net 1,000 goals. The total included regular-season and playoff goals from the NHL and WHA. The game wasn't televised, and there was only a modest amount of media coverage.

"If you equate greatness with longevity and superior play there is no match for Gordie Howe," Neale says. "I think he was the greatest, and under those circumstances I don't even think there is a challenger."

To appreciate Mr. Hockey's durability, consider that Howe played an amazing 96.9 percent of his games in his 26 NHL seasons. In one nine-season period from 1961-1962 to 1969-1970, he missed only two games. Earlier in his career, he missed only six games in one eight-season period, and all of those came in the same season. What makes Howe's durability even more remarkable is that he was a competitor who liked to play in traffic. When there was violence in a NHL game, Howe was usually in the middle of it.

"I would not seriously try to convince anyone that Wayne Gretzky, Bobby Orr or Mario Lemieux weren't as good as Gordie because that's an argument that will go on forever and will never be decided," Neale said. "All I know is that I had Gordie when he was 49 and 50 and he was a phenomenal athlete. I don't know if he had more talent than the guys that I just mentioned. But his passion for the game was unequaled."

Neale says it's "criminal" when Howe doesn't get enough credit for his WHA stats that include 174 goals and 508 points in 419 games. In the season he turned 50 he netted 34 goals, and he was always matched up against the top wingers and defensemen in the WHA.

"We overrated our league, but the NHL underrated our league," Neale said. "When I left the Whalers to go to the Vancouver Canucks, I know the Whalers were a much better team than my Vancouver Canucks. We were a young team, and I know I looked at the team I left and wished I had about seven of them on my Vancouver team."

According to Neale, the league's best WHA teams, such as the Whalers and Winnipeg, was as good, if not better, than the bottom-third teams in the NHL.

Some athletes become mentally worn out near the end of their careers, but that never happened to Gordie Howe. "He always was able to keep the game at the top of his priority for a lot longer than most," Neale said. "He loved to be in a rink. He never took a day off and he loved practice."

Neale had idolized Howe growing up, and when he took the job with the Whalers he had just one worry. "Oh my god," Neale thought to himself. "Don't tell me that I will end up being the one to tell Gordie that he can't play anymore." As soon as he got to the team, he knew that worry wasn't a consideration. Howe led the team in scoring in 1977-1978 and had 10 points in 14 games to help New England reach the Avco Cup Finals where the Winnipeg Jets beat the Whalers.

Even at an advanced age, Howe often seemed like a lion among lambs. "When you played against him, you would say look at the dirty son of a gun," Neale said. "But when he was on your team, you knew that was simply how he played."

Howe was known for counseling younger player not to seek retribution immediately for a cheap shot. He believed it was always more effective to wait until the opposing player had forgotten about the incident. If he hadn't forgotten about it, he would probably spend too much time worrying about when it was coming. And Howe practiced what he preached in that regard.

On New Year's 1978, with New England playing at Cincinnati, Howe's son Marty moved in from defense in an effort to keep the puck in the zone. Robbie Ftorek was coming along the boards, and tipped the puck past Marty and then lifted his stick to get it over Marty's stick. In the process, Ftorek's stick came up and caught Marty in the cheekbone. It was immediately clear that Marty was severely hurt.

Marty suffered a fractured jaw and Gordie stayed in Cincinnati to be with him the next day when his cheekbone was wired back together. Ftorek certainly hadn't hurt Marty on purpose; he was Cincinnati's best player and that season he finished the season third in the league with 59 goals.

Many, but not Mr. Hockey, forgot the incident. On the second to last game of the season, the Whalers were trying to secure the trophy for the fewest goals against by a team. The Whalers' opponent was the Ftorek-led Stingers. In the third period, the Whalers were holding a 3-1 lead and trying desperately not to give up any more goals. Neale vividly remembers seeing Ftorek going into the corner and Howe going in after him. "I heard the crowd go 'Ohhhh,' and the referee put his hand up and Gordie was given a five-minute penalty."

Howe had cut up Ftorek, and the Whalers had to kill off the power play and preserve their goals against average. Even though the Whalers were able to accomplish that, Neale felt he still had to say something to Howe after the game. "Gordie," Neale said. "You can't take a penalty like that in a situation like we were in."

"You're right Harry," Gordie said, "but you know what he did to Marty on New Year's."

Neale understood. "A lot of young guys tried to make their mark running Gordie and that was his philosophy," Neale said. "He was mean, there was no doubt about it."

Howe was known for waiting forever to even a score, but Neale said the best illustration of Howe's patience in that regard was told to him by former NHL defenseman Bobby Baun. Baun was a predatory body-checker, solidly built and overflowing with spit and vinegar. In 1959, Baun was playing for Toronto and had caught Howe taking a shot from just inside the blue line. "He didn't knock him out, but Baun told me that Howe didn't know where he was at," Neale said.

In 1967-1968, Baun was lost in the Expansion Draft to Oakland, and he was playing for the Seals against Detroit. He spotted Howe coming over the blue line in a vulnerable position. This time, Howe saw him coming.

"He got his stick up and caught Baun under the chin and in the throat," Neale said. "Baun told me he was lying on the ice, and he didn't know if his head was coming off. He couldn't breathe. He couldn't talk and there was Gordie coasting over to him. He stopped, looked down at him, and said, 'Now we are even.'"

Neale laughs. "He waited eight years."

"Not many people took a healthy run at him in the WHA because the word was out," Neale said. "Everyone knew you were apt to get a stick or elbow down the throat."

Howe had his own code of justice, and he served as both judge and jury. One of Gordie's pet peeves was crosschecking. If you crosschecked Howe, you paid a price.

The Whalers played the Edmonton Oilers in a playoff series in 1977-1978, and Neale was a friend of Oiler's defenseman Dave Langevin. In Game One, Neale noticed Langevin was trying to move Howe away from the net by using his stick against Howe's back.

Neale remembers the conversation.

Neale said, "I'm not telling you to let him score, but tie him up, don't crosscheck him."

Langevin said, "Screw off, Harry, what's the old guy going to do? He's 50 years old."

Neale replied, "I'm telling you to be careful, tie him up, don't crosscheck or Gordie will turn on you."

The next game, Langevin didn't heed Neale's warning. "He was crosschecking Howe from behind, and Gordie put his stick over his shoulder like he was shoveling snow and he cut him up."

As tough as Mr. Hockey was, he had a sense of humor about his reputation. "He would skate by the bench and say he was sorry," Neale said. "Right, I'm sorry this is the 900th guy I cut in my career."

Neale also respected Gordie because he wouldn't use his superstar status to interfere with the management of the team.

"I'm sure there were times when he wanted me to play Marty more than I did or Mark on a different line, but I never heard it from him."

Neale had never encountered an athlete with Howe's natural level of conditioning, strength and desire. By the time Howe played for Neale in 1977-1978, he had been playing professional hockey for more than 30 years. Yet Neale recalls Howe telling him that he was actually three pounds lighter than he was at the launch of his career.

Howe had only one limitation, as Neale recalls. Mr. Hockey wasn't much of a runner. At least he wasn't at that stage of his career. Neale used two-mile runs to get his troops in shape at the start of training camp and those training sessions seemed to be taking a toll on Howe. Neale had tried to make him exempt from the running, but Howe refused to be given special treatment.

As the running continued, Neale noted that Gordie's shins, ankles and knees were becoming quite sore.

Howe was expected to be the New England Whalers leading scorer that season and Neale couldn't afford to have him hobbled before the season even began. He told Howe that he wasn't going to allow him to run with the team any more. Howe protested again on the grounds that team morale can be undermined if players are given special consideration.

Neale asked Howe to trust that he would know how to handle the situation properly.

Word spread among the players that Neale had a "special announcement."

"Gordie Howe no longer has to run because he has some chronic injuries," Neale said. "But this isn't special treatment because I'm making a deal with all of you. If you play for me within the season you turn 50, you won't have to run either."

Neale is quick-witted, and enjoys Howe's dry sense of humor, particularly Howe's playful ribbing. Neale is an analyst for Hockey Night in Canada, and one of his colleagues Scott Oake asked Howe once on camera how he rated Neale as his coach.

Impishly, Howe said, "I thought he was the second best coach I ever had, and all the others were tied for first."

Neale seems to enjoy telling that story. "I consider myself one of the privileged few that ever had a chance to stand behind a bench and yell, "Howe, your line is up next."

Editor's Note: At age 52, Gordie played his last NHL season. He was the oldest player and the only coach older than Howe was Fred Shero.

Harley Hotchkiss

Calgary Flames Owner
Chairman of the NHL Board of Governors

Although Harley Hotchkiss is one of the owners of the Calgary Flames, he could be forgiven if the mention of number 9 brings up images of Gordie Howe and not Lanny McDonald whose number 9 was retired by the Flames.

The son of a tobacco farmer, Hotchkiss grew up in southern Ontario as a fan of the Production Line of Ted Lindsay, Sid Abel and Howe. After World War II service in the Canadian Merchant Marine, he attended Michigan State University and always managed to carve out some time to make the 90-mile trip from East Lansing to Olympia to watch the Production Line dominate. That line was so dominant that Lindsay, Abel and Howe finished one-two-three in the scoring race in 1949-1950, and then Howe won the next four scoring crowns.

Hotchkiss said it is impossible to have been a fan in that era and not be an admirer of how Howe played the game.

"Hockey is a fast moving, physical game, and Gordie combined great skill and durability with great strength in a way I don't think anyone else has at that level. He played the game in a way that was unique to Gordie Howe," Hotchkiss says.

As chairman of the NHL Board of Governors, Hotchkiss has become acquainted with Mr. and Mrs. Hockey. He considers them among hockey's greatest ambassadors.

"They have done a lot for the game that no one knows in terms of their charity work," Hotchkiss said. "I don't know how many hundreds of thousands of autographs that Gordie has signed, but he and Colleen are symbols of what's really great about our game."

Hersh Borenstein

President of Frozen Pond Inc.

Before hockey memorabilia dealer Hersh Borenstein first began working with Power Play to utilize the services of Mr. Hockey in 1998, he could not have had a true understanding of the notion of mixing business with pleasure.

One year after they began working together, Gordie and Colleen rented a condominium in Florida and invited him down for a few days.

"They wouldn't let me reach into my pocket the whole time I was there," Borenstein says. "They wouldn't even let me pay for souvenirs. Colleen and Gordie, and their associates Aaron Howard and Del Reddy made sure that I thoroughly enjoyed myself. In fact, I had my own condo and this was during the peak vacation season. I've dealt with hundreds and hundreds of athletes and no one has ever treated me like that."

When he opened a new store, Mr. and Mrs. Hockey, along with Howard and Reddy were at the grand opening. The Howes were not there as celebrities, but as Borenstein's friends. Borenstein brought in a Zamboni and Gordie drove it through the ribbon to signify the grand opening. "People ask me how much I had to pay them to do that, and I say nothing," Borenstein says.

Borenstein continues to work with the Howe's business managers Reddy and Howard on the sale of Mr. Hockey autographed memorabilia. As someone who has witnessed hundreds of athletes sign autographs, Borenstein is appreciative of the pride that Howe takes in the items that are created with his signature. "If someone is nice enough to ask or want his autograph, he makes sure they can read every letter," Borenstein said.

Many modern athletes have a non-decipherable signature, presumably so they can sign autographs at the rate of 700-800 per hour. Howe can't sign that many per hour, but it's also not necessary to hire a hieroglyphics expert to determine what is written.

"He signs, 'Mr. Hockey, Gordon Howe'on every item. There is a great pride in his signature and the collectors love it," Borenstein says.

Borenstein says Howe's image in the memorabilia world is "surreal."

"He transcends the game," Borenstein said. "No heads turn quicker than they do when you are with Gordie," Borenstein says.

Greg Wolff

Insurance Agent and Friend

When Greg Wolff met the Howes for the first time as a consultant 27 years ago, Gordie was chopping wood with the ease of a man pushing a knife through butter; and Colleen was dissecting the complexities of insurance coverage. It was difficult for Wolff to determine which sight was more impressive.

Before that meeting, Wolff had known the Howes from working with them on the Greater Hartford March of Dimes Walk-a-Thon. Wolff had been on the March of Dimes board of directors, but he also was in the insurance business and Colleen had invited him to their house in Glastonbury, Connecticut, to discuss their coverage.

"I was amazed as I dealt with Colleen at how business savvy she was and how she believed in life insurance as a means of protecting the family," Wolff said.

Colleen's understanding of how to use insurance and tax planning as a means of improving the family's financial strength impressed Wolff. "Colleen also wanted to purchase insurance for her grandchildren as a gift from Gordie and her," Wolff said. "I learned that besides being a very good businesswoman, she loved her family and that was number one in her life."

Dressed in a coat and tie, Gordie had excused himself from the insurance meeting after 30 minutes because he had chores to accomplish. When Wolff was leaving, he found Howe outside with his coat off and his tie tucked into his shirt. He was splitting wood for the fireplace.

"He had his sleeves rolled up and his arms looked like Popeye," Wolff recalled.

There seemed to be no resistance from the logs of wood as Howe swung his ax down upon them. Howe offered Wolff a swing, and he accepted. He took a mighty cut and the ax traveled only halfway down the log. He tried again with the same result.

"I couldn't believe how difficult it was," Wolff recalled. "It was then I realized how strong he was."

Wolff remembers that near the end of Gordie's management tenure with the Whalers, Mrs. Hockey would call Wolff and use him as a sounding board for business issues. He was impressed by how the Howes weighed business ventures in terms of the challenge it presented more than the money it could offer.

"He wasn't going to be a figurehead if there wasn't something of importance that he could do for the Whalers," Wolff said. "This is the type of integrity that they have. They have shown that although money is important, doing the right thing is more important."

Through the years, Wolff said he worked with a variety of Whalers and athletes from the University of Connecticut and "Colleen was as good as an agent as I had ever seen."

Wolff witnessed Colleen's business acumen, and noted that her stewardship was often the difference between success and failure of a business venture.

"At one point, they purchased the Gallery Restaurant in Glastonbury, Connecticut, and put Gordie's memorabilia on display and the restaurant did real well," Wolff said. "But when Colleen moved away from the restaurant to attend to other business affairs, the restaurant was not able to sustain itself."

Wolff considered the Howe marriage a perfect partnership because each partner complemented the other.

"Each has strengths and weaknesses," Wolf said. "But as a team, there were no weaknesses."

Vic Stasiuk

NHL Player

Vic Stasiuk played for the NHL for 14 seasons, six of which were with Detroit. He played left wing and is the only person who can say he was with Gordie Howe when Gordie met a very pretty woman and scored his prettiest goal.

He was bowling with Howe at the Joe Evans Lucky Strike Lanes, near Olympia Stadium, when Howe had his first conversation with Colleen.

"I was busy bowling, but I remember he said, 'I sure like the looks of that girl,'" Stasiuk recalled.

Howe ambled up to the counter to find out who she was, and the manager introduced them. Gordie had offered Colleen a ride, but she had her stepfather's car and had to decline. Nevertheless, it was clear there had been a spark in their first conversation.

Stasiuk certainly wasn't surprised that Howe won Colleen's heart. Howe was the superstar who behaved like an average Joe.

"Often I would be sitting in the lobby, and he would ask what I was doing and when I said 'nothing' he would say, "Come with me," Stasiuk said. "He did that with many young rookies. He also loaned me his car on occasions."

Stasiuk became a golfing enthusiast, and he was always fascinated with the reverence Howe had for the maintenance of the course.

"When you hit the green, not only would he fix his own ball mark, he would fix those of the members who had neglected to fix theirs," Stasiuk said. "It was like he was the greens-keeper of the course."

What Stasiuk remembers most is that "Gordie always had time for you."

"At training camp everybody would rush to look at the list to see if they played with Gordie Howe," Stasiuk said.

Stasiuk remembers one Edmonton Flyers farmhand saying once, "If I could just play one game with Gordie Howe, I would die happy."

Stasiuk said Howe was a humble and gracious man until the game began. "When you irritated or bothered him, he would turn from a gentle giant into a mean hockey player," Stasiuk recalled.

With 2 Stanley Cup Championships and 183 NHL goals on his resume, Stasiuk owns the qualifications to assess players and hockey feats. He netted five goals in 11 games during Detroit's 1955 Stanley Cup Championship run, and made a nifty backhand pass to help set-up Alex Delvecchio's first goal in Detroit's 3-1 win against Montreal in Game Seven. Howe scored the game-winner in that contest. Stasiuk also coached four seasons in the NHL with Philadelphia, California and Vancouver.

He views a one-handed goal by Mr. Hockey scored against Boston as perhaps the most spectacular things he ever witnessed. Howe gained control of the puck near his own goal line and he carried it coast-to-coast to score.

"Boston's Milt Schmidt, picked him up through the center zone," Stasiuk said. "Milt was tapping him with his stick, and interfering with him," Stasiuk said. "Schmidt was still on his back, and a defenseman was on his back in the Boston zone. Gordie went in one-handed with the stick (straight not curved) in his right hand. He cut into the goal crease and flipped the puck into the top corner for a big goal."

Stasiuk vividly remembers Schmidt "on his knees in the crease looking up at the heavens or the gallery gods and saying, 'What are you going to do?'"

Throughout his years at the game, Stasiuk never saw another goal like Howe's one-hander. He has no reservations about saying Howe was the greatest player in NHL history.

"If you take five Wayne Gretzkys and five Gordie Howes and played a game, the Gretzkys wouldn't touch the puck," Stasiuk said.

He says Howe taught him many lessons in hockey and altered his breakfast habits.

Stasiuk remembers staying at Howe's home and realizing, that Mr. Hockey included oatmeal as part of his daily routine.

Since then, he has had a bowl of oatmeal every day. Says Stasiuk, "If it is good enough for Gordie, it's good enough for me."

Reg and Ronnie Sinclair

Former Teammate and His Wife

Reg Sinclair played only one season with Gordie Howe on the Detroit Red Wings and yet he has the distinction of being able to say that he knew Gordie was going to marry Colleen before Gordie even knew it.

The New York Rangers traded Sinclair to Detroit before the 1952-1953 season. He and his wife, Ronnie, quickly became close to Howe and his new girlfriend, Colleen. "They did a fair bit of their courting at our house," Sinclair recalls.

Sinclair recalls that Howe didn't tell Colleen immediately that he was an NHL player, and thinking that "she must have been concerned that every bar and restaurant they were in everyone would say, 'Hi Gord. How are you Gord?'"

"You have to wonder if Colleen might have thought her new boyfriend was a bit of a tippler," Sinclair says, laughing.

One day Gordie and Reg were out with Reg's nine-month old son, Jimmy, while Colleen and Ronnie were shopping. When the Howes left, Ronnie had some nothing-but-fun gossip to share with her husband.

"At dinner time, Ronnie told me that Colleen had told her that Gordie doesn't know it yet, but she was going to marry him," Sinclair says, chuckling. "I thought that was kind of spiffy to have that kind of confidence, but he was pretty smitten with her."

Sinclair remembers being with Gordie when he was first wooing Colleen "and he used all of his charms." Sinclair jokes, "I just wish to hell that he would have been that gentle and that nice when he played hockey."

Sinclair had been a 20-goal scorer for the Rangers the season before, and had crossed swords against "The Production Line" of Ted Lindsay, Sid Abel and Gordie Howe on more than one occasion. "You could hit Gordie, provided you hit him pretty clean," Sinclair recalled. "But you didn't want to make the mistake of getting a stick up near his head, not after the operation he had when we nearly lost him. If you got the stick up near his head, you were in for a bad night."

When Sinclair was traded to Detroit with John Morrison for Leo Riese Jr., on August 18, 1952, he wondered how Howe and the Red Wings were going to receive him. "When I walked into the training-camp hotel in Sault Ste. Marie, there were two guys sitting on a couch. They came up and welcomed me to the team," Sinclair said. "It was Ted Lindsay and Gordie. Boy, that took a weight off my shoulders and they both became dear friends."

Even though Sinclair played only one season with Howe, the Howes and Sinclairs remained close through the years. "When Colleen came to visit us in Savannah, Georgia, she was always laden with gifts," Sinclair said. "The last time she was in our home she came with a box full of hockey memorabilia—some of which I had never seen. She had pictures of Gordie and me as well as team pictures. They were all beautifully framed. She was a special person in her ability to be kind to other people."

Ronnie Sinclair said Colleen was a prolific gift giver. "She was very generous," Ronnie said. "You wouldn't get one lovely gift; it would be several lovely gifts. She thought about her gifts carefully; whether it was a really good book, or at Christmas, we would get a lovely fruit basket. She was a very caring person." Ronnie says she has fond memories of watching games with Colleen and Lindsay's wife, Pat. "Colleen was an interesting woman always," said Ronnie Sinclair. "We believed her when she said she would marry Gordie. They always had a lot to say to each other, and they were always very compatible. Colleen was a grand girl."

In many ways, according to Sinclair, Colleen was like Gordie in that "she was strong but very kind."

Even though Mr. Hockey was the league's most dominant offensive player, Sinclair said. "He was so unselfish and he never expected anything, You always wondered 'Would I be that kind and gentle if I had his status?' Howe was the best hockey player you could ever see."

"When you played against him, he would do things and you would say, 'That lucky SOB, the puck bounces for him,'" Sinclair said. "Then when you start to play with him every night, you realize there isn't a great deal of luck attached to it."

Sinclair recalls that when Gordie was on the ice and Detroit defenseman Bob Goldham was on the bench, he would often say, "Reg, this is the best. We eat pretty well. We travel pretty well. And twice a week we get the best seat in the house to watch the best hockey player in the league."

Tom Webster

Former Teammate
Detroit and New England

Tom Webster spent time as Gordie Howe's roommate and his linemate, but his first duty for Mr. Hockey was to be his secretary.

Before the 1970-1971 season, the Detroit Red Wings traded Roger Crozier to the Buffalo Sabres to land the highly-regarded youngster Webster for the purpose of playing him on right wing with center Alex Delvecchio and left wing Frank Mahovlich. This was GM/Coach Ned Harkness' plan because he wanted to move Gordie Howe permanently to defense. At the time of the trade, Webster had only 11 games of NHL experience.

If that was not enough pressure, the 22-year old Webster shows up at training camp and discovers that he has also been assigned to be Howe's roommate.

"I check in and got into the room and the phone starts ringing," Webster recalls. "I would have to say I took close to 100 messages, and I'm the guy that doesn't want to take any numbers or addresses wrong. I didn't want to screw up anything."

Finally, Howe enters the room and Webster calls him "Mr. Howe" and introduces himself. Howe tells him that he's "Gordie and not Mr. Howe." Then Webster hands Howe the 100 phone messages, proud and relieved that he took great care in making sure each name and number was correct.

Webster's laughter is deep and long as he tells the story of his first meeting with Howe.

It took Webster time to overcome his nervousness about being Gordie Howe's roommate. He always took all of Howe's phone messages to assure that Howe was well rested for games.

However, Webster admits he would have trouble getting enough sleep. "I'd be nodding off, then I'd roll over and look at the guy in the other bed and think, 'Holy cow, that's Gordie Howe,' and I'd be wide awake."

Webster was quite impressed that Howe was willing to move back to defense. Throughout his career, Howe would spend some minutes on defense at various times, particularly if the Red Wings needed a goal. The prevailing wisdom was that Howe would be more dangerous than any forward on the ice would even if he had also had to get back to cover his zone. Nevertheless, asking Howe to move to defense permanently was too much.

"But Gordie being the consummate team guy said he would give it a try," Webster said. "It certainly helped me get my start, I was so appreciative."

The Red Wings didn't have much success, and Howe moved back to forward. However, Webster took advantage of the opening Howe gave him to score 30 goals that season and finish second to Buffalo's Gilbert Perreault in the NHL rookie-of-the-year race.

Webster recalls that Howe actually enjoyed defense and had no difficulty adjusting to the position, and he wonders if that is why his son Mark had such an easy transition from left wing to defense.

That wasn't the only time that Webster benefited from Gordie Howe switching positions

In 1977-1978, Webster was traded to the New England Whalers in the WHA and Howe moved to center so Webster could play right wing on his line with Mark on the left side.

"I remember Gordie said 'Webby, don't worry about going into the corners. You get into the slot and you can shoot the puck, and I will go get the puck.' I said, "Gordie, you just made my day and my year. I had the best start I ever had. I love him to death."

Webster also was very glad Gordie liked him because he saw what Howe did when he didn't like a person. Gordie's revenge against Robbie Ftorek for cutting Marty is well documented. But Webster's version of the events told to *Windsor Star* columnist, Bob Duff, provides more insight into the Howe-Ftrorek feud.

"We were in Cincinnati one night and Robbie Ftorek was cheap-shotting everybody," Webster said. "He crosschecked Mark in the face and when Gordie got back to the bench, he slammed his stick down and said, 'That's it. I've had enough.'"

"He didn't do anything the next shift or the shift after that. The third time we're out together and he goes behind the net with Ftorek. He brings his stick up and slices him right across the face. Ftorek's just lying there behind the net in a pool of his own blood."

If an opponent did something that Howe didn't like, he would pay a severe price. Howe had his own code of justice, and most of Howe's opponents understood that. Apparently, Ftorek didn't understand it, or chose to ignore it.

While it is true that Howe's strength was natural and not created with weight training, it is false to suggest that Mr. Hockey didn't work out to keep himself fit and conditioned.

Late in Howe's career, Webster remembers visiting Howe in the off-season and being stunned by Howe's training methods. He saw him run up hills with what seemed like a winter's worth of chopping wood.

"He would put a log on his shoulder and then get two big pieces of wood, maybe weighing 20 or 25 pounds, and he would hold those outstretched like they were dumbbells," Webster recalled. "He would do all sorts of exercises with them. In those days, there were no fancy gyms. It was his creativity and imagination that allowed him to stay in shape."

Webster said Howe worked even harder as he got older. "It was almost like he was embarrassed that he was training," Webster said. "He would keep this to himself. He did it because of the pride he had in his performance. He knew people were coming to watch him; he prepared himself to meet the expectations that people had for him."

Howe played at about 204 pounds for most of his career. With today's training methods, his playing weight probably would be at least 220 or 225. People who played against him when he was 204 shudder to think how devastating he would have been if he would have been even stronger.

Webster was coach of the Los Angeles Kings when Wayne Gretzky was there in his prime. However, he says his former line mate, Howe, is the best player he ever saw.

"There is no hesitation, no question in my mind," Webster said. "He was the ultimate power forward with great skill. I don't even think he had shoulders. I think everything just went into muscle-mass in arms and forearms."

Chuck Kaiton

Broadcaster, Carolina Hurricanes

Chuck Kaiton is amused that the world has become "so politically correct" that some NHL arenas number standing room spots to make sure even those ticket holders have rights.

A ten-year old Kaiton had no rights more than 40 years ago as a standing room ticket holder at Olympia Stadium on the night Gordie Howe tied Rocket Richard's National Hockey League record of 544 career goals. It was essentially hand-to-hand combat in the standing area behind the balcony seats, and the chaotic nature of his environment seems to have made Kaiton's memory of the event more exciting.

"I remember barely seeing the goal because I was short," Kaiton recalled. "I was short and my dad had lifted me up and I saw the goal over two tiers of standees. I was in the third row of standing room. There was pushing and you could still smoke in the arenas back then and I remember the smoke. There were no replays back then, either you saw it or you didn't. I saw it. I lived it. It was incredible."

Growing up in Detroit, Kaiton became a huge fan of Mr. Hockey. It was a dream-come-true for Kaiton when he was named as the play-by-play broadcaster for the Hartford Whalers in their first NHL season of 1979-1980.

Kaiton and the Howes, maybe because of the Detroit connection, became instant friends and remain so to this day.

"I thought Colleen was a brilliant woman," Kaiton said. "She was perfectly matched for Gordie. He's such a good person and people took advantage of him; and as a loving wife, she essentially said, 'I will protect you.' She was a mother hen, very protective of Gordie as well as her sons and daughter."

Kaiton was behind the microphone January 6, 1980, when Howe made his first appearance back in Detroit playing for the Hartford Whalers. Not counting the preseason game for the Houston Aeros in Cobo Arena, Howe hadn't played in Detroit since he had retired from the Red Wings in 1971. There was a buzz in Motown because the expectation was that Howe would play on a line with his two sons.

Famed Red Wings public address announcer, Budd Lynch, announced the starting lineup, and Kaiton recalls that Lynch waited until the end to announce, "center Gordie Howe." However, it's doubtful anyone actually heard the words because right after he had announced Mark Howe on the left wing and Marty on the right wing, everyone in the building knew what was coming next. The crowd arose in unison and produced a thunderous roar that was deafening.

"The ovation was two or two and half minutes," said Kaiton who has a penchant for remembering details.

One forgotten detail about that memorable night that Kaiton offers is Howe overruled his coach, probably for one of the few times in his career, to make sure that Detroit fans got what they wanted.

Hartford coach Don Blackburn had reluctantly agreed to start the game with the Howe family playing on one line, but he had ordered Marty to jump off the ice right after the face-off.

"Marty was not one of Blackburn's favorite players and he was a defenseman and Blackburn wanted another wing on the ice," Kaiton said. "Gordie got wind of it and told Marty to stay on the full shift."

Gordie Howe was not one to be insubordinate to his coach, but he was somebody who had great respect for the fans of Detroit and great appreciation of how well Detroit fans had treated his family.

"I have a classic photo of the face-off and you can see the leg of a Whalers player over the boards as he gets ready to make the change," Kaiton said. "But Marty stayed on the ice for the full 45 or 50 seconds of the shift."

The Whalers won that game 6-4.

"I'm biased, but I think Gordie is the best of all-time," Kaiton said. "No disrespect to Wayne Gretzky or Mario Lemieux, but I saw the man play. I think he combined strength and finesse. He was a gentleman off the ice and a fierce competitor on the ice."

Kaiton clearly believes Howe's ferocity is one element that separated him from other NHL legends.

He remembers that in Howe's final season in the NHL, Los Angeles Kings player J.P. Kelley sent Howe "ass over teacup" into the penalty box. It was clear that Howe was angered by the hit because he cut Bert Wilson in retribution. Moreover, it was clear what the Kings and Kelley wanted.

"Kelley apologized," said Kaiton, "He said, 'Mr. Howe, I didn't mean to check you like that.' He was shaking. Gordie was 51."

One of Kaiton's favorite Howe intimidation stories came from Kaiton's good friend Jimmy Roberts, the former NHL player who came into the league as a rookie with the Montreal Canadiens in 1963-1964.

In Robert's first game against Detroit, Toe Blake assigned him to check Mr. Hockey.

"Gordie drove him right through the boards," Kaiton said. "And Gordie said to him, 'Welcome to the NHL.'"

Aaron Howard

Business Manager, Personal Friend of Gordie and Colleen

On one of Aaron Howard's first assignments working for Gordie and Colleen Howe, he discovered that crowd control was an important and challenging aspect of his job.

Howe was signing autographs at the San Jose convention center, and Howard was trying to keep fans organized when a "pushy" newspaper reporter essentially wanted to run Howard's roadblock to get to Howe.

"Move out of the way kid," he told Howard, "just get out of the way."

Gordie overheard the reporter, and quickly told the reporter, "That's my son you're talking to."

The reporter was surprised and apologetic. Howard learned that instant that when you are part of Gordie and Colleen's team you become part of their family.

"I saw Gordie's soft-spoken nature and how easy going he can be, relaxed and confident," Howard said. "He didn't want to be treated any different even though he's hockey's greatest player."

It's almost as if fate was trying to tie Howard together with the Howes. When he was 11, he was riding his bike when he saw hundreds of people lined up to get into a pizza parlor. Told that Gordie Howe was signing autographs, Howard got into line. "By the time I was in the front of the line, I was almost speechless," Howard recalled. "I could hardly say my name. I still have that treasured first autograph card."

When Howard was 20, he met Del Reddy who was friends with Howard's brother Matt. Reddy had just become the Howe's representative. He asked Aaron to help prepare and organize some *and...HOWE!* books at his apartment so the Howes could autograph them for an upcoming appearance. "Little did I know that meeting Del would open the door for my career. It has allowed me to befriend and work with two of the greatest, most wonderful people I have ever met," Howard said.

While Howard was attending the University of Michigan, Colleen hired him part-time. He lived with the Howes for three consecutive summers before being hired full-time by them in 1999.

Howard says he had never even flown on a plane before Colleen hired him to assist with their hectic schedule. Nevertheless, Colleen always had a knack for seeing an acorn and envisioning the oak tree. She was always a good judge of character and talent.

"She obviously saw something in me that I couldn't see," Howard said. "I was a nervous 20-year old kid lacking in self-confidence. I didn't have a clue of what was expected of me. Colleen knew I would do well."

The education Howard got working for the Howes may have been as valuable as the one he received at Michigan.

"Colleen shaped me as a person and taught me some of the most important lessons in my life," Howard said. "I learned most from just observing her from a distance. If you know Colleen, you can't help but quickly recognize her as a most generous, kind and caring person. Colleen taught me that the little things in life are so important. I learned to respond and treat people with kindness and care. I learned to help others and still be firm. I learned that money is not the most important thing in life."

Gordie had greatness, but Colleen had charisma, Howard insists.

"She won my lifetime respect," Howard said. "She was the ultimate hockey mom, entrepreneur, crusader and just a great lady. Talk about visionaries, Colleen Howe is the biggest visionary of all. Her ideas were simple, amazing, and simply amazing! She would entertain any idea, none ever too big or too small."

No one enjoys surprising people with gifts more than Mrs. Hockey did. Howard remembers the Howes were appearing at a Hallmark store in Oscoda, Michigan, when Colleen heard there was a firefighter in the back of the line with a touching history. He had lost vision in one of his eyes in a dramatic rescue. Before the hero could make it to the front of the line, Colleen had purchased a Hallmark ceramic collector's edition Fire Station and she and Gordie had signed it.

When he made it to the front of the line, Colleen gave him the gift. The firefighter was so shocked and overcome with emotion that he broke down and wept in front of everyone.

"Colleen understood," said Howard, "that little actions like that can make a huge difference."

Don and Pam Howard

Parents of Aaron Howard and Friends

Don and Pam Howard aren't usually at a loss for words, but they admit they were short on words when they met Gordie and Colleen for the first time. It was during a personal appearance at a furniture store on a hot July day in St. Clair, Michigan. The quiet was broken when Colleen extended her hand and said, "Hi, I am Colleen and this is Gordie." The Howard's said in a written tribute, "That day started a relationship for us that will never be forgotten."

"From that day when we first met, we sensed a certain charisma and an indistinguishable magnetism that only comes with maturity." The Howard's believe that their son's association with the Howes has dramatically changed his life. "The Howes have taken our son Aaron in their confidence, offered him a career, gave him new and important responsibilities, and have worked wonders building his self esteem," the Howards wrote. "He had not worked there long when we noticed all the positive changes taking place."

Even though the Howes had met the Howards for the first time at the furniture store, the Howards noted that the two couples talked as if they had been friends for years. "From that first day our relationship grew, and we came to know Colleen and Gordie as personal friends," the Howards wrote. "We learned of their unselfish giving of their time, their tremendous financial support to those who were in need and how much they cared about others. We had the opportunity to meet their whole family and many of their friends. We have spent several holidays with Colleen and Gordie in our home together with our son. So many great times that we will never forget."

"Gordie's gentile manner, unbelievable world record hockey career and Colleen's intellect and perseverance have made them the most memorable people in our lives," the Howards added. "We are blessed to have Colleen and Gordie as our friends.

Mike Jaszcz

Volunteer for mrandmrshockey.com

Fan memories of Gordie Howe often involve a special goal he scored, or a spectacular play or even Howe giving a rookie his initiation along the boards. However, one of Mike Jaszcz's favorite Howe memories is eating take-out Chinese food with Mr. Hockey in the front seat of a mini-van.

Jaszcz began working with the Howes as a volunteer at the invitation of the Howe's business managers Del Reddy and Aaron Howard. One of his first assignments was helping at a signing at Joe Louis Arena. Per his tradition, Gordie had insisted on making sure they were early. With time to spare, Gordie suggested they get a bite to eat.

"Now you would think someone of Gordie's stature would walk into some fancy restaurant and have a seat waiting for him," Jaszcz says. "At least that's what you would think. That was not the case. Gordie and I walked into a Chinese fast food restaurant with no fanfare whatsoever. The man is so down to earth."

Still with more time to kill, Gordie took Jaszcz to the Southfield neighborhood where he and Colleen had purchased their first home.

"Here I am, just a nobody in the world to Gordie, and he was showing me around his old neighborhood and telling me stories about raising their children there. As we continued our drive down the Lodge toward Detroit, I kept asking questions about his playing days, and in Gordie's low quiet voice he kept telling me memory after memory of his many trips down that very same route. That was a very exciting day."

Jaszcz says his association with mrandmrshockey.com has provided him the opportunity to introduce countless numbers of people to Gordie. Howe has treated each of them as if they were a friend. According to Jaszcz, not once did Gordie ever just shake their hands and leave. He always had a story to tell, or a question to ask.

"We can only wish that the athletes of today were a fraction like the man Gordie is," Jaszcz says.

Nevertheless, Jaszcz's best Mr. Hockey memory came in June, 2003 when Howe and Howard came out to a local golf course to visit with

Jaszcz's wedding party. Jaszcz had been looking for a special gift for his wedding party, and Howe's friendship helped him create that gift.

"Here is the greatest player in the history of the NHL, taking time out of his hectic schedule to come golf with us," Jaszcz said. "Needless to say, everyone was in shock. It was truly a special day for my friends, family and me. We took some priceless pictures with Gordie that day. Soon after, he autographed each picture taken and personalized it to everyone who was there. Talk about a wedding gift."

Jaszcz's friends and family were shocked that Howe showed up for the golf outing, but Jaszcz was not. He had witnessed how Mr. Hockey treats the fans that line up for his autograph, particularly children.

"Gordie always makes them feel very special," Jaszcz says. "He will kid around with them and bring a smile to their face if for only the few seconds that they may be around him. Some are very young and may not ever remember meeting him, but I'm sure when they get older they will have a story to tell about meeting the greatest to ever play the game."

The first time Jaszcz met Colleen she gave him a hug. He had been invited by Reddy to assist with a private party/fundraiser for Children's Hospital in Detroit. He was nervous, and she made him feel like a life-long friend.

"Talk about feeling impressed and important at the same time," Jaszcz said. "She made everyone around her feel just as important as any celebrity during the night. We first started out in the hotel and then made our way to Children's Hospital to hand out gifts to some of the sick children. This is when Colleen really made the kids feel very important. I don't think all of the kids knew who she was, just that she was a very caring person who was there to brighten up their day.

Jaszcz offers one poignant moment that seems to summarize how Mrs. Hockey's compassion and sentimentality often intersected with her love of surprising people with gifts.

Nearly a decade ago, Colleen and Gordie attended a charity auction in New York City. Bidding aggressively, she won a stunning portrait of Joe DiMaggio that was painted by Curt Flood, the famous baseball player. Upon winning, Colleen announced that the portrait was too beautiful to hang in their house and that it should really hang in the home of Joe DiMaggio.

I have seen the photo of Colleen presenting the painting to Joe DiMaggio," says Jaszcz. "You can see a tear in his eye. He was deeply touched by her unexpected generosity. "Only Colleen could make that happen."

Jeanne Gallagher

Consultant with USA Hockey In-Line

Jeanne Gallagher grew up in the Philadelphia area where the NHL isn't just a trivial pursuit. "Hockey is life," Gallagher said. "And Gordie Howe is a god. Bobby Clarke and Bernie Parent are gods."

That's why six years ago she decided to take advantage of the opportunity to meet Mr. Hockey at an event that would clearly change her life.

Former Philadelphia Flyers player, Ed Hospodar, was hosting a charity event and Gordie and Colleen Howe were among the celebrities that agreed to give a helping hand. She enjoyed meeting the Howes, but it was the receipt of their book *and...HOWE!* that actually put her on a new career course.

"I read the book and what was shocking to me was that I was more touched by Colleen's story than I was Gordie's story," Gallagher said. "I found that odd for me because I'm a hockey fanatic and yet I was touched more by the difficult time she had gone through as the agent for her husband and children. How she drove her kids to Canada for practice. Her whole story just touched my heart."

Gallagher says she remembers thinking, "what a terrible time this woman must have had."

"Everyone thinks she had a great life, but people gave her a hard time many times," Gallagher said.

Gallagher decided to write to Mrs. Hockey to express her admiration. And per Colleen's custom, she wrote back. They corresponded for months and in those letters Gallagher revealed that even though she was enjoying a successful career in the shipping industry, she had always longed to have a job in hockey. She had satisfied some of those desires by volunteering and working on the game-day staffs for the NHL Philadelphia Flyers and baseball's Philadelphia Phillies. Nevertheless, she longed for full-time work in hockey, even though she believed it to be an unrealistic goal.

"I told her thanks for touching my soul and over the course of six or eight months she kept telling me, 'Don't give up your dream. You can do anything,'" Gallagher recalled. "I had heard that my whole life from my parents, but she was so encouraging. She kept telling me to put feelers out there and see what I could do."

Gallagher says Colleen "helped me find the strength" at age 34 to quit a $60,000 per year job as a regional manager to accept a $17,000 job in the East Coast Hockey League.

Gallagher laughs. "Everyone in my life thought I was absolutely crazy and that I was going through my mid-life crisis early."

When Gallagher began a telemarketing job for the Trenton Titans in 1997, she remembers Colleen was very proud of her. "She said it was only the beginning, and it was just the door opening," Gallagher said. "She told me to just hang in there and the money will come and in three years I was a director with the New York Islanders."

Today Gallagher is a Director of Sports for the USA Hockey inline facility in Toms River, New Jersey.

"I never would have done that without the encouragement of Colleen Howe," Gallagher said. "She was just amazing. Since then, I have been blessed to do things that women could have never done 15 to 20 years ago in this industry. She proved to me that a woman could make a difference in this industry and not to be afraid."

Ralph Mellanby

Former Producer of Hockey Night in Canada

Hockey Night in Canada guru Ralph Mellanby always appreciated that Gordie Howe had a strong-willed, business-minded wife because he had one himself.

Ralph and his late wife, Janet, were close friends of the Howes for many years because they had so much in common. Mellanby actually got his start in television in Windsor, Ontario, just across the river from Detroit, and had known Howe since he was a young player. They were both courteous, talented, funny men, and their wives were both smart and confident.

"Colleen reminded me of my wife Janet," Mellanby said. "I had other business interests beyond my television work and Janet was running my businesses and Colleen was doing the same thing for Gordie."

Howe had seen Mellanby in the lobby of the Queen Elizabeth Hotel at an All-Star game and invited him and his wife to dinner. "My wife Janet was from Saskatchewan and I said it was about time that the two great legends of Saskatchewan met each other," Mellanby said.

They kept in touch and got together whenever possible. Furthermore, they were both amused and thrilled that coincidentally the Howe's son, Mark, and the Mellanby's son, Scott, would end up playing together on the Philadelphia Flyers in the late 1980's.

"Colleen would always call me and say she was doing this or that and wanted to make sure it got on Hockey Night in Canada and she would ask for my help," Mellanby said. "I would always give it to her."

Mellanby said he loved dealing with Colleen, even though it would always cost his company a few extra dollars.

He would hire Gordie to serve as an analyst during the playoffs, and inform Colleen that the going rate was $500, or whatever it would happen to be at that time.

"She would say Gordie won't work for that," Mellanby said, laughing. "I always gave Colleen her way, not because I was intimidated, but because I liked her."

Whenever Howe had a media deal or an endorsement possibility involving television work, Colleen would call and ask Mellanby for his opinion.

"She had the smarts and she always knew who to go to find out what was going on. She would say, "What do you think of this deal with NBC or whatever she had going," Mellanby said.

He laughs. "I was always flattered that she asked my opinion, and then I found out that she was calling everyone else too to get their opinion."

Mellanby admired Colleen's thoroughness in obtaining information, and he enjoyed the way she and Gordie meshed socially.

He remembers when Mr. and Mrs. Hockey stole the show during a restaurant meeting with a then well-known Montreal Expos baseball player. Their agent had set up a dinner with him because the Howes had not met him and Gordie had always been an avid baseball follower.

"He of course talked all about himself," Mellanby recalled, laughing. "He had a nice blonde with him. He had played in a golf tournament and he was saying he almost got a hole in one. He was doing this and doing that. And we were all just listening."

The Howes and Mellanby listened to the former Expo star's stories for what seemed like an eternity. He might still be talking about his golf if Howe had not become too warm and removed his sports jacket. It was the middle of winter, but Howe was wearing short sleeves, and the sight of his muscles overpowered the room.

"The guy just stopped talking. In fact, all conversation stopped," Mellanby said. "Everybody was looking at Gordie because you couldn't help it. He was such a beautifully built guy, especially his upper body. His muscles were rippling

The baseball star was a terrific major league hitter, but he was a pudgy athlete. He was nearly left speechless by the sight of Howe's physique. "It was like he didn't know what to say so he asked Gordie when he golfed what brand of ball he used," Mellanby recalled.

Mellanby said, "After Gordie provided the answer, Colleen added, 'It doesn't matter what brand he uses because Gordie can only hit any ball once or twice because he flattens them."

"This guy never said another word the whole night," Mellanby recalls, laughing.

Mellanby always found Howe to be an entertaining dinner companion and friend. He enjoyed Howe's sense of humor, and his ability to tell a story or to make a point.

He recalls that the HNIC crew interviewed Howe in-between the first and second periods of the 1970 All-Star game after Howe had scored what turned out to be the game-winning goal.

After the interview, Howe kept sitting in the chair, sipping a soft drink.

Mellanby told Howe he could go back to the dressing room, but Howe insisted he wasn't going back in the room with Claude Ruel who was coaching for the Western Conference.

"Why?" Mellanby asked, "Claude Ruel is a pretty good guy."

"Do you know what his instructions were?" Howe said, "Stay up, stay up, come back and don't tear the sweaters."

Players had been given a freshly designed sweater with stars on the front, and Mellanby looked down at Howe's sweater and it was torn.

"He didn't want to go back because Claude would have been mad at him," Mellanby said, laughing.

When the Howe's son and the Mellanbys were on the same team, Gordie would often joke, "I'm surprised about Scott, not about Mark, you have to have hockey genes to produce a player in the NHL."

Ralph Mellanby played a little baseball, but never played in the NHL.

It's not difficult for Mellanby to come up with other stories Howe told him, like about the edge he had in his famous fight with New York Rangers tough guy Lou Fontinato on February 1, 1959.

"Gordie told me that he saw Fontinato coming in the reflection of the glass," Mellanby said. "He said, 'It was perfect timing when I flattened his nose. I turned and let him have it, and he just ran into my fist.'"

Mellanby also recalls Howe telling him that when Howe was a young player a veteran slashed his ankles, and he told him if he did it again he would "take his head off."

He did it again, and Howe knocked him out. "When he came to, Gordie told him, 'I didn't take your head off, but I loosened it,'" Mellanby recalled.

Mellanby believes Howe was the best all-around player the game has ever known.

Mellanby pauses, "And he was certainly the funniest player."

John Stanzik

Michigan Hockey Arena Owner and Operator

When John Stanzik offered space in his Canton, Michigan, ice arena for the proposed Mr. and Mrs. Hockey museum, he was partly reliving his childhood.

Growing up in the Joy-Greenfield area of Detroit in the 1960's, Stanzik viewed Howe as the embodiment of what was good about sports.

"To any kid growing up in Detroit, Gordie was number one and Al Kaline was number two," Stanzik said.

He knows precisely where he was in 1963 when Mr. Hockey passed Maurice "Rocket" Richard to become the NHL's all-time leading goal scorer. He was listening to the game on a department store issued transistor radio.

"I was listening to Budd Lynch and when he scored I jumped up and down and my dad came in and said turn off that damn radio and do your homework," Stanzik, said laughing.

At the invitation of his friend DC Sports memorabilia dealer Steve Graus, Stanzik was involved in using the Mr. Hockey signed bobbleheads for a charity fundraiser. While Gordie and Colleen were at his Arctic Pond Arena in Plymouth, Michigan for the appearance, the Howe's agent Del Reddy asked Stanzik about the other ice facilities that he and his partners owned. During their discussion, Reddy mentioned that the Howes were looking for a special place for their museum because a recent offer in Frankenmuth, Michigan, had fallen through. For 50 years, Colleen had preserved their family's memorabilia. It was her dream for the last three decades to find a museum home for their special keepsakes.

Weeks after the signing, the Howes, along with Reddy and Aaron Howard, met with Stanzik and his partners Craig O'Neil and Deb Jewett at the Arctic Edge Ice Arena in Canton. The group previewed the proposed museum site that offers 10,000 square feet on the second floor of the arena. Stanzik is hopeful the museum will be operational by the end of 2005. It has been Mrs. Hockey's vision and dream for so many years.

One Saturday morning, Stanzik's son Chris said it was "Gordie Howe on the phone." Stanzik didn't hurry because he presumed it was one of his friends playing a joke. That was standard procedure for his friends.

"But as soon as I heard his voice I knew it was Gordie and then it was, 'Yes Sir, Yes Sir,'" Stanzik said.

Stanzik's wife Kim could tell by his politeness on the phone that it was a special call, but when she asked who it was and Stanzik said, "Gordie Howe" her response was, "Yeah, right."

However, his family came to understand Stanzik's admiration for Howe after meeting him. Stanzik was with his 17-year old son at a Red Wings game at Joe Louis Arena and Howe took the time to say hello to his son. "And he treated my daughter Courtney like gold," Stanzik said.

When Howe visits the Canton arena, Stanzik is amazed that he has the patience to talk to everyone who addresses him. "Guys bring up things they saw and he's always got a story," Stanzik said.

Stanzik met Colleen after the dementia had started to tighten its grip on her. "But I also got to feel a little bit of the drive she has," Stanzik said.

He's never going to forget the time he ate with Mr. Hockey at a restaurant.

"It was like eating with Christ," Stanzik said. "People would come by and touch his arm or shoulder, and just say hello. It's just amazing the type of draw and aura he has."

Carl Lindstrom

Detroit Junior Red Wings Coach

Carl Lindstrom's memory seems blurry on what Colleen's official title was on the Detroit Junior Red Wings in 1970-1971, but he is very clear on what her role was.

"She was the architect of the whole thing," said Lindstrom who was coach of the first American team to play in the Ontario Hockey League Junior A League.

Mark and Marty Howe had played for Lindstrom's National Champion Midget team sponsored by Olympia Agency Insurance. When the team was coming back from the National Junior Championships in Fort Wayne, Indiana, Lindstrom recalls saying to Colleen, "I don't know where we are going from here because Mark and Marty are going to waste another year playing Midgets."

Lindstrom recommended that they find better competition, and Colleen promptly organized a Junior B team.

The team won the Junior B National Championship in San Diego that following year, and on the plane ride back, he had a similar conversation with Colleen. The team needed to advance and play Junior A, and that meant playing against the Canadians.

Lindstrom remembers getting a call from Red Wings General Manager Jimmy Skinner shortly thereafter.

He said, "Do you think we have enough players to compete in the Junior A League?" Lindstrom said. "I said I thought we could."

Lindstrom is convinced that the team would have never become a reality without Colleen's influence. She was a woman who knew how to put together sponsorships and build coalitions to accomplish tasks.

"She was very, very involved," Lindstrom said. "She was a good businesswoman and one great lady. She knew what she was doing. She took a lot of criticism, but she hung in there. She was fair and if you did it her way, it usually worked out."

Larry Stockwell

Long-Time Youth Coach and Hockey Fan

When the Howe's business manager and promoter, Del Reddy, was telling Gordie about one of Reddy's favorite coaches from his youth sports days was struggling with his recovery from heart surgery, Mr. Hockey asked how he could help. Reddy called Stockwell at the hospital and spoke with him about his recovery. Reddy told him, "Before we hang up, someone wants to say hello."

"As soon as I heard the voice, I knew it was him," said Larry Stockwell, who had coached the St. Mary's Catholic Youth Organization sports in Wayne, Michigan for more than 40 consecutive years until retiring a few years ago.

Stockwell was still sick from the impact of double bypass and valve replacement surgery at the University of Michigan hospital in 2003 when Howe delivered the best inspirational talk Coach Stockwell had ever received. The phone conversation lasted 20 minutes. "I was down completely," Stockwell said. "I was ready to jump. I was sick all the time. It pepped me up. It was like a miracle. I completely changed. I was awesome after that," Stockwell paused. "I was very negative until I talked to him. He made my day. He's a wonderful person."

Stockwell says Howe talked about sports and other subjects, but his message was clear. "He said I had two things going for me. He said I was in a good hospital with the greatest doctors in the world and I had God on my side. He said keep a positive attitude and you'll be okay."

Howe was introduced to Stockwell by Reddy a few years before and had been impressed with Stockwell's commitment to youth athletes. As one would expect, Howe has a special appreciation for longevity in sports. "He talked about how we had introduced hockey to Del and he said he was impressed with our interest in kids," Stockwell said. "And I said I hadn't done anything compared to what he has done for people."

Stockwell was touched that Howe connected with him at a time when Howe was going through a difficult period in his own life because of Colleen's illness. How quickly after Howe's talk did Stockwell start making strides in his recovery? "Five minutes," Stockwell said. "I didn't have any problems after I talked to him."

Maureen Reddy

Employee of Wayne-Westland School District

As much as Maureen Reddy admired Colleen Howe, she didn't understand her full impact until a visitor spotted an autographed Mrs. Hockey photo on the shelf behind her desk at the Stottlemeyer Pre-School in Westland.

The school nurse, Carol Haas, had spotted the photo when she came in to talk about a student and she became quite animated, "What is Mrs. Hockey doing on your shelf?" she asked.

Thinking Maureen did not hear her, she repeated, "What is Mrs. Hockey doing on your shelf?" Haas said. "Do you know her? Do you realize that she is the person who inspired so many kids, like my grandson, to play hockey? How do you know her?" Haas asked.

Struck by how excited Haas was, Maureen explained that she had met Colleen at a few fund-raising events and immediately liked her because she was so positive. She also was there when Colleen and Gordie carried the Olympic torch together in 2002. At that event, she had a picture taken with Colleen.

Haas went on to tell Reddy that she believed Colleen Howe was the most influential woman in hockey. As an example, she told Reddy that Colleen had founded the Detroit Junior Red Wings, which was the first Junior A Hockey Club in the United States.

Before she left the office Carol said, "That lady deserves all the accolades bestowed on her. She is my hero! She is not only a beautiful woman; she has done more for kids and sports than she will ever know. She inspired my grandson Jacob to play hockey!"

Ken Daneyko

Long-Time NHL Defenseman

Ken Daneyko played 20 years in the NHL and one of the highlights of his career actually happened on water, not ice.

He went snorkeling with Gordie Howe on a summer cruise that combined active players with retired greats.

"I had been in the league eight or nine years then, but it was like I was a little boy again," Daneyko said. "I kept thinking, *I'm snorkeling with Gordie Howe*. And he was so engaging, so down to earth, especially given that he is Mr. Hockey and a legend. And he showed me great respect because I was a player and really you don't see that in sports today."

Daneyko remembers spending much of his time with Howe during that cruise. "We talked hockey and the differences in eras," Daneyko said. "How he treated me had a big impact on me. You don't think about that when you are playing, but when you get closer to the rocking chair you think about it. I know if I talk to a kid or at a school, I remember how he treated me."

Given hockey's back seat status among the major sports, Daneyko says Howe's work as an ambassador for the sport has been crucial.

"Absolutely his name is magic," Daneyko said. "Gordie is Michael Jordan to us because of the world-wide attention he gets. Only a select few in our sport can get that attention. In football you can name 50 guys that have that kind of impact, but the uniqueness of Howe makes him more special."

Bob Resch

Produced Mr. and Mrs. Hockey CD

When Bob Resch was composing the song *Mr. Hockey,* the phrasing he enjoyed most was his creation of Gordie Howe being "a lean, mean, scoring machine."

The trick of song writing is to be catchy using compact verbiage. It's an art form and it can be agony when a writer can't find the proper wording. Resch was struggling to find a lyrical description of Colleen when he decided to talk to Colleen and Gordie with the hope of finding some inspiration. That's when Gordie's impishness took over. He said he had the answer.

"Colleen," Howe said, grinning, "is a lean, mean, blonde machine."

Colleen, Bob and Gordie nearly fell out of their chairs laughing so hard.

The line wasn't used, but Resch said that moment gave him insight into the relationship of Mr. and Mrs. Hockey. This couple had been in love for almost half a century. They knew how to elicit laughter from each other. They knew how to tickle each other. They knew how to have fun. They understood and appreciated their roles within their relationship.

"He's a really down to earth guy and you could tell how their whole relationship worked when you saw them together," Resch said. "Like Gordie always says, the reason he could fully commit himself to his sport is that she took over the reins when it came to taking care of the family and the business."

Resch, now in his early 50's, idolized Howe growing up in Plymouth, Michigan. Money was tight and he didn't attend a lot of Detroit Red Wings games at Olympia, but Howe is paramount in his hockey memories.

He remembers sitting once behind the net at Olympia and seeing Bobby Hull drive toward the goal with the power of a locomotive with a wide-open throttle.

"Roger Crozier was in the net, and Hull was sent into the post," Resch said. "Bodies were flying everywhere and I remember Howe skating away with a look, like *did I do something wrong?* They carried Hull off."

After Resch got married, he was visiting his mother-in-law in Florida when she told him that Gordie Howe could often be seen walking the beach, collecting seashells.

"I said, 'you had better put a little less vodka in your sea breeze drink,'" Resch said, laughing. "I'm thinking, *she is pulling my chain.*"

However, much to Resch's surprise, he did see Mr. Hockey walking on Siesta Beach. At first he was so much in awe, he couldn't even get himself to speak to Gordie. He would just watch him from afar.

Then he literally ran into Howe at the Sarasota K-mart and decided to introduce himself.

"I remember thinking he's a sports legend, but he must know the value of a buck if he shops at K-mart," Resch said, laughing.

They struck up a conversation, and they saw each other on the beach a few times. Resch had some pictures taken and he wanted to get them signed. He took them to the Howe's condo office to drop them off and the manager called Colleen. She said to send Resch down to their condo.

"When I got into the condo, I realized how dedicated she was to his career," Resch said. "Every flat surface in that condo had a picture, lithograph or piece of memorabilia on it. They would be down there three to six weeks and that became her office."

Resch laughs. "Gordie would be down on the beach having a good time and she would be in the condo working."

Resch had already produced *Hockeytown Rocks*, which was used by UPN television for the Stanley Cup celebration. One of his favorite lines in that song was *Remember Mr. Hockey wearing Number 9, tearing it up with the Production Line.*

The Howes liked it as well. Because there were many projects in development at the time, the alliance with Resch was postponed for a couple of years.

One day the Howe's business associates, Del Reddy and Aaron Howard, were discussing new product ideas with Colleen. It was suggested to give Resch a call and see about collaborating with him on marketing a new musical CD.

Reddy phoned Resch. They began discussions about the new "Mr and Mrs. Hockey's Greatest Hits" CD. "Resch is such a talented guy and his Music Town Group with song writer Jim King and singer Dick Fidge are top rate," said Reddy.

Ultimately, Music Town Productions produced the popular music CD, *Mr. and Mrs. Hockey's Greatest Hits*. During the final taping, Colleen, Gordie, Reddy and Howard traveled to Ypsilanti, Michigan, for the finishing cut of the CD at the studio. At the end of the theme song, "they call him Mr. Hockey," Colleen and Gordie taped a message thanking the fans for all their support over the years.

"Thank God that was done," says Resch. "Shortly after, Colleen was unable to participate in things like that."

In working with her, Resch said, "Colleen was one of the most friendly, gracious open hearted people I've ever met."

Like many, Resch appreciates Gordie's sense of humor and his ability to keep everyone guessing about his tricks. One day Resch was walking on the beach with Gordie when Gordie bent over and picked up a camera lying in the sand.

Howe surveyed the beach area for a moment, went over to a group of people, and asked a man if that was his camera.

"The man said it was and I asked him how he knew it was the guy's camera: He just shrugged his shoulders," Resch said, laughing. "I said no wonder he's the greatest player in the world; he's clairvoyant."

Later in their relationship, Howe was re-telling the story, and he asked Mr. Hockey again how he knew whom the camera belonged.

This time Howe laughed and came clean. "I saw it fall out of his pocket," Howe said, chuckling.

"I went for years thinking he was a god," Resch said, laughing. "But what it really shows is the awareness he has. He saw it fall out of his pocket. That's probably the same awareness he used on the ice."

Resch said he also appreciates Howe's ability as a storyteller—of course it helps that Howe's stories have memorable characters.

"I marvel because he can sprinkle his stories with names like Joe DiMaggio, Mickey Mantle, Roger Maris, Rocket Richard and Marilyn Monroe," Resch said. "I'm always freaking out because the closest I've come to knowing another famous person is Bo Schembechler, former Michigan football coach."

Jimmy Skinner

Detroit Red Wings Coach (1954-1958)

General Manager Jack Adams owned such a mastery over hockey strategy and coaching tactics that he could analyze games without actually seeing them.

On the nights that the Detroit Red Wings were on the road, Adams would travel to his office at darkened Olympia Stadium to listen to the game on the radio, presumably because the empty office allowed him to listen to the game without distraction.

"When you came back home, he would say to you, "In that third period, why did you have this player out there instead of Red Kelly?" former coach Jimmy Skinner recalled.

After home games Adams would ask Skinner to come to his office and they would discuss details of the games for at least an hour.

"You never felt like you could make a mistake and you always felt confident around him," Skinner said. "If you did anything wrong, he jumped on you. But he never really openly criticized you. He would say, 'Why did you do this or that?' and I would answer and sometimes he would say, 'That's logical.'"

Skinner and Adams were always in complete agreement that Gordie Howe was the best player they ever saw, and that he should be on the ice at every opportunity.

"He did a lot of amazing things," Skinner said. "He could shoot both right handed and left handed. He could play defense, right wing or center. They all talk about Rocket Richard, however, Richard was a great hockey player from the blue line in. Gordie could check. He could do everything."

Skinner appreciated that Howe had his own personal honor code about how he played the game. It angers Skinner when it's suggested that Mr. Hockey was dirty because he believes nobody saw Howe's true dark side unless they had first done something unsavory by Howe's definition.

"He was never a dirty hockey player," Skinner said. "He was a little chippy, but he did that to make the others players realize they had to respect him."

Through the years, wherever Skinner was coaching, he always started every training camp with a speech in which he implored his players to strive to make their opponents respect them.

"If you don't have respect," Skinner would tell them, "you will be chased out of the league."

According to Skinner, everyone respected Howe, and most of all the fans that witnessed his generosity on many occasions. As a hockey venue, Olympia seemed almost perfect with the low-hanging balcony that seemed to be just a few feet over the player's heads. Those seats, selling for $2.50, often went first. Fans felt connected with their heroes, particularly Howe who would often wink at fans in the stands or smile at a youngster.

"The lights would be dim in the Olympia lobby and Gordie would still be signing autographs after a game," Skinner said. "Other players would come out and walk right by the fans."

At team meetings, Skinner said he would often remind players that fans were the consumers and players owed them more than just a good performance in the game.

"I would say, 'It's going to cost you money if only two or three people are signing autographs and the rest are walking by," Skinner said. "Remember those people are paying your salary."

Howe understood the importance of fans, and with his love of the game, he never did anything half way.

"He used to cost us more for hockey sticks because he would swipe them out of the dressing room for kids," Skinner recalls.

Skinner said Howe did every promotional appearance he was asked to make. In Howe's prime, he was playing more minutes than any forward was in the game. Skinner wanted Howe to skip some practice to assure he was well rested, but he always got an argument from Howe.

With people-person Colleen by Gordie's side, the Howes were truly the Red Wings best advertising.

"She was dedicated to him," Skinner said. "When she first met him she didn't know what a hockey stick looked like. Nevertheless, she made up her mind that she was going to know. She was always there to answer questions for the kids when Gordie was busy, and Gordie was a very busy man."

Art Skov

Legendary NHL Linesman and Referee

The famed Gordie Howe-Lou Fontinato fight on February 1, 1959, actually began with Howe serving as a protector—not a pugilist. This was according to a person who probably had the best view of the altercation.

Art Skov was a NHL linesman that night in Madison Square Garden, and he remembers that hostility began between Detroit's Red Kelly and New York Rangers Eddie Shack. Skov, and his partner Bill Morrison, brought peace to that encounter. But Skov remembers that Fontinato skated in from the blue line as it was breaking up, and Howe said to him, "Hey you big guy, stay out of it."

Order was only temporarily restored because when play resumed Shack was still trying to draw Kelly into a scrap, according to Skov.

"Kelly would have cleaned his clock," Skov insists.

According to newspaper reports, Shack was upset that he had been cut earlier in the game by Howe and roughed up by Pete Goegan.

There is some dispute about precisely what happened next, and there is no film available to collaborate testimony. According to newspaper accounts, Howe became involved with Shack behind the net, presumably because he was continuing to harass Kelly.

Skov says that senior linesman Morrison always liked the younger Skov to enter the combat zone first to break up the fight, but Skov sensed what was about to happen and admits he was less eager to be first man in for break-up duties. That was a tough job, especially when you consider that Skov's starting pay as a linesman was $2,600 per season.

"In from the blue line comes romping Louie," Skov said. "Howe saw him in the reflection in the glass, and he put out his right hand and he busted everything. Everyone formed a half circle and let them fight it out."

Both players were in their prime and Fontinato, 27, already bore a scar from 12 stitches he received in a previous bout with the 30-year old Howe. Fontinato was 195 pounds and he packed a wallop in his right jab, but on this night, he was completely overwhelmed by Mr. Hockey.

"What a powerhouse Gordie was," Skov said.

According to the reporters covering the game, Howe grabbed Fontinato's sweater and brutalized him with savage uppercuts to the face. Estimates on the length of the scrap ranged wildly from 30 seconds to four minutes. The best guess is that it was over in less than a minute.

"Rangers center, Andy Bathgate, was standing beside me and he said, "Art, I think we had better go in and break this up. Louie was tired from getting hit, and Howe was tired from hitting him."

Skov doesn't believe that Fontinato was able to launch any form of attack against Howe, and his face was lost amid the mixture of blood and swelling. Frank Udvari was the referee, and he gave each player a five-minute major penalty for fighting.

"I looked at him and thought, how can you give Fontinato five for fighting when all he did was get hit all the time," Skov said. "He never threw one punch. It was the most one-sided fight I ever saw."

Stan Fischler

Hockey Writer and Television Reporter Since 1955

When Gordie Howe pummeled Lou Fontinato in 1959, he was taking down "the reigning heavyweight champion of the league."

That was the assessment of respected hockey journalist, Stan Fischler, who was on the Eighth Avenue side of the Madison Square Garden press box, right above the action, when the fight occurred.

"If you didn't believe Fontinato was the heavyweight champ, all you had to do was ask him," Fischler says, "because Louie was quite full of himself at the time."

In addition to providing details of the fight, Fischler can offer the context and background that have been lost through the years.

"Shack had been giving Howe a hard time for a couple of years," Fischler said. "If there was anyone who got under Gordie's skin, if that were possible, it was Shack. He was big, and he was sort of like a larger Tie Domi, but he couldn't fight that good."

According to Fischler, the melee started because Shack was involved in "some high sticking against Howe."

"And Louie did what he always did; he butted in," Fischler said. "He came skating in full speed from the left point."

Fischler recalls that Howe "did stare down two or three punches" before he responded. "Then he just destroyed Fontinato," Fischler said.

"Gordie showed what a lot of us knew; that he was the best fighter in the league," Fischler said. "I only saw one guy fight Gordie to a draw, and that was New York Rangers defenseman Jack Evans. Jack was a very tough guy. He was Gordie's size. It was a great fight, but he didn't beat Gordie."

What is also forgotten, according to Fischler, is the traumatic impact the Howe-Fontinato fight had on the New York Rangers who had enjoyed a good season until that point.

"I don't think Fontinato had ever really been beaten before that fight," Fischler said. "And he wasn't just beaten, he was destroyed. It was an embarrassment."

When Fischler got down to the dressing room after the game, it was locked, which was always an indication of something significant happening inside. Reporters could hear shouting and loud banging inside the room.

Fischler said Bill Gadsby, who would later become one of Howe's closest friends, would later tell him that Fontinato had thrown a fit.

"He was so humiliated," Fischler said. "He was throwing skates off the wall and doing crazy things. He was never the same player after that."

More importantly to the New York Rangers, they were never the same team after that fight.

"In a sense, Gordie Howe helped end the New York Rangers playoff run," Fischler said. "The Rangers choked in the homestretch. Fontinato was useless. The Rangers were seven points ahead of the Leafs with two weeks to go, and the Leafs caught them on the final night. A lot of things went wrong, but one of the key things was that Fontinato was useless."

Amusingly, Fischler recalls that the Rangers' press agent, Herb Goren, tried to do some damage control after the fight. Goren had given Fontinato the nickname "Louie the Leaper, and Leapin' Louie," and that helped heighten Fontinato's popularity.

"He had helped build him into a great character and he was beloved by fans," Fischler recalled.

Goren began to tell the New York writers "they had failed to notice all the good body blows that Louie got into Howe."

"It didn't work," Fischler said, laughing. "The picture in Life Magazine of Fontinato's bloodied face erased that alibi."

Fischler believes with conviction that Mr. Hockey was the best player in NHL history.

"There was not a thing that he couldn't do well," Fischler said. "He was ambidextrous. How many guys were ambidextrous? There was nobody else before or since. He had the perfect size. He was a bigger size, but not a cumbersome size. To me, Jean Beliveau was a great, great player, but he was almost too big for the time. Gordie had the absolute perfect size, and he could skate more lyrically and effortlessly than anybody else."

Fischler is amused that some hockey analysts believe Gretzky was a greater player. "I have no arguments about how terrific Wayne Gretzky was," Fischler says. "But his dimensions were limited compared to Howe. Gretzky was a skinny guy. Howe was big for his time. We all know it's a physical game, and so much of Gordie's game was physical.

We didn't keep stats on that. You can't quantify intimidation, you can't quantify the hits, legal or illegal, and you can't quantify a physical presence."

Playing much of his career before hockey television coverage became mainstream, Howe is at a disadvantage in comparisons to Wayne Gretzky, whose exploits were available on videocassette.

"There is not enough video of Howe," Fischler says. "There was not enough media covering hockey when he played. It was a six-team league and so many of the great things he did simply went unrecorded."

Although Howe's intimidation quotient couldn't be statistically defined, it was evident to trained and untrained observers.

Fischler started his television career when the World Hockey Association debuted, and he remembers a night when he said to himself, *I'm now watching Gordie Howe die!*

It was a 1974-1975 game between Howe's Houston Aeros and the New England Whalers, who had a youngster named Nick Fotiu, a Staten Island, New York native who was starting to make a name for himself as a brash, heavy-hitting tough guy.

Fischler was a between-periods host, and he was watching the game at ice level at the Sam Houston Arena. Colleen Howe was standing next to him, and they both saw Gordie retrieve the puck along the boards and Fotiu line him up.

"Fotiu is flying like an out-of-control locomotive and it really looked like it was going to be a devastating check," Fischler said.

This was an era when nobody said much about boarding or checking from behind, and Fichler believed Howe was about to be seriously hurt because it seemed as if he didn't see Fotiu coming.

"He got two inches from Howe and something happened," Fischler said. "The next thing I know, Fotiu is on the ice unconscious. I'm assuming the elbow came up. He probably caught him on his radar just in time. But it was an unbelievable scene."

One of Howe's talents was his ability to physically devastate an opponent without fans or even players truly knowing what he had done.

Mr. Hockey was so dominant that Fischler is convinced that Howe would occasionally play a game within a game to amuse himself.

In 1952, Fischler was in Toronto for Game Three of the Stanley Cup Semifinals between the Maple Leafs and Red Wings. With Detroit up 5-1 late in that game, Howe broke in alone on Toronto goalkeeper, Turk Broda.

"It was as if he was thinking, 'What am I going to do to make this exciting,'" Fischler said. "That's what I interpreted. He faked Broda out to Carlton Street and there was an empty net in front of him. It seemed like he was trying to carom it off the right post, but it didn't go in. I will never forget that. He wanted to make a challenge for himself."

Through the years, Fischler got to know Colleen and he believed she had All-Star qualities in her field.

"She was before her time in a lot of ways," Fischler said. "I remember Colleen pushing certain campaigns that she felt the league wasn't doing right. The league caught on, but they never gave her credit."

Fischler knew Colleen well. "She knew the game and I believe she helped Gordie a lot," Fischler said. "I saw her as an asset to Gordie and she was very well intentioned."

Mr. and Mrs. Hockey both endeared themselves to the media by being overly cooperative. Fischler remembers that *Sport Magazine* hired him to write a lengthy freelance story, about 6,000 words as he recalls, on Howe when he was chasing Rocket Richard's record. He arranged to fly to Montreal for an interview with Howe on a Friday off day. Bad weather forced Fischler's flight to be cancelled. Many athletes may have told Fischler he was out of luck, but Howe met him for breakfast on Saturday and then went on a walk with him around Boston on Sunday.

"He was very amusing, very engaging and he was a great story teller," Fischler said. "What could be better than that?"

Barbara Armstrong

Fan of Colleen and Gordie

When Barbara Armstrong of Otsego, Michigan, was battling breast cancer, she decided that Gordie Howe memories were the best medicine to help ease the distress of chemotherapy.

Her doctor advised her to use "Guided Imagery" to help here cope with her chemotherapy.

"I would close my eyes and visualize Gordie Howe knocking away all of the cancer cells with his hockey stick and elbows," Armstrong says.

Armstrong told her story to the Howes when they met at the "Race for the Cure" in Battle Creek, Michigan, in the summer of 2000.

"I'm convinced through the use of your image that I will remain cancer free," Armstrong told Howe.

Armstrong had followed Howe's career for many years, and had read the *and...HOWE!* book, which chronicled the careers of hockey's greatest couple. She even had personalized license plates that read, "GHOWE9."

When she heard that Colleen had been diagnosed with Pick's Disease, she penned a letter to the Howes saying she appreciated how much they gave of themselves.

Derik Murray

Canadian Television Producer

Ironically, it was at a Wayne Gretzky charity event that Derik Murray came to understand the aura of Mr. and Mrs. Hockey.

"The display of genuine warmth that Gordie and Colleen showed to every person they came in contact with was truly inspiring," Murray says. "They treated everyone from NHL players and Hollywood stars to event staff and fans on the street with an equal amount of respect."

Murray had grown up idolizing Howe. "I thought I knew everything about Gordie after years of studying his stats and attempting to copy his moves in my parent's driveway," he said.

However, he left the event in Brantford, Ontario, with a new perspective of Howe's charm and "an understanding of the key role that Colleen played in his life."

"Gordie and Colleen are a perfect example for anyone in any walk of life," Murray says. "They are a couple who strive for excellence in every endeavor and who are as dedicated to each other as they are to the game they both love."

Five years after the meeting, Murray began production on *Legends of Hockey*, a television series that profiled hockey's greatest players. When the deal was finalized, one of the first calls went to the Howes.

"Their immediate and ongoing support for the project was an important factor in the successful creation of an award-winning documentary series," Murray said.

Bert Webbe

Gordie Howe Hockeyland Student

When Mr. Hockey was running his summer camps at Gordie Howe's Hockeyland in St. Clair Shores in the 1960's and 1970's, it was the equivalent of Frank Sinatra offering singing lessons or former President Dwight Eisenhower teaching a class in foreign policy.

Bert Webbe was a 12-year old Chicago Blackhawks fan in 1966 when his mother signed him up for Howe's camp. But he understood the magnitude of the opportunity that he was receiving.

"I was becoming partial to a player named Bobby Hull, but Gordie Howe was the man," Webbe recalled.

Webbe joked, "He had received every honor that could be bestowed upon a player in the NHL. And now he would have the ultimate honor, he would be charged with the responsibility of honing my game."

Webbe recalls that his parents had barely slowed the car when they dropped him off because he was the youngest child and the only one left at home. His parents were anxious to continue on to Mackinac Island for a vacation without children.

Although the letter of acceptance received from Howe mentioned equipment that seemed foreign to Webbe, he didn't appreciate the problem until he entered the dressing room with other players.

"Prior to signing up for hockey camp, my idea of full equipment consisted of National Geographic magazines wrapped around my legs to serve as shin guards," Webbe said.

As he sorted through the new equipment in his bag, it didn't initially occur to him that there was a sequence that needed to be followed in order to be properly outfitted for competition. After he had pulled his shoulder and elbow pads on, along with his sweater, his new teammates suggested that he was going to look silly if he was going to wear his suspenders over his sweater.

Hoping his wit could cover for his embarrassment, Webbe remembers he joked, "I grew up so poor, I had to wear my mom's Playtex-padded bra before I got shoulder pads."

According to Webbe, who put his Howe memories down on paper in story form in order to preserve them, the laughter accompanied the players out the door."

Howe began the session with a skating drill. Webbe remembers that Howe said, "You will never be a good hockey player unless you become a good skater."

Webbe had only been playing hockey for two winters, and he noticed that most of the other players were wearing sweaters from youth teams. He had considered himself a fast skater, but Webbe was the last skater to complete the first skating drill.

Nobody seemed to notice, except Howe, that Webbe was wearing figure skates instead of hockey skates.

Howe asked Webbe if his parents were around, and Webbe had to tell Mr. Hockey they were on their way to the Upper Peninsula. By then the other campers were starting to see the amusement in Webbe's circumstances.

Leaning over to get closer to Webbe, Howe said, "Go see the fella in the pro shop and tell him that I want him to fit you with a pair of hockey skates. Tell him to charge my account."

Webbe has never forgotten Howe's generosity in buying him his first hockey skates. Years later, Webbe reminded Howe about his memories and Mr. Hockey knew exactly what he was talking about.

"We operated that hockey camp for ten years and no other boy ever showed up wearing figure skates," said Howe, laughing at the memory.

.oto by Lynn Gregg

Canada Post honored Gordie with the first stamp ever issued depicting a hockey player. (Toronto, March 21, 2000)

Colleen and Gordie, with associate Aaron Howard, check out the elbow on the Mr. Hockey® statue in Gordie's hometown of Saskatoon, Saskatchewan.

Photo by Eric Chenoweth

Mr. & Mrs. Hockey® are minority owners of Ron Toigo's WHL team, the Vancouver Giants.

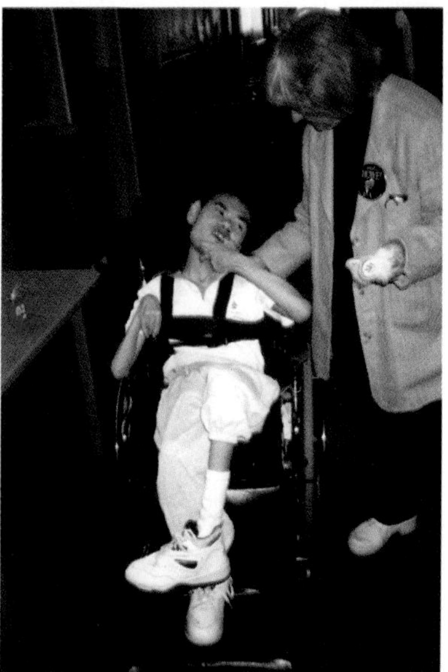
Photo by Helen Cottrell

Colleen has always had a passion to help children. She has spearheaded a number of fundraising activites over the years to help others.

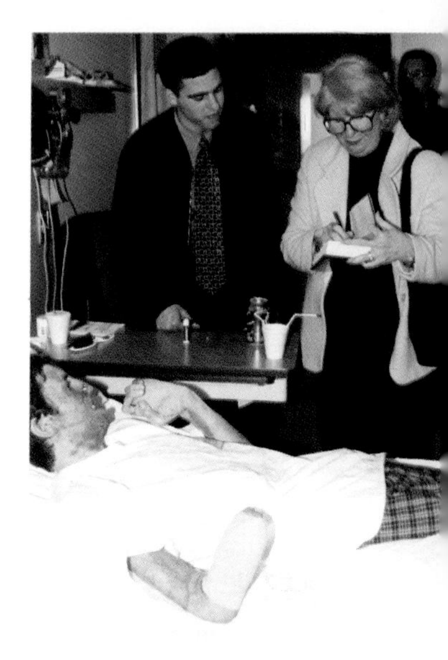

Colleen signs an "and...HOWE!" book for a young man in Saskatoon, Sasketchwan who was severely injured in a farming accident.

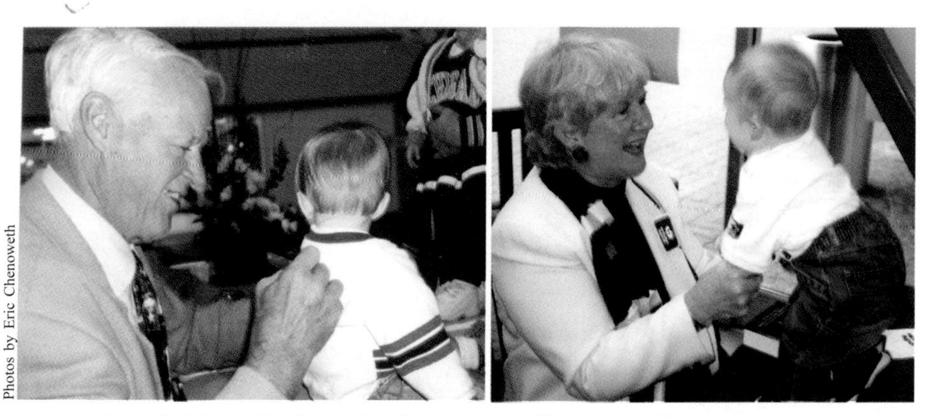
Photos by Eric Chenoweth

Mr. & Mrs. Hockey's® fans span all ages and generations.

Photo by Eric Cheneweth

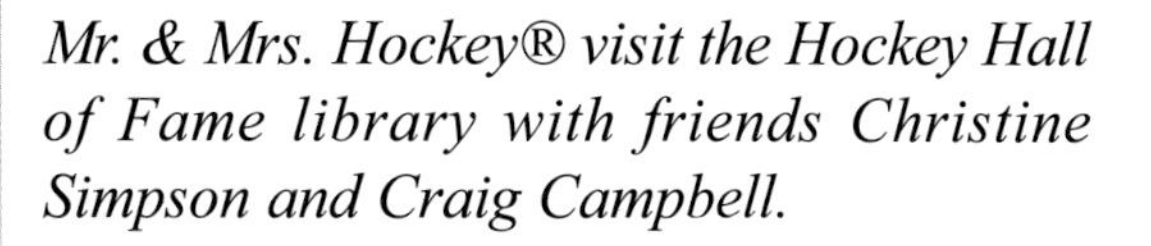

Mr. & Mrs. Hockey® visit the Hockey Hall of Fame library with friends Christine Simpson and Craig Campbell.

Photo by Lynn Gregg

Mr. & Mrs. Hockey®, Bill Gadsby and Red Wing announcer Ken Kal pose for a photo outside of Joe Louis Arena.

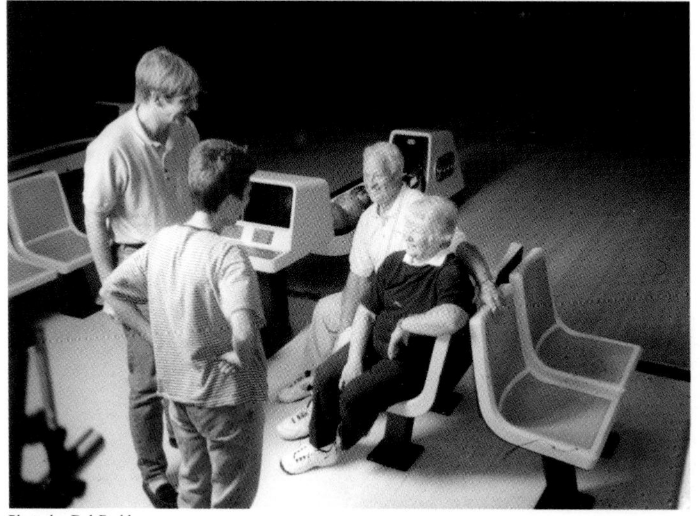

Photo by Del Reddy

Lorien Studio's renowned photographer John Sobczak and his assistant Regan discuss how the Howes first met at The Lucky Strike Bowling Alley in 1950.

Bobby Hull, Gordie, Dick Butkus, Chris Chelios and his famous friends pose with the Stanley Cup before the start of the Chelios Celebrity golf outing.

Photo by Dave Story

Photo by Helen Cottrell

Mr. Hockey ® and Hall of Famer Alex Delvecchio played together in the NHL for 50 years. Alex has always said that Gordie is unquestionably the greatest player in history.

Photo by Aaron Howard

Mrs. Hockey® surprised the Minnesota Wild brass in their innaugural season by purchasing 4 season tickets to be reserved for underprivileged children.

Photo by Lynn Gregg

"Doc" Andrews, his wife Amy, Big Al and the rest of the Dick Purtan crew from 104.3 WOMC pose with Mr. Hockey® during the Walt Disney World Millenium Celebration. (1999)

The Gregg Family receives the famous elbow from Mr. Hockey®

Photo by Del Reddy

Gordie, Dave Hanson, Jeff Carlson and Kick 10's Mark Stein at the Chris Chelios' charity golf outing luncheon.

Photo by Helen Cottrell

Dan Stahl, the developer of the award winning mrandmrshockey.com website.

Photo by Lynn Gregg

Colleen reminisces with special friends, the Bowers, at the Hockey Hall of Fame.

Photo by Aaron Howard

Gordie speaks with Warren Erhart, the President of White Spot Restaurants of Canada.

Photo by Aaron Howard

Mr. Hockey® receives treatment from John Czarnecki of the Training Room.

Photo by Del Reddy

Gordie, Tiger legend Billy Rogell and DC Sport's "Zac" at the Tiger's opening game in 2001.

Gordie receives Canada's Walk of Fame Star. Colleen proudly looks on.

Photo by Del Reddy

'hoto by Lynn Gregg

Colleen and Gordie with business managers Del Reddy & Aaron Howard (not pictured). They are proud to have helped Mr. & Mrs. Hockey® reach new levels of success in business and philanthropy.

Detroit News Publisher Mark Silverman honored Mr. & Mrs. Hockey® as Michiganians of the year. (2002)

Photo by Lynn Gregg

Mr. & Mrs. Hockey® join President Bush at his fundraising dinner in Detroit. (June 2000)

Photo by Aaron Howard

Photo by Lynn Gregg

In November 2000, the Howe family was enshrined into the U.S. Hockey Hall of Fame.

Photo by Del Reddy

D3 Artwork's Rick Murphy and John Littlejohn present Prime Minister Chretien with the Mr. Hockey® Coca-Cola Lithograph.(on the set of the TV show Canada AM)

Photo by Lynn Gregg

D3 Artwork's famous fan scene at Galt Arena honors the Howes with their inclusion in the painting. Additionally, Mr. Hockey® is immortalized in a 14 foot painting by John Littlejohn and Rick Murphy.

Amazing artists Rick Murphy and John Littlejohn of D3 Artworks honor Colleen with a historic painting to be displayed in the Mr. & Mrs. Hockey® Museum.

Photo by Aaron Howard

Mr. Hockey®, the all-time regular season scoring king, with home run king Hank Aaron and Del Reddy at a Super Bowl event in New Orleans.

The first couple of hockey with their VIP friend of 18 years-- Mike Hagen.

Photo by Aaron Howard

Mr. & Mrs. Hockey® with the "King of the Palace," Joe Dumars.

Photo by Del Reddy

Hall of Famer's Colleen and Gordie with coaching legend Al Arbour and wife Claire.

Photo by Aaron Howard

The Great One, Wayne Gretzky, greets Mr. Hockey® in Chicago. Wayne says Gordie is the closest there ever was to being a perfect hockey player.

Wayne Gretzky, Aaron Howard, Mario Lemieux, Gordie and Del Reddy in Toronto for the famous "Pond of Dreams" segment.

Photo by Aaron Howard

Mr. Hockey® drops the puck at the world's largest outdoor hockey game ever. U of M vs. MSU.

Photo by Aaron Howard

Denise Ilitch and her husband Jim with Gordie & Colleen at Tiger Stadium.

Photo by Lynn Gregg

Mr. & Mrs. Hockey® celebrate their Olympic torch run with Maureen Reddy, Del Reddy & Aaron Howard.

Photo by Aaron Howard

Mr. Hockey®, CBC host Scott Oake, producer Michael Drapack & cameraman Mark Punga. They produced a Hockey Night in Canada special on Colleen.

Photo by Lynn Gregg

On Channel 95.5FM, Mojo in the morning crew announced to the world that Colleen and Gordie were being enshirined into the U.S. Hockey Hall of Fame.(Pictured with Mr. & Mrs. Hockey® are Chad, Mojo, Eric, Sara, & Spike)

Hockey's all-time games played leader, Gordie, and baseball's Iron Man Cal Ripken with Del Reddy at Super Bowl 2002.

Photo by Helen Cottrell

Mr. Hockey® with football great Barry Sanders and his wife Lauren.

Photo by Lynn Gregg

Fox Sports Net Detroit host John Keating profiled the "Grateful Gadsby" book signing at Westland Shopping Center.

Photo by Aaron Howard

Trevor Thompson of Fox Sports interviews Mr. Hockey® after he was chosen for the Nextel NHL all-time all star team.

Photo by Aaron Howard

Mr. Hockey® with the CEO of Belfor USA Sheldon Yellen.

Power Play staff with Gibraltor show promoters Wanda O'Brien, Mark Diehm and DC Sport's Steve Graus.

Abbottsford, British Columbia honored the Howes by naming their new middle school "Colleen and Gordie Howe® Middle School."

Mr. & Mrs. Hockey® proudly carried the Olympic torch. They are believed to be the only sports couple in the USA to have had this distinction.(January 6, 2002)

The cast and crew of Mr. & Mrs. Hockey's® Greatest Hits CD. Aaron Howard, Gordie & Colleen with composer Jim King, producer Bob Resch, world class vocalist Dick Fitch and co-writer Del Reddy.

Photo by Mike Hagen

Mr. Hockey® with the President of Frameworth, Brian Ehrenworth, in his office at their world headquarters in Toronto.

Photo by Mike Hagen

Vice President of Frameworth, Brian Ducheck, proudly displays the framed collectible that features Mr. Hockey® and the Great One.

Photo by Mike Hagen

Harry & Brian Ehrenworth, Gordie and Brian Ducheck elbow out some ideas for new products.

Robert Puckett

Former Gordie Howe Hockey Student

Colleen Howe gave birth to four children, but there are hundreds of adults today that view her as their surrogate hockey mom.

According to Robert Puckett, a former Gordie Howe Hockeyland camper, folks in St. Clair Shores, Michigan, haven't forgot Colleen's hands-on management approach to the summer hockey school.

"The hot cocoas at Gordie Howe's Hockeyland are still a pleasant taste we like to savor," says Puckett, now 43.

Puckett couldn't skate at all when he showed up for the camp, and he even put his shin guards over his socks before his first session.

"I need to thank Mrs. Howe," Puckett says. "Mom told me how much Colleen helped her with understanding the rules and the little ways I could help myself off the ice. Of course, I didn't know who she was, nor that she was helping. Mom told me she listened to every word Colleen told her. It was like reading a book."

Meanwhile, Puckett said he remembered Gordie, Marty and Mark Howe "working my tail off" in the summer session. Puckett said he was "big, clumsy and determined."

"But by the end of the first season, I was a hefty defensive forward playing with the drive of a Stevie Yzerman," Puckett said.

When Puckett heard that Colleen was diagnosed with a rare form of dementia, he felt compelled to write a letter to the Howes to express the impact they had on his life.

"The love of Mrs. Howe is one of true compassion for people, not team sports or hockey," Puckett wrote. "We hope a cure can be found so Colleen can live out her days with the memories of our boyish laughter. This was a lady who helped us learn the game we love, never asking for anything except to help; something she did without tiring. Everyone in St. Clair Shores would gladly give anything to allow Colleen to see the things that she made."

Travis Howe

Son of Mark and Ginger Howe

Travis Howe recalls with amusement that he always dialed up his intensity and prickliness when his grandfather Gordie Howe came to watch him compete. "I would always instigate a fight or play much more physical," Travis said. "I guess I felt I wanted to look tough in front of him."

It was always a treat to have Mr. Hockey in the stands proudly cheering for him, but Travis recalls it had a more tangible benefit when he was playing for the Little Caesars Midget Minor team at a tournament in London, Ontario. With Gordie in the stands, Travis became involved in an altercation with another player. Travis wrestled the player down to the ice, and began to swing away. Just as Travis was about to launch another right hand, the referee got in the way and Travis inadvertently struck him in the face. "Needless to say, he was extremely upset and was about to expel me from the tournament for fighting." Travis recalled.

While the referee was at the scorekeeper's box composing himself for the penalty decisions, someone mentioned to him that Gordie Howe had made the trip to watch his grandson play. "Instead of throwing us out he gave us both double minors," Travis recalled. "I was thankful at that moment that my grandfather was there, as was the other player."

Now 24, Travis has fond memories of visiting his grandparents at their home in Traverse City, Michigan. Most fans think of Olympia Stadium when they think of Gordie Howe. However, Travis thinks of fishing, searching for Petoskey stones, playing cards at the kitchen table and eating at the Omelet Shop a few miles from the Howe homestead. "My grandparents taught me the values of family and how important your family really is to you," Travis said. "There was never a minute where my grandparents were not thinking about us. People look at my grandfather as "Mr. Hockey" and my grandmother as the businesswoman behind the scenes. I see them as incredible grandparents who have put all of their time and efforts into their family. There are many laughs and smiles I have shared with them and I will always love them for everything they mean to me."

Azia Howe

Daughter of Mark and Ginger Howe

When Azia was young, she remembers telling her grandmother that her "dream vacation" would be to go to Hawaii. The following year Gordie and Colleen surprised her, along with her younger brother and two cousins, with a trip to Honolulu, Kona and Maui.

As much as Colleen enjoyed the business world, what she enjoyed more was making her grandchildren happy.

"I have gone on many vacations with them," said Azia, now 22. "They have taken me and my cousins to Canada, the Poconos, and even to Russia. We also vacationed in Sarasota, Florida, with them every spring while we were growing up. But my most memorable vacation with my grandparents was a 10-day trip to Hawaii."

Since Azia's cousins liked horses, the Howes planned two days on Kona to visit a ranch. Unfortunately, for the party, it rained for 48 hours. They drove around to look at the sights, but all they found were miles and miles of sugarcane.

The endless acreage of sugarcane became a source of amusement for their grandmother.

"Anytime someone complained about being bored in the car, my grandmother would just say, "Hey, look at all of that sugarcane," Azia recalls fondly. Grandmother and the children would howl with laughter.

The Howe grandchildren benefited from having active grandparents. Before leaving for Maui, Azia and her grandfather went exploring. They saw tons of molten lava and hundreds upon hundreds of white rocks. All along the way, people had put rocks together to spell their names.

"So to make sure people knew we were there, we stopped and wrote "The Howes 1994," Azia said.

The most memorable day of the trip was one that has provided years of stories and laughter for the family and it involved Azia's chance encounter with a giant sea turtle.

Azia and a cousin had just finished snorkeling, and were trying to find a passageway through a large patch of seaweed. They decided to separate, with the plan of whomever found a path would show the other.

"I picked the wrong way because after a few seconds of swimming," Azia said. "I looked up and there was a giant turtle head that was bigger than me staring me right in the face."

Azia immediately started screaming. She swam as fast as she could in the opposite direction until she finally found an exit from the seaweed.

"When I finally had enough courage to tell my grandpa what I just saw, he got so excited," Azia recalled. "He and the rest of my cousins went off to see the turtles. If only I wasn't so scared, I would have been able to share in watching the beautiful sea turtles. Now I am just scared of the ocean, which is quite unfortunate since I live on a boat every summer!"

"My grandparents have never let me forget that day," says Azia.

At every holiday, Azia received a turtle figurine. "Now every time I see some form of turtle, I am reminded of my grandparents," Azia says. "It isn't that I remember looking into the turtle's face necessarily, but I remember how wonderful my grandparents are for allowing me to witness something so fantastic."

According to Azia, it wasn't the Hawaii vacation she remembers as much what it meant to her that her grandparents were willing to put the work on hold for their grandchild.

"Then again, they always did everything for their grandchildren," Azia said. "I am very fortunate to have grandparents like them, ones that are always there for me and have showed me how much they love and care for me. I will never forget that trip and the many great memories my grandparents have given me. I just want them to know how much it means to me."

Nolan Howe

Son of Mark and Ginger Howe

Nolan Howe says he has had more special moments with his grandparents "than a whole book could ever capture."

He remembers his grandparents rented a condominium every year in Sarasota, Florida, and would fly all of their grandchildren, in first class no less, for a visit over Easter.

"Those were, to this day, the greatest vacations ever," Nolan remembers. "I just always look back at the generosity they showed us to give up their little vacation time each year to spend with us." How much fun was it? "Come on, 12 years old, beaches, pools, basketball nets," says Nolan, now 17. "No parents, just grandparents; who you know always let you stay up a little later or bought you the extra piece of candy. It was Heaven on Earth."

Grandpa would take the kids on a seashell-collecting exhibition that would last about two minutes. "We all gave up and went running into the water," Nolan said. It was movies every night with popcorn and blankets. In the day, Nolan could be found playing soccer on the beach with his sister, Azia, and Mr. Hockey.

"The most special time of every year though was when we would all get up really early on Easter Sunday to attend the morning service held on the beach. Just walking there with my grandparents and all the grandchildren and watching the sunrise. It was beautiful."

Nolan treasures those moments as much as or maybe even more than Red Wings fans treasure their recollections of No. 9 coming over the blue line and ripping a wrist shot past Montreal goalkeeper Jacques Plante.

"My grandparents have given me so much, and I love them with all my heart," Nolan said. "This is my story to them to let them know how much, now and forever, those trips meant to me. Thank you for being such great grandparents to us all."

Cathy (Howe) Purnell

Daughter of Gordie and Colleen

Unparalleled hockey achievements, awards and trophies packed away for safe keeping, countless hours of charity work, Colleen's run for Congress, formation of the Howe Foundation, restaurants, the ahead-of-her time businesswoman, the goodwill, press clippings and photos; no one understands the public image of Gordie and Colleen Howe better than their children.

"But it is the private moments, the ones witnessed through an adult child's eyes that are the greatest tribute to my parents," says daughter Cathy.

She calls her mom and dad the "rocks of my foundation."

"They were the parents who made sure that every night we went to bed knowing we were loved unconditionally," Cathy said. "I don't know how, but somehow they found the time to be involved in our daily lives, our schools, checking homework, meeting and welcoming new friends, especially those high school dates."

Cathy jokingly adds, "It's a wonder that after the first date's interrogation by Marty and Mark that I ever got asked out again."

According to Cathy, her parents guided her in every phase of her life.

"In early childhood, they were there for every scraped knee, every ballet lesson, skating lesson, and every magical birthday party. Mom somehow pulled together, plus tolerated and even encouraged, what must have seemed like endless screeching viola practice," Cathy said. "Then came what I now know is the toughest job—the teenage years.

Cathy insists she was responsible for her parent's gray hair.

"Mom says there was one for every time I worried them," says Cathy. "They were there with patience and wisdom that I didn't appreciate until now. Always asking where I was going, with whom, when would I be home and how they could find me if needed.

"They were true poster parents for *The Responsibility Is Yours* anti-drug campaign. One of them was always up and waiting for my safe, and on time, arrival home. They shared every smile, wiped away every tear, listened patiently to all the teenage traumas and talked me through each heartache I was sure would never end."

As parents, the Howes were disciplinarians, but always generous with the hugs and kisses.

"And much to my frustration they were always one step ahead of me," Cathy says.

When Cathy became an adult, she said her parents became her closest friends.

"They are the first phone call for every bit of news, good and bad," Cathy says. "Until the past year, I couldn't imagine a week going by without talking to Mom. There was never anything I couldn't share with her. Now Dad gets to listen to my bragging about Bob, Jaime, and Jade. They are still the first smiles to greet me everyday as their picture sits on my nightstand. I love, admire and respect them more than I could ever put into words."

Cathy calls her parents "an amazing couple" because they illustrate what it takes to make a marriage and partnership last for more than 50 years.

"They have been through the 'for better, for worse, for richer, for poorer, in sickness and health,' and have been caught holding hands walking down the beach," Cathy says. "What a shocker that was for the grandchildren! I have been truly blessed to have the parents and family I do, and thank the Lord for each and every one of them everyday. Mom and Dad's unwavering commitment to family and love for each other is the truly their greatest story."

Bob Purnell

Son-in-Law of Gordie and Colleen

When Bob Purnell married Cathy in February 2000, he quickly discovered that Colleen recognized no statutes of limitation, and would allow no age discrimination when it comes to mothering her children.

A few months before they were married, Gordie and Colleen invited Bob and Cathy to join them for Wayne Gretzky's Hall of Fame induction in Toronto that year. The crowd was overflowing that night and everyone became separated. Eventually Bob and Cathy stumbled upon Colleen talking with her dear friend Edna Gadsby, wife of Hall-of-Famer, Bill Gadsby. The two ladies were enjoying a glass of wine, and as Bob walked up from behind Colleen he heard her say, "I wonder where the kids are?"

"What makes this so funny," says Bob Purnell, "is I am only five years younger than Colleen and it has been quite a while since anyone called me 'kid.'"

Bob came to realize that Colleen always had time for her children, always wanted to help and would move mountains to be part of their lives. Bob and Cathy were married in the Jefferson County Courthouse in Montana, and he had only met his perspective in-laws twice before the marriage. The Purnells had planned a two-week Caribbean cruise for their honeymoon, and invited Gordie and Colleen to join them on their second week. Gordie had previous commitments, but Colleen wouldn't miss a chance to be with her family. She met them in Miami.

"She checked into a suite on the ship. When we sailed that evening, much to her surprise, Cathy and I had our stateroom and Colleen couldn't believe that we didn't stay with her in her suite," Bob said. "I was very well aware of Honey's reputation of being generous, but this was generosity above and beyond. We still love to tell this story."

Bob says he considers himself "the luckiest man alive" that he discovered Cathy and her daughter Jade. He says he feels blessed that the Howe family accepted him with "love and respect."

"Every one of Gordie and Colleen's children are an example of how all children should be raised," Purnell said. "What a testimonial to what hard work, discipline and education will accomplish."

Jade Roskam

Daughter of Cathy (Howe) Purnell

Jade Roskam remembers that the mile-long walk to the ice cream parlor from her grandparents home on Lake Michigan could be rewarding in more ways than one.

When she was six and seven years old she remembers walking with her grandmother, known to her as Honey, 50 feet behind the remaining family members, including her grandfather who is known to the grandkids as Pee-Paw. The walk by itself would have been a great memory, but much to Jade's amazement she would find money every time she would go for ice cream. Primarily, it would be spare change, but every once in a while a dollar bill would be located, and once she found a 50-dollar bill.

"Honey" always told me that a lot of joggers ran down the road early in the morning and must lose money out of their pockets," said Jade, now 16.

It wasn't until she was nine that her mother slipped and revealed that it was actually her grandfather who was purposely dropping the money that she was finding. He had accidentally dropped the $50, thinking it was $5.

"That's how 'Honey' and 'Pee-paw' acted, always trying to give to others," Jade remembered. "They love their family and are always there to help us out and to talk to us. I thank them for being such great grandparents and I love them both."

Jaime Greer

Daughter of Cathy (Howe) Roskam

Jamie was the first granddaughter of Gordie and Colleen Howe. Now 23, she wrote her own tribute to them.

"Luck can be defined in many ways. Throughout all of our lives, we encounter lucky people, lucky things and lucky places. But few can say that they are truly lucky."

"The two most amazing people in the hockey world are the two most amazing people in my life. Gordie and Colleen Howe are not only the best grandparents, but are my idols, my heroes and my family. In 24 years, I have experienced things with them that have not only made me a wiser individual, but also made me the person I am today. From family vacations to hockey functions to my horse shows, there is not one moment that I have not loved and will treasure in my heart forever.

"Through ups and downs, they have always been there holding my hand and giving encouraging words when they were needed. They have opened my eyes to so many places, people and things that I could never thank them enough. It is very difficult to find words for a feeling that is so full of love and admiration. It almost seems impossible to get the words out, but in the end, what always seems to be consistent is that I am truly the luckiest person to have been blessed with them as grandparents.

"'Honey' and 'Pee-Paw', time may pass, our lives may change and we may always seem to head in different directions, but please always know that I love you both more than words could ever say and feel blessed to be able to call you my family. I love you both."

Ken Kal

Detroit Red Wings Play-By-Play Broadcaster

Some fans wear their hockey allegiance on their sleeves, but Detroit Red Wings broadcaster Ken Kal carries his in his wallet in the form of an Olympia Stadium ticket stub from January 25, 1969. "It was my first NHL game and Gordie Howe scored a goal and mixed it up with Carol Vadnais," Kal said. "He didn't fight, but I think he cut Vadnais. Terry Sawchuk started that game, and I always wondered if it was his last game as a Red Wing."

Kal said Howe's name is one of the most "magical" in Detroit sports lore. "I grew up listening to Budd Lynch and Bruce Martyn calling Howe's name all the time," Kal recalled. "Then you would tune in Sunday and hear Dan Kelly calling Howe's name. For so many years you heard Howe this and Howe that, and I can tell you as a broadcaster, it hasn't gone away." He pauses, "When someone says the Howe name, you just listen. After all, he is one of the greatest, if not, the greatest player, who ever was."

One of Kal's treasured hockey mementos is a photo he had snapped of him standing beside Mr. Hockey. He enjoys telling the story of why his face is contorted in the photo. Right after the Red Wings 1997 Stanley Cup Championship parade, Kal was with Mark Howe, who is a professional scout for the Red Wings. When he spotted Gordie, he asked Mark if he could get his picture taken with Mr. Hockey. Mark offered to operate the camera. "Right before the picture I'm smiling real nice and I got my arm on Gordie's shoulder," says Kal, laughing. "Right before the shot, Gordie gives me the elbow and I suddenly look like Lee Harvey Oswald in that famous photo."

Kal has had only one conversation with Colleen, but he came away from it understanding Mrs. Hockey's reputation as a people person.

As a board member of the Michigan Polish Sports Hall of Fame, Kal had called Colleen to discuss the fact that Gordie Howe has some Polish lineage. "It was almost like I was talking to one of my aunts," Kal said. "We talked about 45 minutes on the phone and she told me about Gordie growing up. I remember thinking this is a great phone call."

Rich DeLisle

Publisher of USA Junior Hockey Magazine

When magazine owner, Rich DeLisle, first witnessed Gordie Howe's legendary status in person, Mr. Hockey had a pen in his hand, not a hockey stick.

"They say Gordie Howe was a great hockey player, but he is even greater as a man," DeLisle says. "That was evidenced in the first time I met him."

The event was the U.S. Junior A National Tournament in Green Bay, Wisconsin, and Howe was signing autographs, just like he had been doing for more than 54 years.

"People were lined up there for three or four hours," DeLisle said. "And everyone got the same attention from the first person to the 4,000th person."

That didn't surprise DeLisle because he understands that the Howes had helped shape the landscape of junior hockey. There are 4,000 players and more than 200 teams in Junior A hockey today, and DeLisle believes Colleen played a role in that as the driving force in the formation of Detroit Junior A Red Wings

"She spearheaded the development of junior hockey in the United States," DeLisle says. "That was just the beginning of what she has done for hockey in the United States, particularly with establishing rinks and programs."

DeLisle remembers the Howes sponsored "some sort of Mite program and that was in the 1960's."

"What the Howes have done for hockey is nothing new," DeLisle said. "They have probably done more off the ice than Gordie did on the ice."

Mark Hacala

Master Chief Hospital Corpsman

After Colleen Howe was diagnosed with Pick's Disease, Gordie received a letter of support from a U.S. military man who said in essence that Mr. Hockey was a gift for all occasions.

Keeping in the Howe's tradition of wanting to share their lives, Master Chief Mark Hacala has made it a habit of giving Gordie Howe signed Detroit Red Wings pucks as gifts. He is always humbled by the response he receives.

Here are some of his gift stories:

A friend of his works for the Department of Veterans Affairs in Dearborn, Michigan, and his daily mission is to help combat veterans recover from the emotional trauma of war. A combat wounded veteran himself who deals with his own pain, he played hockey in an adult league to relieve the tension of his job. "Getting the puck you signed brought him to tears," Hacala wrote to Howe.

He gave another Howe-signed puck to a dyed-in-the-wool Boston Bruins fan. He was a master chief petty officer in the Navy and a former youth hockey coach. "He put forth a lot of effort to get personnel and tons of supplies to the World Trade Center site," Hacala said. "He even went there himself to dig through the rubble. I could not think of anything else that would demonstrate my esteem for his dedicated service than a Howe inscription to him."

Howe had signed "Happy 40th" to Hacala's brother and that puck had become a special birthday gift.

When another friend, a diehard Torontonian and Leafs fan, completed her PhD, Hacala gave her a Mr. Hockey signed puck. According to Hacala, she had said, "That was the coolest graduation present I got from anybody."

Hacala had repaid acts of kindness with pucks, like when a family friend who had twice given up his Red Wings season tickets to Hacala and his brothers over the Christmas holiday. "He had a lot of nice things, but he did not have a puck autographed to him by Mr. Hockey," Hacala wrote.

Not long before Hacala wrote his letter, he had coordinated with Aaron Howard of the Howe's company, Power Play, to arrange for his wife's parents to meet Mr. Hockey at a Gibraltar Trade Center show.

Hacala inadvertently discovered a couple of years before that his in-laws were devout Howe fans.

Hacala had made the mistake of mentioning that he liked the phrase "Gordie Howe Hat Trick" as meaning a goal, an assist and a fight.

"My mother-in-law, Heidi, immediately went off on a rant describing how you were not a constant fighter, but were known more for your use of your elbows," Hacala said. "She knew this from seeing numerous games at Olympia. His father-in-law, Jim, leaped in saying how you'd wait patiently for weeks to get someone back for a dirty hit."

Hacala had not told his in-laws why they were going to Gilbratar. They were stunned when Howe stepped out of a mini-van followed by Aaron Howard carrying his camera. His father-in-law, who grew up a fan of Rocket Richard, but believed Howe was the best, stood almost at military attention, holding out his hand and saying, "Sir, it's an honor."

Howe smiled, and said, "It's Gordie."

Howard snapped some photos from the special encounter and as is his custom, Gordie began telling stories. Hacala's father-in-law, a Chatham, Ontario, native, loved all of them, especially the tale of why Howe named his dog Rocket.

In that meeting, Howe had talked openly of the sadness he felt over Colleen's illness. It is clear to everyone that in addition to being husband and wife, Gordie and Colleen are best friends.

That's why Hacala said he felt compelled to write so he could remind Howe that he had thousands of fans that would like to share his pain because they had shared his joy.

"Throughout my life you've given me thrills and excitement on the ice," Hacala wrote. "To all the people who have received a puck you've autographed, you've given them something to cherish. Thanks for the memories, your time, your humor and for giving me a name to say with enthusiasm and reverence."

Jim Gray

Photographer and Wayne State University Professor

As much as Mr. Hockey earned a reputation for the creative use of his elbows and as an athlete willing to play a tad naughty to gain an advantage, he also enjoys having fun with his image.

Photographer Jim Gray learned that the first few times he captured Howe on film interacting with fans.

"I would say, "Okay. Everyone ready? One...Two...," Gray recounts. "The count of three was rarely heard as Gordie would thrust his left elbow beneath the chin of a fan. Click! Everyone would be laughing."

There are thousands of photos of Gordie poking fun at his tough guy reputation by throwing a fake elbow toward a fan's face or ribs, making contact but not hurting his admirer.

After being introduced to the Howes by their agent Del Reddy, Gray became friends with Mr. & Mrs. Hockey by photographing book signings, Red Wings Alumni games and even the induction ceremony for the Michigan Sports Hall of Fame. Gray became aware that Colleen and Gordie were bound by their playfulness and impishness.

When Gray was a young biology teacher at Lincoln Park High School in the late 1960's, he would sometimes find himself the victim of student tomfoolery. He remembers telling the Howes about how he once found his name on a graffiti-infested bulletin board in a school hallway.

"Along with my name, there was a witty, off-color comment suggesting that I was having a relationship with a rabbit," Gray said. "Colleen loved the story."

At a subsequent dinner with Gray at The Palace in Auburn Hills, Michigan, Colleen presented Gray with "a huge stuffed rabbit" as a gag gift.

"Colleen is the unifying factor throughout the Howe family and she possesses a sense of humor to match that of Gordie," Gray says. "We have shared many laughs."

As someone who seems to enjoy the twists and tumbles of life, Gray seemed to enjoy the irony of "a guy who can't skate hobnobbing with Gordie and Colleen Howe."

He appreciated that hanging with the Howes afforded him many opportunities to explore the joy of life through his 35mm.

"To me, a camera is somewhat like a microscope," Gray said. "Through the lens, I am able to concentrate on the subjects and filter out potential distractions. I enjoy candid photographs capturing people laughing and truly enjoying life. My friendship with the Howes certainly provided me with ample opportunities to capture such moments. Their love for each other, their family, close friends and ever expanding fan base is evident in my photos. They exude a fondness for their fans and truly enjoy sharing time and stories with them. Their sincerity and enthusiasm for the well-being of others remain intact behind the scenes in private moments."

Mel King

Former Michigan Foster Parent of the Year

In 1992 Mel King was flying from Ohio to her home in Kingsley, Michigan with a terminally ill baby she had just adopted. A stranger in the Detroit Metropolitan Airport befriended her.

"I was real nervous, and she had noticed," King recalled. "She patted me on the shoulder, and said 'do you realize that your baby is blue?' I said 'I do' because she has a real rare heart condition."

They talked for a few hours, and the woman clearly was moved by King's story of being a foster parent and her willingness to open her home to an extremely ill child. When it was time for King to board her plane, the woman gave King her business card and said she wanted to help.

A few weeks later King found the card in a diaper bag and began corresponding with the kind stranger and informing her about the condition of her daughter.

"Months later I was writing another card out to her and addressing it when my girlfriend came in," King recalled. "She asked who I was writing to, and I told her it was the woman I met in the airport. She grabbed the card and said to me: 'Do you have any idea who these people are?'"

The woman in the airport had been Colleen Howe.

"My husband is the biggest hockey fan in the world and he had just never paid any attention to who I was writing to," King said, laughing at the memory. "When I called her I said, '*Why didn't you tell me who you were?*'"

Colleen replied, "Because Mel, I wanted you to like me for me."

Mel and husband John got to know Colleen and Gordie extremely well, but Mel says after Colleen said what she did "I always had trouble seeing them in any different light."

To the Kings, the Howes weren't superstars, just friends who shared their desire to be helpful. The Kings were foster parents for 20 years, and the last 12 of those years they specialized in terminally ill or medically fragile children. Colleen was particularly touched by the work that the

Kings did. They had four biological children of their own, and adopted six others, and three of those died.

The Kings were named Michigan Foster Parents of the Year, and Colleen and Gordie, along with their associate Del Reddy, surprised them by flying to Lansing for the awards ceremony.

"I was scared to death to begin with and then I walk in and they are there," King said. "Oh my goodness. And I heard that it was quite the story getting them there, because they were off somewhere else."

Colleen had wanted to be there. "And she moved mountains to be there," King said, laughing.

At Christmas time, the Howes and Reddy brought presents to the King children. The Howes were financial backers as well.

"We were putting an addition on our house, and Gordie happened to come through and was looking at it," King said. "He asked when it was going to be done, and I said 'not for a little bit, because we have to save some money to do it.' And the Howes helped pay to finish the addition."

Nelson "Freckles" Little

Former Minor League Goalkeeper

In a letter to the *Hockey News* in 1994, Tulsa, Oklahoma community leader Nelson Little penned, "if hockey gave out a top award equal to the Nobel Prize it should definitely go to the great Gordie Howe."

Gordie and Colleen had just visited Tulsa as part of the Mr. Hockey 65th birthday 65-city birthday tour, and they had raised $12,000 for Easter Seals and a local youth hockey program. During the entire year, the tour raised over $1 million for charity throughout North America.

Even though Gordie was combating the effects of the flu, he fulfilled his day-long duties in Tulsa, including a picture and autograph party that lasted well into the early morning hours at his hotel. Freckles was impressed that Howe approached his promotional obligations with the same durability he had as a player.

"The job he is doing for youth minor hockey in this country and Canada is commendable," Little wrote. "And I might add the name of his wife, Colleen. They have touched so many hearts and minds."

The 65th birthday bash wasn't Little's first encounter with Howe. Freckles Little had been the goalkeeper for the Fort Worth Rangers of the United States Hockey in 1945-46 when Gordie Howe made his professional debut for the Omaha Knights at age 17.

"He could really skate and he was big," Little recalled. "And he could take a hit and he could give a few."

Howe's bloody brawl with Lou Fontinato at the NHL level is well documented, but few know that Howe had a similar reputation-building scrap in the USHL in 1945-46.

Harry Dick seemed to be to the USHL what Fontinato was to the NHL. He was a 210-pound defenseman for the Kansas City Pla-Mors. He was a rugged competitor who was among the league's penalty minute leaders. He never advanced to the NHL, but he had a noteworthy minor league career as a rough-and-tumble tough guy.

"He would run the guys and one night he was running Gordie and Gordie beat the heck out of him," Little recalled. "Nobody fooled around with Gordie after that."

Little said "once that story got around" opponents gave this Saskatchewan teen-ager plenty of room. That helped him score 22 goals and add 28 assists in 51 games for Omaha.

As tough as Howe was, Little knew even playing against Howe that he had a sense of humor. One night Howe parked in front of the Fort Worth net like he was a stonewall.

"I'm only 5-8, but I pushed Gordie down and the referee gave me a penalty for it," Little said, chuckling. "And there is Gordie on the ice, looking at me and laughing."

Little's team didn't make the playoffs that season, but he was designated as the emergency goalie should any of the playoff goalies become injured. Teams only carried one goalie in those days, and it was prudent to have a spare ready. He remembers that famed NHL coach Hap Day was scouting the USHL during the playoffs that season and he asked Little's opinions on players.

"I told him this kid named Gordie Howe was going to be really good, and the next guy was Ray Powell who played with me at Fort Worth," Little recalled.

Powell of Timmons, Ontario was a 19-year-old center with good size (6-0, 170) and a nifty scoring touch. With 19 goals and 29 assists in 33 games Powell ended up winning the USHL scoring championships in 1948-49 and 1949-50.

But Howe became Mr. Hockey® and Powell played only briefly with the Chicago Blackhawks in 1950-51, even though he had seven goals and 15 assists in 32 games that season.

"Management got mad at him for something," recalled Little.

Powell even won a scoring championship while playing for the Providence Reds in the American Hockey League in 1951-52, and the Blackhawks still never recalled him.

In the Original Six era, general managers always seemed to be looking for reasons to dump players or to disqualify them from consideration for promotion. The competition for jobs was fierce, which is why Howe's promotion to the NHL at 18 was quite remarkable for the times.

In hindsight, it wasn't just Howe's talent that intrigued management. There was something about him that everyone found fascinating. He was beastly on the ice, and "Mr. Congeniality" off the ice.

"He was a real young gentleman even back then," Little said.

Little and Howe had sat in the stands together when Howe was injured one night in 1945-46, and Little was struck by how pleasant and humorous that Howe could be. Even though they played against each other only one season, and Little never wore a NHL sweater, Howe treats him with the same measure of respect he treated his NHL adversaries. Little has always appreciated that Howe always treated him like a former teammate, even though they never played together.

"He grew up in a poor family like I did," Little explains. "He was in Saskatchewan and I was in Manitoba."

He believes that Howe's contributions as a role model are often overlooked. "If you look back on the history of hockey, he and Colleen did more for young hockey players than anyone," Little says.

Little believes that Eddie Shore was the greatest teacher of hockey in history and that Gordie was the game's all-time greatest player.

Little says Howe's stature was as much about his personality as his point totals.

"I never heard Gordie say anything bad about anybody," Little said. "He was such a wonderful gentleman. If he could have run for Prime Minister of Canada or Saskatchewan, he probably would have won."

Editor's Note: In 1993 Mrs. Hockey established the Howe Foundation whose mission was to preserve and protect the welfare of children. In an unprecedented example of good will and fan appreciation, she established a 65-city tour for Gordie to thank the fans for all of their support over the years. Their daughter Cathy also helped coordinate the many appearances as the Howes traveled to over 65 cities in North America. All the money raised went to charity and good causes. Colleen produced commemorative t-shirts, pucks, sticks and a tour program sponsored by Upper Deck that paid homage to Mr. Hockey's unprecedented career. He signed these at hundreds of venues. When the tour concluded toward the end of the year in 1993 in Traverse City, Michigan, nearly one million dollars for charity was generated. It is estimated that Mr. Hockey signed for over 100,000 fans during the birthday tour and the Howes helped keep a few airlines in the black.

Bill Dow

Freelance Writer

When Bill Dow was researching story ideas for the Detroit Free Press sports section, he excitedly noticed that March 31, 2003 was a particularly noteworthy day. The special significance for Dow and many sports fans was that date would be the 75th birthday of Gordie Howe. Dow received approval for a birthday anniversary profile from his editor, Alison Boyce, at the newspaper. He then set upon his quest to talk with Mr. Hockey. After contacting Power Play's office, Dow corresponded with the Howe's business managers Del Reddy and Aaron Howard. They facilitated the meeting for Dow to visit the office and speak with Gordie on the occasion of his 75th birthday. While there, Dow realized he would be interviewing two different subjects.

"One of my biggest fascinations is that he was two different people on and off the ice," Dow says. "I had relatives in Toronto who watched him play in the 1950's and 1960's and they told me how dirty he was when the referee wasn't looking. But they respected him as a hockey player because he was so great."

Dow wanted to meet that Gordie Howe, along with the other Gordie Howe who "sees some stranger stuck in the snow and gets a shovel to get him out."

As a journalist, Dow was trained to approach a story with detachment in order to present an unbiased report. But it was difficult for Dow to divorce himself from his emotions because he had grown up in Dearborn, Michigan, in the 1960's and he remembers viewing Howe and Detroit Tigers star Al Kaline as "larger than life" figures.

"I thought Gordie Howe was the Babe Ruth of hockey," he says.

In Dow's office is a folding chair from the defunct Olympia Stadium, plus a Red Wings yearbook from the second game he attended at Olympia in 1967. He was a sixth grader at Greenfield Village Schools and his gym teacher Mrs. Elaine Heaviland had been a classmate of Colleen Howe years ago at McKenzie High School. Colleen coordinated a student field trip with Heaviland so that her entire sixth grade class of 25 students, with Dow included, could attend the Red Wings vs. the Toronto Maple Leafs game. The class, along with Dow's mother,

Heaviland and Colleen sat in the mezzanine section for the game. Dow still has a newspaper clipping that reports that legendary King Clancy was behind the Toronto bench in place of Punch Imlach who was battling an ulcer.

Howe scored in that game, but it was what Dow witnessed after the contest that had a more lasting impact on Dow.

"Gordie had huge stitches in his head," Dow recalled, remembering that Howe had also been pictured in the newspaper days before proudly wearing his stitches while being awarded the Lester Patrick Trophy for contributions to hockey in the United States. "These were really ugly stitches."

"What truly made this trip even more special was that Colleen arranged for our class to visit the players and Gordie after the game." We were excited when we went down near the locker room and Gordie had all the school children line up. "And he made sure everyone had their autographs," Dow said.

Earlier in the game, between periods, Dow stood along the rail separating players from fans when they walked through the concourse to the dressing room, a father held up his young son to give him a better look at the Red Wings. A smiling Howe paused for a moment by the wide-eyed child. "Gordie ran his stick up through his glove and stopped it right by the kid's nose," Dow said. "I was fascinated by him."

Thirteen years later Dow was in the top row of Joe Louis Arena at the 1980 NHL All-Star Game watching Howe receive what may be the longest standing ovation in NHL history. He estimates the ovation lasted about 20 minutes.

He was focused on Howe after the game and he recalls that Mr. Hockey threw one of his gloves into the stands, and that he gave his stick to another player.

Through the years Dow has read much about Colleen and reached his own conclusion about her place in the game. He considers her "a pioneer" for the work she did in promoting youth hockey, rink development and junior hockey in particular, and for rising to become an agent for her family.

"I sometimes wonder if it was because she was a woman that she was criticized for it," Dow said. "If she was a man doing what she was doing, would she have been looked at differently?"

Dow said it was "a big thrill" to spend 45 minutes asking questions of Howe about his exploits over a 32-season career in the NHL and World Hockey Association. While interviewing legendary players who played with Gordie, he was impressed with the number who tagged him as the all-time greatest. When I called to interview Bobby Orr about the feature, he called me back immediately," Dow said. His comment was, "There is no question that Gordie is the all-time best player."

Coming into the interview, Dow's vision of Howe was that he was two different people with one a more aggressive persona on the ice and a much more docile one off.

His impressions weren't altered much after his interview. "His sense of humor is the other thing I love about him," Dow said. "He is such a great ambassador of the game. As a player he had this profile and outside his job he was someone else."

Editor's Note: Mr. Hockey was the first player ever to receive the Lester Patrick Trophy in history! Coach Jack Adams was the first ever recipient.

Felix Gatt

Personal Friend

In the late 1940's, Gordie Howe was the warm-up act for the *Three Stooges* and *Laurel and Hardy* on the Mediterranean island of Malta.

"At the old movie house, the big treat was the newsreels," recalled Felix Gatt who was born and raised in Malta. "Before the movies, they showed us hockey clips, and the way Gordie Howe played impressed me."

When Gatt was sitting in the darkened theater watching No. 9 playing a game that was completely foreign to his area of the world, he had no idea that fate would allow him to become one of Howe's close friends 50 years later.

Gatt was one of nine children, and his father couldn't make a decent living in Malta and decided to find a better life by moving his family to Detroit.

"I could not wait to see Gordie Howe," Gatt said. "I was a big hockey fan before I even got here."

He was at Olympia April 14, 1955 when the Red Wings captured the Stanley Cup championship by defeating Montreal 3-1 in Game 7 with Howe netting the game-winner, and Alex Delvecchio scoring a pair of goals. Howe set two NHL marks with 12 points (five goals and seven assists) in the Finals and 20 points (nine goals and 11 assists) in his 11-playoff games that season. "Gordie played great," Gatt recalled.

Gatt earned his degree from Detroit School of Business and his master's degree from the University of Detroit. Today he owns Creative Impressions, a successful printing business. Through the years he has celebrated his interest in Howe's career by putting together a monumental collection of Howe memorabilia. His basement is a shrine to Mr. Hockey. He has a 1947 Howe game-used skate, and a game-used Houston Aeros jersey that he bought for $15,000. One of his favorite artifacts is a six-foot wax statue of Howe that he purchased from an Indiana wax museum that was closing its doors.

Today, his granddaughter, Mikayla, who calls Howe Uncle Gordie, will stop and ask the statue where her grandfather is hiding when they play hide-and-seek.

But Gatt's most important treasure is that he has become one of Howe's close friends. They were first introduced at a memorabilia signing that Steve Graus of DC Sports had organized. Aaron Howard of Power Play was impressed with the quality of the materials that Gatt was printing for DC Sports; he asked Gatt to produce some promotional material highlighting some upcoming Mr. Hockey events. Soon after, Gatt began helping out at the appearances and became friends with Howard and buddies with Gordie. He often attends events around the country with Howard and Howe, especially since Colleen has been diagnosed with dementia. He assists with the Colleen J. Howe Foundation, and plans on being involved in the creation of the Mr. & Mrs. Hockey Museum, which was one of Colleen's visions.

"I was always in awe of him and followed his unbelievable career," Gatt says. "Today I know what a great person he is."

Gatt seems to enjoy seeing that Howe's aura remains as strong, if not stronger, today as it was when he was playing.

"At the All-Star game (in St. Paul in 2004) Gordie drew the biggest crowds," Gatt said.

Gatt has been introduced to many of Howe's adversaries through the years, and he recalls Keith Magnuson, who has since died, telling him that he had hit Howe once and then promptly apologized right after. "He told me that he told Gordie, 'Mr. Howe, I will never do that again,'" Gatt says.

But Gatt says their friendship goes beyond hockey. "When he needs someone to talk to, he calls me," Gatt says. "I talk to him everyday. It's just a shame. Colleen is a great lady."

He wants to be there for Mr. & Mrs. Hockey because Howe has been there for him. Five years ago, Gatt broke his hip and suffered complications that resulted in a need for a transfusion. He received contaminated blood, and he has faced life-threatening illnesses since then. Having Howe as a friend has helped him find the energy to fight.

"My wife Rita told Gordie that he was the best thing that happened to her husband," said Gatt. "And I believe that."

Dr. John Finley

Red Wings Team Physician from 1957-2003

During almost five decades of taking care of Detroit Red Wings athletes, Dr. John Finley liked to joke that the late cartoonist Al Capp had used Gordie Howe as his model for L'il Abner. "He was built just like L'il Abner," Finley said. "He had such a remarkable physique."

Entrusted with the job of making sure that Mr. Hockey remained healthy, Finley probably had the greatest appreciation of what a marvelous physical specimen Howe was. His appreciation came as much from conversations as observations. Over time, Finley learned that Howe probably benefited from a unique fitness program during his younger days, though it would clearly be considered non-traditional by today's standards.

As a young man, Gordie worked as a laborer. "Someone asked him to get two 80-pound bags of cement," Finley said. "They expected him to make two trips. He came back with an 80-pound bag under each arm."

Finley started to appreciate Howe's stamina on a team bus ride during a playoff series when Howe told him a story about how he used to race a school bus when he was a youngster. Every morning Howe liked to rise early and shoot pucks off the side of the house. "He told me the school bus would come and pick up his brothers and sisters," Finley recalled. "He said he would say 'goodbye' and then he would take off and run seven miles to school." When the bus would arrive at the school, Howe's siblings would find Gordie shooting pucks off the side of the school.

"He did so many things naturally that contributed to his great strength and physique," Finley said. With a narrow waist and jackhammer-sized forearms, Howe was probably the most imposing player in the league.

"Back in the six team era the guys liked to go to Montreal and have their suits done by Tony the Tailor," Finley recalled. "It was always such a chore for Tony to outfit Gordie because he has such a remarkable physique. He had those sloping shoulders that were different than the rest of us."

Finley said Howe was the most remarkable all-around athlete that he had ever witnessed.

"He was always self conscious about his lack of education, but he was so intelligent on the ice," Finley recalled. "Gordie was the perfect description of a superstar. He had a super physique, super intelligence and a little bit of meanness on the ice. He was so strong he could take advantage of that."

Finley remembers that in 1961, the day after Gene Littler won the U.S. Open at Oakland Hills in Michigan, Howe and Finley were invited to play on the same course, which was nicknamed the Monster. "The club was just cleaning up the course and the pin positions were exactly the same as the last day of the U.S. Open," Finley said. "Gordie was absolutely remarkable. He shot par 72. He had six pars, six birdies and six bogeys." When Howe would get ready to strike the golf ball, according to Finley, "he would get into a crouch like a baseball player in a batting cage."

"He would hit the ball and it would go a mile," Finley said. "It was one of those balls that would take off and gradually rise as you see with the great hitters."

As Howe's doctor, Finley knows better than anyone the amount of pain Mr. Hockey endured to play 25 seasons for the Red Wings, "He took his lumps," Finley says simply. In addition to the serious head injury that Howe suffered early in his career, Howe had surgeries on his knees and groin. He had hernias repaired on both sides. Finley remembers that one of Howe's most aggravating and painful injuries occurred in a pre-season game in St. Thomas when he damaged his ribs. He was checked against the boards near the bench because the door wasn't shut properly. Howe was jammed into the opening. It required a fair amount of moxie to play through his discomfort for the start of the season. It was even hard for Howe to breathe when he played.

Finley and his wife, Genevieve, became friends with the Howes. Many of Finley's memories of the Howes involved social occasions. In addition to being a great player, Gordie was a humorous dinner companion. They would often dine at the Clam Shop with the Howes, and Gordie would amuse Genevieve by cracking his lobster with his bare hands.

Colleen once threw a surprise baby shower for Genevieve, inviting about 30 or 40 of the Finley's closest friends. They lured the Finleys to their home under the pretense that Gordie and Dr. Finley would play golf and Colleen and Genevieve would spend time together. Gordie had all the cars parked elsewhere to make sure the Finleys didn't suspect anything when they drove up. "It was a total surprise and one of the greatest events of our young lives," Finley said.

The Finley's son, Mike, and the Howe's son, Murray, who both ended up becoming doctors, played on the same youth team. Finley recalls that Gordie would end up on their backyard rink giving hockey tips. He can still envision Gordie passing the puck back and forth to the boys on that rink. "I remember Gordie said to Mike, 'You are a little guy; if someone gives you a cheap shot just rap them just above the boot in the back of the leg. That will get them to behave,'" said Finley, chuckling.

Being with the Howes always created humorous moments. Once, when Mike and Murray's team was playing on the road, Murray was missing for a couple of minutes when it was time to go home. "We are all on the bus after the game, and we found Murray back there signing autographs," Finley said laughing.

Finley always marveled at the patience Gordie had with autograph seekers. In that time, one of Finley's Oak Park, Michigan, neighbors, Charlie McCarthy, was producing penny postcards depicting pictures of NHL players. Finley said Gordie and Colleen were buying McCarthy's cards "and they were sending an autographed postcard to everyone who sent them a letter. It was absolutely remarkable." McCarthy postcards, especially those signed by Howe, are treasured today.

Finley remembers he and his wife, Geneviere, attending an RV show at the Detroit armory and seeing Howe being interviewed in a draped off area by Detroit sportscaster Dave Diles. The Finleys walked into the area just in time to hear Howe being asked, *Who had the hardest shot in hockey?* "Gordie said he wasn't sure, but in my opinion the guy who just walked in, meaning me, has the hardest shot because I had given him a number of antibiotic injections through the years," said Finley, laughing.

Howe's sense of humor was front and center in another interview that Finley recalls with great delight. Here is Finley's version of what was said:

Interviewer: "I've heard that the NHL has many bi-lingual players. Are you bi-lingual?

Howe: "Yes I am. I speak English and profanity."

Editor's Note: Many believe that there should be a section in the Hockey Hall of Fame for legendary physicians and trainers. When this happens, Dr. John Finley will be a first ballot inductee.

Genevieve Finley

Wife of Former Detroit Red Wings Physician John Finley

Genevieve Finley recalls with great amusement that the first time she met Colleen Howe she asked her, "What does your husband do?"

"He plays hockey," Colleen said simply.

That Colleen-Genevieve meeting came 47 years ago at a Detroit Red Wings luncheon, and it has been a source of humor for the Finleys and Howes ever since.

"Even after all these years Gordie occasionally will ask me what my husband does," says Genevieve, the wife of Dr. John Finley who was the Red Wings team physician for 46 seasons before retiring in 2003.

In 1957, Genevieve was the new bride of Dr. Finley and was excited to receive "a beautiful hand lettered invitation" from Helen Adams, wife of Red Wings General Manager Jack Adams, to attend a luncheon to meet Gloria Abel, wife of the Red Wings new coach Sid Abel. He had replaced Jimmy Skinner who had resigned while the Finleys were on their honeymoon.

"We all wore suits, hats and gloves in those days and as I slid into my chair the stunning blonde next to me grinned ear to ear as we were both wearing the same suit," Genevieve recalled. "She (was) in blue, me in brown and we each had made the suit from the same Vogue pattern."

The bond was instant, and their friendship ongoing.

"To this day I remember how comfortable she made me feel," Genevieve says. "She graciously introduced me to all the wives and it was a great beginning to a treasured friendship. She knew I was the new wife of one of the team physicians and never flinched when I asked her "what does your husband do?"

Colleen was taking some night classes at the Highland Park Junior College and as our apartment was right across the street, she would come over to wait for Gordie or he would come by and wait for her if she was running late.

Genevieve learned how much Gordie enjoyed pranks and jokes when he offered to tutor her on the strategy of hockey.

"He told me when you scored shorthanded it counted two points, the bench emptying brawls were not as frightening as they appeared to be and he always was hoping to find a better pair of gloves when the equipment was all in a pile." Genevieve recalls. "After embarrassing myself by standing up and yelling that the scoreboard was "wrong" and asking Jack Adams why the team did not buy better gloves for the players, I learned that Gordie possessed one of the greatest senses of humor of anyone we've ever met."

According to Genevieve, Colleen was a "creative and a very accomplished" dressmaker.

"We would make dresses for the annual Ruth Alden dress drive and she taught me how to do the very difficult English hand smocking details," Genevieve said. "We made hats, craft projects together and went to art and craft shows together. Every year we would exchange a Christmas creation."

"The only time I ever remember Gordie saying anything about our projects was when he opened the garage in Lathrup Village and he was furious as the whole garage was covered with a mist of gold paint. Aerosol cans were the rage and we had dozens of wreaths made from macaroni glistening all over. Because it was cold we had decided this was an inside project."

As years passed, growing families made it more difficult for the Finleys and Howes to enjoy as many social outings as they would have liked, but their friendship endured.

"The hockey wives did not have their own room in which to gather so we settled for hugs in the hallway after the games," Geneviere recalled.

When they did find the time, they enjoyed the moments and replayed the history they had together.

"The Howes are a fabulous couple. They are devoted, talented, great parents and role models," Genevieve said. "Our lives and our family are richer for having known them and we are honored to have them as true friends."

Gerald R. Ford

38th President of the United States

If anyone understands the marvel of Mr. Hockey's longevity as a pro player, it's former U.S. President Gerald R. Ford who was a U.S. congressman from Michigan for almost the entire duration of Howe's tenure with the Red Wings.

Ford was elected in 1948—two years after Howe's rookie season, and remained a Congressman until he became vice president in 1973. That was two years after Howe had left the Red Wings.

"My relationship with the Howes came about because Gordie was such a fantastic hockey player with the Red Wings," said Ford. "I was always sympathetic to the Red Wings success, but also to his particular career."

Ford had many charity golf tournaments, and Howe always tried to attend. A former University of Michigan football player, Ford admired Howe's athleticism.

"I can tell you he hit the ball, as far as any pro in the country," Ford said, "Those sloping shoulders must have had special muscles when he teed off. He could hit that ball a long way."

Ford also knew Colleen, aware that she had run for Congress in Connecticut as a Republican.

"They obviously had a wonderful marriage," Ford said. "They symbolize what is good about a marriage."

Editor's Note: As a Republican, Colleen took her opponent to the primary in a Congressional election in Hartford, Connecticut in 1981.

Dave Ponzi

Retired Ford Motor Company Executive

As masterful as Colleen always was performing under the glare of the spotlight, she was probably never more creative than she was the morning she became the sunrise poet.

Through years of vacationing in Sarasota, Florida, Gordie and Colleen became friends with Dave and Fil Ponzi , a husband-wife team who lived in Michigan but wintered in Florida. One night Gordie and Colleen happened to stop by the night before the Ponzis were packing for the return trip to Michigan. They talked about a variety of topics, including an aggravating lawsuit Ponzi had going with the condo association over the length of his deck.

When the night was over, Colleen told Dave that they would be there in the morning to see them off.

"You don't have to do that because we are leaving at five o'clock in the morning," Ponzi said.

But as Ponzi was loading the car before daybreak he heard someone whistling and walking up the road toward their condo.

It was Colleen and Gordie. Colleen informed the Ponzis that they had to go back into their home because the night before she had written a poem that they had to hear.

It was called "The Saga of the Ponzi Deck" and it was a satirical rendition of the trials and tribulations that Ponzi had endured trying to keep his deck.

"She had put this together," Ponzi said. "She did it in the music trend of hip hop. As she was saying this, she was wiggling back and forth. It came out so nice. It was unbelievable."

Dave Ponzi had known many sides of Colleen, but the five a.m. poetry reading remains one of his favorite Colleen memories.

Typical of most of Colleen and Gordie's friends, they had discovered each other by simply being friendly. Dave Ponzi was celebrating his birthday on the deck overlooking the gulf, and he noticed Colleen with her granddaughter, Azia. What he really noticed was Azia eyeing his birthday cake.

"I went over and told her, 'I have a big problem because I am an old man and I have so many candles on my cake that I need help blowing out these candles. Can you help me?' Azia said, 'well yes', and Colleen and Azia came over. We blew out the candles and we had cake and ice cream."

Dave has celebrated many of his birthdays with the Howes through the years, and the Ponzis even helped with a surprise 65th birthday party for Mrs. Hockey at the Italian American Club in Livonia, Michigan. Gordie, along with their associates Del Reddy and Aaron Howard, brought Colleen to the club under the pretense that she and Gordie would be making a charity appearance.

But most of their memories center on Sarasota, walking along the beach, watching Gordie engrossed in his hobby of seashell collecting. Sometimes Gordie would find shells that he would like, but he knew he had to leave those on the beach because they contained living sea life.

"Colleen would say, 'Never bring a live shell home, "Ponzi says, laughing. "Gordie wanted to keep some of them but he would give them away before he got home. Otherwise, Colleen would take them back."

On one occasion Ponzi's daughter had a friend from Michigan visiting and she proclaimed she would like to take some seashells home with her. Howe volunteered to lead her on a hunting expedition. They had a delightful couple of hours together, and the Ponzis documented the hunt with photographs.

The Ponzis had pictures developed of Howe and their daughter's friend "shelling" on the beach. When she returned to Michigan, she apparently showed them to her father and brother.

"She was saying, 'This is when I was in Florida and I went shelling with a man named Gordie Howe," Ponzi says, clearly amused by the tale. "Her father said, *'Gordie Howe! Do you know who he is?'* Apparently the whole time she was down in Florida with us she had no idea who he was."

Jim Bates

Promoter and Television Consultant

In an era when sports journalists are forever debating where athletes in a multitude of categories rank, long-time marketer Jim Bates puts Gordie Howe No. 1 in a category without fear of being challenged.

"Gordie is without question," says Bates, "the most accommodating celebrity I've ever seen anywhere at any time."

Bates' association with the Howes dates to April 4, 1984 when he negotiated with Colleen for the hiring of Gordie to be a color analyst with Home Team Sports in Washington D.C. for a Washington Capitals vs. Philadelphia Flyers game. Famed CNN interviewer Larry King was the studio host.

Through the years he has had many dealings with Mr. and Mrs. Hockey, and he has the utmost admiration for the professionalism they bring to sports marketing.

"From the hockey standpoint, Colleen probably invented the whole marketing game," Bates said. "Arnold Palmer and Mark McCormack started it, but she was one of the earliest people in hockey to get it off the ground, getting endorsement dollars for Gordie and the family."

Bates believes Colleen's work paved the way for other hockey players to gain endorsement dollars that were previously not available. "I can't remember people going gangbusters before the Howes came along," Bates said.

Negotiating with Colleen meant negotiating with someone who understood what the market could bear, and understood the value of the Howe name. "Colleen was absolutely very fair," explains Bates.

What Bates appreciated about Howe is that his approach to marketing was the same approach he brought to the ice. He wanted to work harder than everyone else and he wanted to be the best at his craft.

"If you said to Gordie you don't have to be there until 10 o'clock, he would say 'what time are you going over?'" Bates said. "I would say 8:30 and he would say, 'I will go over with you.'"

Bates says, some athletes are easy to work with, but he has learned through the years that with others "you never know what's going to happen on a day-to-day, minute-to-minute, hour-to-hour basis."

With Howe, the only problem was that sometimes he wanted to stay too long. He remembers a specific instance at Atlantic City when Howe took his duties seriously enough to turn it into a traveling show.

"He's at the booth and finally I said, Gordie we have to go and he told the people to come with us," Bates said, laughing. "And we ended up walking down the boardwalk with him. That's the kind of guy he is."

He organized Howe's 65th birthday tour stop at Nassau Coliseum on Long Island, and he remembers that Mr. Hockey spent three hours signing autographs after the game. "Every kid got his autograph and a knock on the nose with the pen," Bates said.

According to Bates, the Howe name is golden in the marketing world.

"When you are with Gordie and Colleen they set you at ease so quickly," Bates said. "There is not the hero thing. Gordie is just a wonderful, warm, friendly guy and everyone I knew in business who dealt with them had the exact same thing to say about them."

He organized a cruise with NHL Hall of Famers in 1993, and the highlight of that cruise came on the last day with Gordie and Boom Boom Geoffrion sitting on the top deck telling stories, playing a game of "Do you remember when."

"Denis Potvin was no slouch himself on the ice, but he was up there listening with his jaw bouncing off the deck as he watched these two guys telling stories," Bates recalled.

Bates says, "Howe is the true definition of a hero. So many athletes forget where they came from, but not Gordie."

In the course of his association with Mr. and Mrs. Hockey, Bates got the opportunity to play some charity alumni games with and against Gordie. Several times he was Howe's defensive partner, and Gordie would always say "Jimbo, we are going to use my brain and your legs."

"I didn't know whether I was getting a compliment or not," Bates said, laughing.

Bill Sobel

Entertainment Lawyer in California

When attorney Bill Sobel was contacted by the Howe's business manager Del Reddy to help negotiate the deal for the proposed movie about the Howe's World Hockey Association exploits, it was as if his fantasy world had merged with his reality.

He grew up in Toronto idolizing Mr. Hockey. He had a backyard rink, and the words 'Gordie Howe, he shoots, he scores' were spray-painted at one end and at the other end it was, "Dave Keon he shoots, he scores."

But Bill's idol was Howe because his dad's idol was Howe. "Being able to share an idol with your father is really special," Sobel said.

There was no cable television in those days, and Sobel fed his interest in Howe by listening to games on the radio. "I had no idea what the inside of the Olympia rink looked like but I would fantasize," Sobel recalls. "Gordie was Mr. Hockey and he was bigger than life."

He remembers meeting Howe when he was four years old and then again when he was six at an autograph signing session at Eaton's Department Store. Mr. Hockey did promotional work for Eaton's for many years.

"I meet and represent a lot of famous people and it's never quite the same as when you are a young child and you have that kind of idol," Sobel says.

Sobel said his interest in Howe has certainly influenced how he views celebrities today.

"I think then and now the expectation of the Howes is honest, hard working and with integrity," Sobel said. "Today, money drives so much of what we do in the athletic world and the entertainment world. You think back to that era, you know that Gordie was excelling because of the passion of his sport, not maximizing his revenues. I don't think they make athletes like that any more."

Sobel didn't know Colleen, but his background and profession gives him an appreciation of what she accomplished.

"Colleen was someone known to any hockey fan, as someone who was very visible in Gordie's life," he says. "She was a role model for women. Gordie was out there doing his work, but she was the businessperson behind him.

Sobel married a Texan, and it never occurred to him that her parents would be hockey fans. But they live in Houston and were keenly aware of the Howe's history with the World Hockey Association's Houston Aeros.

"With my in-laws, what do we talk about?" Sobel says, "it's Gordie Howe, Mark and Marty. Geez, they say, it would be great to get a hockey team, but it would never be the same without the Howes. Houston is a huge sports city, but 30 years later they still talk about the Howes."

Ron Cantera

Detroit Red Wings Public Relations Director
Former NHL and WHA Broadcaster

As a New England Whalers broadcaster in 1978-1979, Ron Cantera was the first to report that Gordie Howe was the first grandfather to score a goal in a professional hockey game.

Upon hearing that Mark's wife, Ginger, had given birth to his first grandson, Travis, Gordie promptly went out and scored a goal in his honor.

"On the air we said it was the first by a grandfather," says Cantera who has the game on video. "He scores the goal and then gets slammed by someone on a late hit. Nothing developed, but Gordie was pretty hot."

Although Cantera was with the Howes briefly in the WHA, much of his perspective came from working with them as a Red Wings public relations director. He saw many career highlights:

- Howe scoring against Gump Worsley for his 544th goal to tie Rocket Richard's NHL career goals record on October 27, 1963.
- Fourteen days later Howe breaks the all-time scoring record by scoring against Montreal's Charlie Hodge.
- On November 27, 1965, Howe scores his 600th goal. This one also coming against Montreal's Worsley.
- Mr. Hockey netting his 700th career goal, against Pittsburgh goaltender Les Binkley, on December 4, 1968.

Cantera was also doing broadcasting work then and interviewed Howe for the Detroit audience between periods after the goal.

Cantera believes Howe's exploits over almost a quarter of a century laid the seeds for the Hockeytown image that Detroit owns today.

"Detroit had the greatest player in the history of the game," Cantera says. "And that built the foundation for everything that is going on today."

As someone who spent years promoting the game and the Red Wings in Detroit, he also understood that Colleen played a significant role in that endeavor. Colleen was probably the best friend to our PR Department," Cantera says.

According to Cantera, Colleen had a clear understanding of the relationship that athletes should have with their fans. “She is very dynamic,” Cantera said. “She was a woman who got things done so it was always a pleasure to work with her. She was always very supportive of our efforts in public relations. She understood the value of it. Some other folks didn’t see it that way.”

The Howes appreciated Cantera’s professionalism enough that they attempted to woo him to Houston after Gordie became President of the Aeros. Cantera was broadcasting for the Boston Bruins at the time, and it never came to pass. “I know how flattering that was and I’m sure Colleen had a lot to do with it,” Cantera says.

Cantera would argue that Colleen served Howe’s interests as well as any of his linemates. She had assists for every season he played.

“People knew what a great player he was, but he wasn’t appreciated to the degree he should have been,” Stated Cantera, now an instructor at Southern Utah University. “She spearheaded the effort to get him that kind of long lasting recognition. He’s Mr. Hockey because of her.”

Cantera says he gets “a bit upset” when he hears someone suggesting that someone other than Howe is hockey’s greatest player. “He’s the greatest athlete I’ve seen in any sport,” Cantera says. “He has the longevity to prove it. (Modern challenges) didn’t have to compete the way he did as tough as the league was back then. And who plays into their 50’s?”

Howe’s showmanship also earned him extra credit with Cantera. “Gordie was so playful with the fans,” Cantera recalls. “Even playing exhibition games, he had his favorite trick. He would have a nail in his stick and he would pop it down on the puck and zig zag around the ice with it.”

According to Cantera, the union of Mr. and Mrs. Hockey was a marriage of exceptionally talented people.

“They were a perfect combination,” Cantera said. “Gordie loved hockey so much. The business and marketing side didn’t matter a lot to him. He was the king of the ice. Colleen brought the other dimension to him.”

Would the legend of Gordie Howe have been as well known without Colleen?

“I don’t think it would have been the same if she hadn’t come along,” Cantera said. “It almost seems like destiny that they got together.”

Andra McLaughlin Kelly

Champion Figure Skater
Wife of Hall of Famer Red Kelly

An amused Andra Kelly enjoys telling the story that a falsely rumored romance between Gordie Howe and World Skating Champion Barbara Ann Scott led to her marriage to then-Detroit Red Wings player Red Kelly.

Gossip columnists had suggested that Howe might even be engaged to the Canadian athlete Scott who had won the World Championships in 1947 and 1948. "Gordie didn't even know her, but it was something that had been just put into the paper willy-nilly," Kelly recalled. "He said to Red, 'I want to go down to Carl's Chop House to meet Barbara Ann, will you go with me?' 'Of course,' Red said." The mistake was that it wasn't Scott who was going to be at Carl's Chop House. It was American, Andra McLaughlin, who was the other principal skater in the ice show. "That's how Red and I met. In reality we met through Gordie," says Andra, who finished sixth at the World Championships in Paris in 1949.

Andra had placed 11th at the World Championships in London in 1950 and seventh at Milan in 1951 before joining the ice show. "It was our love of ice that brought Red and I together," she says.

Shortly thereafter Gordie met Colleen, and Andra became acquainted with Colleen. "She was the first of the hockey wives to invite me to her home," Andra recalled. "She barbequed some wonderful steaks. She was such a good mother that she seemed like a special person for any hockey wife to emulate."

Red Kelly was traded away to Toronto before Andra could develop any lasting relationship with Colleen. "But the favorite story that Red likes to tell tongue-in-cheek is about the first game he played against Detroit after the trade," Andra says. "The two were fighting for the puck in the corner and Gordie said, 'How's the family, Red?' Red turned to tell him and Gordie hit him. Red says his imprint is still on the boards at Maple Leaf Gardens."

Chuck Robertson

Long-Time Family Friend

It's been said the true test of a healthy friendship is the answer to the question, 'Would you leave your child with this person?'

The fact that Gordie and Colleen allowed their youngest son Murray to live with the Robertson family and continue his hockey career in Michigan when they moved to Houston to join the Aeros speaks to the bond that Mr. and Mrs. Hockey have with Chuck Robertson. Gordie and Chuck have been friends for almost half a century.

Robertson first met Howe when he came to Houghton, Michigan on a promotional tour in 1954. "It was like God coming to Copper Country," Robertson said. "Every kid in the UP was there."

Their friendship blossomed in the Detroit area a few years later, and Robertson views Colleen as the best linemate Gordie ever had. In the hockey world, Gordie was relentless in the corners and a true star in every sense of the word. In the real world, Colleen was equally relentless in the corners and a true star in every sense of the word. Robertson, involved in hockey with Paddock Pools, believes junior hockey benefited immeasurably from Colleen's drive.

"They were a good one, two punch combination," Robertson says. "Collectively they could do a lot of things, even after hockey, they worked well together running a business. They were good as a team. One of the greatest things they did was the book, *and...HOWE!* They worked so hard on that book."

Robertson was such a good friend that the Red Wings asked him to put together Gordie Howe Day when Mr. Hockey's jersey was retired on March 12, 1972. Among the special guests was vice president Spiro Agnew. Gordie's former coach Tommy Ivan was there as well. The game was against the Blackhawks so Bobby Hull was playing one of his last games in a Chicago uniform. He would jump to the WHA the following fall.

Friendship aside, Robertson believed Howe was the greatest athlete he ever saw.

"He could play every phase of the game," Robertson said. "He could put the puck in the net. He was a good defensive player and we all knew if he wanted to play rough there is no one better than him. He was an all-around player and he played when there were only six teams and every team was an All-Star team."

All of Colleen and Gordie's accomplishments aside, according to Robertson, the private side of the Howes is even more impressive. "They do so much for people that people don't know about," Robertson said. "It's a privilege to know them. They are super, super, super people."

One of Robertson's favorite Mr. Hockey moments came 30 years ago when he accompanied Howe on a trip to Canada. They were at a banquet together, and Robertson was sitting on a chair. A photographer came up and asked Robertson who he was. "Well, could you get off the chair so I could use it to take a picture of Gordie with this young kid," the photographer said.

The kid was 12-year-old Wayne Gretzky and the photo became the famous photo of Howe hooking the stick under Gretzky's chin.

Nova Lanktree

Vice President of Player Marketing
Lanktree CSMG International

Mrs. Hockey didn't officially mentor Nova Lanktree and yet Lanktree says she viewed her "in that capacity."

Lanktree entered the "sports marketing" world in 1985 before it was even referred to as sports marketing. It was a baby industry then, with sporadic use of major sports figures, but there were no shoe companies paying millions of dollars for athletes to squeeze their tootsies into their brand of gym shoe. It took aggressive salesmanship to marry an athlete with a company in those days.

"I was a little out of context," Lanktree said. 'There weren't too many women, and I don't think there are many now, doing what I was doing."

Lanktree was attempting to broker deals between advertising buyers and sports celebrities for commercial projects. Today, Lanktree is one of the most respected movers and shakers in the industry. When she started to call Colleen to discuss how she might use Gordie, she was still a novice.

"In a way it was almost an instant bond with Colleen and me, because she was establishing herself as a power person in hockey and she understood some of the obstacles," Lanktree recalled.

According to Lanktree, all of the many conversations she had with Colleen "were morale boosting for me and very encouraging."

The mentoring came from witnessing how Colleen conducted herself as a businesswoman in that field.

"She was a statement of how it could be done, without aggressiveness, without feminism, without ball busting," Lanktree said. "You just had an obligation and responsibility to know what you were doing. You had to earn your trust and earn your respect by showing that you deserved it. It was a pretty good example to have for someone starting out in the industry."

Lanktree was fascinated by Colleen's style. Even though they talked about several endorsement deals over a 15-year period, they never were able to finalize anything. That wasn't uncommon in the industry since many discussions take place before a buyer even commits to a project. In essence, Lanktree is like a casting director, looking for the right fit for the right producer.

"I called her on various things and no matter when I called her—and keep in mind we never finished a deal—there would be a book in the mail to me signed by Gordie or some kind of poster," Lanktree said. "She was relationship oriented, so attentive. She was saying, Even though it didn't work out, 'thanks for thinking of us. Thanks for putting him in the mix.' It always impressed me. It is a very significant tool that I use in how I do business today."

Lanktree said she "would not discount the possibility" that Colleen's work on enhancing Gordie's profile opened doors for other hockey players.

"Hockey was never part of mainstream advertising," Lanktree says. "Somehow through her efforts she maintained a high profile for Gordie. She did this in a very professional way. The fact that any perspective buyer would get these tokens of appreciation…what she was doing was keeping his name out there, keeping his face out there and keeping his legend out there. That was important because one of the main variables in choosing a celebrity spokesperson is name and face recognition."

Ironically, four years ago, Lanktree was able to find a promotional fit for Mr. Hockey as a celebrity endorser for a national advertising campaign. Colleen was just starting to feel the effects of Pick's Disease and she had turned over the negotiating duties to Del Reddy.

"He is devoted to the Howes, and he did a great job," said Lanktree. "But it was kind of sentimental because we both knew that something was missing."

Lanktree pauses. "I hope," she says, "That Colleen knows, at some level, that something got done."

Kevin McCrory

Charter Member of Disabled Athletes Hall of Fame

When Mr. and Mrs. Hockey's close friend Steven Kirkpatrick made hockey history by starting a Central Hockey League game as a goaltender in a wheelchair on April 1, 2000, there was no one prouder of the moment than Kevin McCrory.

McCrory, a member of the Disabled Athletes Hall of Fame, had inspired Kirkpatrick to become involved in sports and help foster his interest in Gordie and Colleen Howe. McCrory, from Fostoria, Michigan, and Kirkpatrick were both stricken with muscular dystrophy. One of the ironies of McCrory's life is that he had worked at a muscular dystrophy camp before he was actually diagnosed with the disease as an adult. He befriended many people with the disease through the years, but he and Kirkpatrick developed a special bond. Kirkpatrick didn't travel much out of his hometown of Sandusky, Michigan until McCrory started driving him to various sporting events.

"Finally I said to him one time, 'Why don't you go to (wheelchair) basketball with me,'" McCrory recalled. "He said, 'Why do I want to go to basketball because I can't make a basket.' I told him you can block for a person like me that can make a basket."

Kirkpatrick did accompany McCrory, and McCrory said it was instantly clear that Kirkpatrick was a very smart player.

"There was no one I would rather have in front of me going down a court than Steven because he knew how to set a pick and do the little things," McCrory said. "I might have scored 30 points in a game but it was because of him that I scored those 30 points,"

Once McCrory was asked to give a speech about Kirkpatrick, and he said, "He never scored a point but he was the ultimate team player because he made things happen behind the scenes that you only knew if you were a teammate."

Wanting to pay back McCrory's kindness, Kirkpatrick would always ask McCrory who his favorite player was and McCrory would say it was Gordie Howe. He educated Kirkpatrick about Howe's exploits, and told him that Colleen was actually from Kirkpatrick's hometown of Sandusky. "He never believed me," McCrory said, chuckling.

McCrory frequently drove Kirkpatrick to Port Huron Border Cats, Flint Generals and Detroit Vipers minor league games. One night, at the invitation of the Detroit Vipers special events coordinator Lynette Shady, Colleen and Gordie participated with Santa Claus in a promotion. Before the start of the game, children would come up and have their photo taken with the famous trio.

Later during the game, Kirkpatrick happened to be in the concourse when he spotted the Howe's agent Del Reddy wearing an *and...HOWE!* book button that pictured Colleen and Gordie. He asked Reddy if he was with the Howes. Reddy was struck by the man's enthusiasm and friendliness and invited him up to the Howe's suite, but Kirkpatrick insisted that McCrory had to accompany him for the Howe visit.

Months before Kirkpatrick had managed to persuade the Hall of Fame to bring the Stanley Cup to Sandusky. "And Steven kept saying he wanted to top that," McCrory said.

He figured he was topping that when he accompanied Reddy and brought along McCrory to meet the Howes.

"Colleen gave me a big hug," McCrory said. "Steven told Colleen, 'Kevin thinks you are from my hometown of Sandusky.' And Colleen said, 'Are you from Sandusky, Ohio or Michigan?' and Steven said 'Michigan.' She said, 'I am from there.' Steven's mouth dropped."

The Howes, Reddy, and their associate Aaron Howard, bonded with Kirkpatrick and McCrory that evening. The relationship grew to the point that when Kirkpatrik hatched an idea to be the first athlete to start a professional hockey game from a wheelchair Mr. & Mrs. Hockey added the weight of their name behind the project.

"Steven's motto was it never hurts to ask," said Reddy. "He told us that he got his inspiration from the movie *Rudy*." "I had many, many talks with him about his dream to play pro hockey. There were many obstacles that were surmounted for him to fulfill his amazing feat."

The idea was first rejected by another minor league, but CHL Commissioner Tom Berry gave approval for Kirkpatrick to play for the Indianapolis Ice in a game against the Huntsville Tornado.

"Tom Berry had neighbor children who had muscular dystrophy and he saw the positives of this," said Ice general manager Brad Beery.

Before the game, Kirkpatrick, 22 at the time, said, "I don't think I'm Michael Jordan or anything, but maybe someone out there will say, 'if he can do that, I can do anything.'"

Kirkpatrick was signed to the CHL's standard player contract of $275 per week, and it was pro-rated to one day's pay. He didn't cash the check. He framed it.

Thanks to an agreement before the game, players from both teams skated full speed to assure that Kirkpatrick got the feeling of real game action. After the opening faceoff, Tornado player Chris George, on a breakaway, skated in on Kirkpatrick. Wearing jersey No. 78 plus 35 pounds of goalie gear, Kirkpatrick motorized out of the crease about 20 feet to cut down the angle. George snapped a hard shot into Kirkpatrick's goalie pad. History was made! It was important that he make a stop because that would be the only way he would be officially credited with playing the game according to the Howe Sports Data, which kept the official league statistics.

The Howes, Reddy and Howard and Steven's friends were there to support Kirkpatrick. Mr. & Mrs. Hockey dropped the ceremonial puck for the opening face-off.

Some players were crying on the ice when Kirkpatrick made the save. George was selected to shoot the puck because he and his wife had done charity work for the Muscular Dystrophy Association.

"It was about a 40- or 50-mile-an-hour shot," Kirkpatrick told the media afterward. "I used my right kick pad, and kicked it away and that was it. I stopped it."

McCrory said he remembers Kirkpatrick admitting to him that he had been scared, but he didn't show it. Kirkpatrick told the media that the 10 seconds of action "seemed like an hour."

"It was just crazy. I didn't think it was that fast," Kirkpatrick said. "When you're on the ice and they're coming at you, you're just like, 'Oh, man, I'll go hide behind this net here.' I didn't think it was going to be that fast, but it was," he said.

The Howes were so proud of Kirkpatrick that they posted his story on the mrandmrshockey website. He remained very close with their group until his death of cardiac arrest on September 6, 2001.

"It's a sad, sad, sad day," Gordie Howe said about Kirkpatrick's death. "Thank God he got to fulfill his dream of playing goalie in a professional hockey game. He will be remembered for his sense of humor and his drive."

Kirkpatrick will also be remembered for aggressively spearheading the naming of the hockey rink in Sandusky after Colleen J. Howe.

McCrory remembers how proud Kirkpatrick was about his appearance in a game. He remembers that while driving home

Kirkpatrick's ventilator became clogged and they had to stop at a Fort Wayne, Indiana hospital. The doctor recognized him from the television coverage of the game the night before. Kirkpatrick ended up autographing newspaper accounts of the game for the doctor and the nurses.

When he got home he called McCrory to say that his statistics were on the website and he had 1.000, which he reported was at the top of the goalie leaders. "Better than Patrick Roy," as he put it.

McCrory remembers that Kirkpatrick was hospitalized once when their wheelchair basketball team was in the state tournament and they won in his honor. They went to visit him at the hospital and lied initially about the results. "We told him we had come up short and he said that he was sure we had done our best," McCrory said. "Then we showed him the three-foot trophy."

The following year Kirkpatrick was on a ventilator, but he petitioned to be allowed to play in the tournament. Tournament officials allowed him to play, and the team finished off back-to-back state championships.

The Howe Foundation had purchased a van for Steven and they were trying to assist him in the pursuit of his goals. "He told me he wanted to do something in every major sport," Reddy said. "He wanted to umpire in a pro baseball game next."

But his life ended before he could complete his objectives. The night he died Reddy had talked to Kirkpatrick four hours earlier. He mentioned that another dream of his was to be portrayed on an authentic hockey card.

Two years after his death, Upper Deck issued a special hockey card with Kirkpatrick in the set. He is pictured on the card wearing his famous Indianapolis Ice jersey. On the day he created history, his friends, Howard, Reddy, Mr. & Mrs. Hockey and McCrory, surround him.

"Steven was like a son to me," McCrory said. "He made the best of his last years and he did more than a lot of people will do in their whole lives. Once he got something in his head there was no stopping him."

Peter Jennings

Anchor and Senior Editor for ABC News

As a Canadian, a hockey fan since the 1940's and a journalist, ABC broadcasting legend Peter Jennings can offer a perspective about Mr. Hockey that is rooted as much in emotion as observation.

"Every sport has its legends, and hockey has other legends, but for me and for his generation there is nobody else but Gordie Howe," Jennings says.

Jenning's father, Charles, was a journalist, announcer and later rose to the rank as General Supervisor of the Canadian Broadcasting Company. That meant Hockey Night in Canada was under his watch and Jennings has vivid memories of Maple Leaf Gardens, and Foster Hewitt doing play-by-play from the Gondola.

"As a young kid in Toronto I was a Maple Leafs fan and when Gordie, Ted Lindsay and Sid Abel came to Maple Leaf Gardens they were among the most despised, feared, hated characters on the ice," Jennings, recalls with great fondness. "I think the rivalry between Detroit and Toronto was almost as strong as Toronto and Montreal."

Howe, in particular, Jennings recalled was thought of "as being a fearsome figure."

Now 65 and in his 40th year with ABC, Jennings says Howe "represents a great deal about what hockey, in its purest sense, really meant."

"He stands for two things about hockey," Jennings says. "He stands for absolute determination. He played the game hard, hard, hard all the time. And his longevity is astonishing. It's all about endurance, and Gordie stood for endurance. I watch players get hurt in other sports and they seem to get off the field quickly. In hockey they go back on the ice as soon as they can—and Gordie represented that attitude."

Although Jennings has spanned the globe, he never lost his interest in hockey. In his later years he has become a fan of the Detroit Red Wings and somehow he believes it has strengthened his ties to Howe. They have run into each other through the years, and there is a mutual respect. Clearly Jennings views Howe as a Canadian treasure.

"Gordie also invokes the ambition and the struggle that kids had out on the prairies and in Quebec to become a hockey player," Jennings says. "It's very difficult for Canadians to explain how hockey is part of the national ethos. "

Jennings says he likes hockey because "it's not a touchy, feely game." He admired Howe's physical presence and his aura.

"He represents an era when we recognized our hockey players," Jennings says. "My wife has introduced me to (New York) Mets baseball and I have introduced her to hockey and her greatest complaint is how hard it is to identify with the athletes because you don't know what they look like without a helmet. I think if Gordie played today he would still try to play without a helmet."

According to Jennings, the respect that Howe has in his field crosses all generations. He remembers watching a biography of Wayne Gretzky in which Gretzky spoke eloquently about Howe's aura and contributions.

"I love the relationship between Gretzky and Howe," Jennings said. "When Wayne talked about Gordie Howe, he is so touching."

As the child of a Canadian broadcaster, Jennings says, "hockey's broadcasters and players were as heroic to me as anybody I've met in similar fields in my whole career and I have had a long career."

Remember this is a man who has interviewed presidents, statesmen, kings and heads of state. In 1974, he won a Peabody Award for his profile of Egyptian President Anwar al-Sadat.

Told that Gordie has insisted for caring for dementia-stricken Colleen in their own home, Jennings tells of learning during his travels that Africans have a measure "of respect for the elder member of the tribe because there is always something to be learned from the oldest no matter what the circumstances."

Jennings says longevity doesn't always bring wisdom, but in Howe's case it certainly does.

"You can always learn something from Gordie," Jennings says. "His affection and respect for his wife involves a longevity that we hardly see anymore."

Terry Perrelli

Bookkeeper for Colleen and Gordie

When former Howe Enterprises bookkeeper Terry Perrelli talks about her relationship with her employer/ mentor Colleen Howe it's difficult for her to fight back the tears.

"She was like a sister to me," says Perrelli, "I would say she's like a mother but we are too close in age."

Perrelli, who worked for the Howes in Connecticut, said Colleen's influence has made her more adventurous. "She showed me that if I wanted something that it can happen," Perrelli said. "She was never afraid to try."

It's difficult for outsiders to appreciate how busy the Howes kept themselves with charity work, Hartford Whalers promotional work and endorsements. Perrelli was always amazed about how Colleen could juggle so many endeavors.

"She had a file for every trip and there were hundreds of them," Perrelli recalled. "She was always on top of her game. Everything was under control and she always had time for everyone."

Colleen Howe liked free enterprise ventures, and business that involved people and networking. She has said often that she and Gordie's time spent working with Amway were among their best because of the positive people associated with that type of work. The Howes enjoyed Connecticut and only moved back to Michigan when their contract with the Hartford Whalers expired.

Perrelli remembered that like any entreprenuer Colleen had many successful business ventures and some that were not, but if they were failing, she would move on and not dwell on the past.

"I learned from her that you can always make it happen if you work hard enough," Perrelli said. "And she worked harder than anyone I know."

Bernie Geoffrion and Marlene Geoffrion

Hall of Fame Player and Wife

When it was revealed that Colleen Howe was suffering from Pick's Disease, Bernie "Boom Boom" Geoffrion was among the first to call Gordie to express his concern.

They were intense NHL rivals for many years when Mr. Hockey played for Detroit and Geoffrion wore Montreal colors, and yet these two Hall of Famers respected each other like they had been teammates.

"One game in Detroit Gordie hit me and I fell into the boards and dislocated my shoulder," Geoffrion recalled. "He came over and apologized. I never see that in hockey today. Then he said, "Hey kid, next time keep your head up."

Geoffrion said all players from the Original Six era view Howe as being one of the symbols of the essence of the game. "They just love the guy," Geoffrion said. "Every time after a game he would be there signing autographs for the kids. Do you see that today? No you don't."

On the ice? "I didn't like Gordie on the ice because he was too good," Geoffrion said, laughing. "Gordie played the game to win, he never cared about records."

When Howe tied Rocket Richard's NHL goal scoring mark in Montreal some fans booed him, but Montreal players respected Howe.

"Can you imagine that he never scored 50 goals?" Geoffrion said. "He could have scored a 100 goals. But he was a team player. He didn't care about records."

Geoffrion said he admired Colleen because she was willing to stand up to Detroit General Manager Jack Adams about Gordie's contract. More than 40 years ago Mrs. Hockey was criticized for acts that today are part of an agent's job description.

"We all had children but we were making peanuts," Geoffrion said. "They used to give us a contract and we would sign it because all we wanted to do was play the game and wear the sweater."

Geoffrion paused to come up with the right words. "Colleen paved the way," Geoffrion says, finally.

Through the years Geoffrion would jokingly ask Colleen to be his agent, but he was serious about the respect he had for what she accomplished. He noted that she had an uproarious sense of humor. "But when it came time for business, then it was business for her," Geoffrion said. "There was no fooling around."

Colleen involved both husbands and their wives in the book *After the Applause,* and that featured the Geoffrions.

"She was a real warrior," said Marlene Geoffrion. "But always very charming and very nice. We loved them both. That was a couple that really loved each other."

For years Colleen tried to convince Marlene to do a book because she is the daughter of NHL legend Howie Morenz.

Marlene always appreciated the Howe humor. For years Marlene had been attempting to ask Gordie for an autographed picture. About 10 years after she started asking, Boom Boom finally remembered when he saw Gordie.

"He wrote, to Marlene, best wishes, Gordie, and just say hi to the other one," Marlene said.

Geoffrion said he always marveled that although Howe was a superstar, his "family was first and career was second."

When he heard about Colleen's illness, he said, "She is in good hands with Gordie."

Mark Primeau

Hockey Fan

When Brighton hockey fan Mark Primeau was reviewing the list of past winners for the *Detroit News* Michiganians of the Year award in 2001 he thought that it must have been a mistake that Mr. & Mrs. Hockey had not yet been chosen.

Realizing that the Howes had never been nominated, Primeau figured it would be an honor to correct what he considered an injustice. "It was kind of a disgrace that they hadn't been nominated," said Primeau who immediately sent in a nomination letter.

"I knew it would be a hands-down victory," Primeau said. "I compared all the past winners, I knew they would win and they should win."

The Howes were chosen for the honor, along with former Detroit mayor Dennis Archer, Detroit Pistons owner Bill Davidson, and Dr. Alexa I.Canady who was a pioneering female neurosurgeon in the United States, plus a few others.

Primeau had met the Howes at promotional autograph signings but he really didn't know them when he nominated them. But he said he believed they deserved the honor because of the work they did in building the game, especially at the youth level, and for their charitable work.

"They are definitely Michigan's most charitable couple," Primeau said, who said he was bothered that some of the past winners weren't even Michigan residents anymore.

The Howes were made aware that Primeau had nominated them. The Howe's business manager Aaron Howard asked Primeau to meet him for breakfast before a public signing of the new Mr. Hockey, Coca Cola lithograph that was created by D3 Artworks John Littlejohn and his partner Rick Murphy. At the restaurant, Howard and the Howe's other business manager Del Reddy, positioned Primeau so he wouldn't see the door. Suddenly, there was a tap on Primeau's shoulder and it was Mr. Hockey asking him to scoot over.

Gordie, Colleen, Murphy and their associates joined Primeau for breakfast to thank him for thinking of the Howes.

"I would have paid to be there," Primeau said.

Primeau also sat next to the Howes at the dinner to honor the Michiganians of the Year. Primeau is an autograph collector, and he remembers his brother said to him "if you want to get all the people's autographs sit next to Gordie and Colleen and they will come to you."

That was exactly true and all of the dignitaries and special guests stopped by the Howe's table to pay homage to Mr. and Mrs. Hockey.

"What an honor," Primeau said. "I think we had the table most desired to sit at."

Jay Barrymore

President of Handplay Productions

When Jay Barrymore says that he had the best seat in the house for a Detroit Red Wings practice session in Port Huron, Michigan in the late 1960's it is a literal interpretation. Thanks to Mr. Hockey, he was actually sitting on the Red Wings bench as an astonished eleven year old.

Watching training camp on a daily basis at McMorran Arena, Barrymore remembers that he kept inching closer to the Red Wings bench on each passing day until at one point he was standing next to it during a scrimmage. Howe jumped over the boards and sat on the last seat next to Barrymore, and much to Barrymore's shock, Howe started to talk to him. "I was awe struck and tongued tied," Barrymore said. "He started asking me questions, what I was doing there, whether I played hockey. He was incredibly friendly. Then he invited me to sit on the bench next to him." Howe would take his shift, then go back, and sit next to Barrymore. "And he would point out what was going on on the ice," said Barrymore.

At one point, Barrymore had Howe sitting on one side of him and the legendary Alex Delvecchio on the other. "He was talking to me like someone's dad would be talking to me," Barrymore said.

Thirty-five years later Barrymore with his partner Marley Blood became involved in an entrepreneurial venture called *Handplay*. The catch phrase was "preserving the handprints of history." Barrymore and Blood collaborate with celebrities to provide handprints for sale for charity and for sale to the public. Who did they recruit first?

"I went back to my roots," Barrymore said. "The first person we wanted was Gordie Howe." Barrymore and Blood traveled from Maryland to Michigan to meet with the Howe's business manager's Del Reddy and Aaron Howard of Power Play. Soon after, Barrymore and Blood were at Power Play's office in Commerce Township, Michigan. They preserved Mr. Hockey's famous hand and autograph in the historic first "Handprint." "It was great." Says Barrymore.

Dave Duran

United States Mail Carrier

What Dave Duran discovered is that acts of kindness directed toward the Howe family can sometimes come back ten fold.

Steven Kirkpatrick had come to the Sandusky area hockey association with a suggestion to name a new proposed hockey arena after Colleen Howe who was raised in Sandusky. Kirkpatrick wanted to honor Mrs. Hockey for her contributions to the development of the game at many levels—and for her passion to help others less fortunate.

"I was treasurer for the first three years of (the arena's) birth and the Howe name was such an asset that I can't even put words on it," Duran said.

Once the hockey board decided to name it the Colleen J. Howe Arena, the NHL Players Association Goals and Dreams fund (administered by Devon Davis and Hall of Famer Mike Gartner) donated $45,000 for the purchase of a Zamboni. There was no arena within 60 miles of this facility, and the NHLPA donated the money to encourage hockey growth in rural areas. There are now 12 different leagues in the arena, and open skating usually has at least 50 participants.

"(The arena) affects everyone in the community," Duran said. "It was an asset we really needed. Our theatre burned down, they took the roller rink out of town. The community tried to pull this together for a tribute to Colleen."

The arena was dedicated on March 17, 2002, after Kirkpatrick had passed away on September 6, 2001, at age 23 from cardiac arrest.

"One day I was delivering Steve's mail and he knew I was involved with the hockey board," Duran said. "He approached me and said he knew the Howe's well and that Colleen was a great woman and Gordie was a great guy. He thought it would be a great idea to honor her with the name on the rink."

With Duran's help, Kirkpatrick made his pitch to the hockey board. He even invited the Howe's business representatives, Del Reddy and Aaron Howard, to demonstrate their support of the project and Kirkpatrick's connection with the Howes. The Howes, Reddy and

Howard had met Kirkpatrick at a Detroit Vipers game and they had become friends.

At the time of the dedication, Colleen already was feeling the effects of dementia, but she could still appreciate the honor. She gave the scissors to Duran's son, Jonah, for the ribbon cutting so he could be included. After the ceremony, two teams comprised of boys and girls, Mrs. Hockey's Heroes and Mr. Hockey's Heroes, played a scrimmage game.

In the arena, there is a case honoring Colleen Howe and Steven Kirkpatrick. The Howes helped finance Kirkpatrick's headstone which reflects his accomplishments, including playing in a Central Hockey League game in a wheelchair. The headstone is shaped like a puck.

"Steven was quite an individual," Duran said. "He had half the body of a normal person and yet he accomplished more than 90 percent of those around me."

Editor's Note: During the dedication of the Colleen J. Arena on March 17, 2001 Board Secretary Sharon Bush wrote in the commemorative program: "So...with the help of God, we have arrived at our first goal...ICE! We may now formally dedicate our arena to "Mrs. Hockey," our own Colleen Howe, and also to the people of our community. We have other goals, such as figure skating classes, league hockey, and more, but today, I present to you...THE COLLEEN J. HOWE ARENA!"

Mort Greenberg

Retired Television Cameraman and Fund Raiser

As a CBC cameraman for decades, Mort Greenberg was masterful at framing his subjects. He could capture an expression or a gesture that would allow his viewers to look inside a person's soul. He could sum up an athlete's entire career with 24 seconds of film.

But Greenberg struggles to find his focus when talking about Mr. and Mrs. Hockey.

There are too many memories, too many wonderful moments. There is too much love and admiration in his heart to bring any objectivity to the telling of this story.

"Colleen has a generosity of spirit that in my experience was unmatched in a woman," Greenberg says.

The Howes have been friends with Greenberg for more than 35 years. Colleen would call Greenberg and use him as a sounding board on a variety of issues. At many major events in their lives, Greenberg was invited. When Colleen was dealing with a problem, she would call Greenberg because he was much like her, strong and supportive, full of fun and energy.

They met in 1968 when Greenberg was assigned to shoot a hockey instructional film that Colleen produced. The special session was filmed at Bowling Green University with Gordie, Terry Sawchuk, Bill Gadsby, and the Howe's two sons.

Early in the session, Greenberg was on the ice trying to capture the two sons in a skating exhibition when one of their skates kicked the feet out from under him. He went splat on the ice and his Bolex camera seemed to hang in the air like it was in suspended animation. While on his duff, Greenberg was able to reach up and grab the camera before it crashed to the ice.

A grinning Gordie Howe came over and said, "Al Kaline could not have made a better catch."

Greenberg began to believe Howe was a fun-loving guy during the shoot. It was really brought home that night at three in the morning when the phone rang and it was Gadsby. He was pretending to be a doctor inquiring about the injuries he suffered in the fall.

When the joke was over, Gadsby told Greenberg to come upstairs "because we need a fourth for pinochle."

Greenberg didn't even know how to play pinochle, but that didn't matter to Howe and his buddies.

"Howe got the call early in the morning that he had to go home to be a pall bearer at Jack Adam's funeral, and he hadn't had any sleep," Greenberg said. "But he drove home."

He pauses. "I fell so in love with this family immediately and it never lapsed. When I read *and...HOWE!* I cried all the way through it. Gordie learned about his mother dying while he was at a golf tournament. He came over to me and told me. I remember thinking that he shared such an intimate detail with me...I felt so privileged."

Colleen would call Greenberg and they would have some terrific in-depth conversations. For many years, they both exchanged letters and cards. When it was decided to delay making Colleen's illness public, while she was in her early stages of dementia, it hurt to keep it from Greenberg. After Greenberg had called a number of times, the Howe's agent Del Reddy reluctantly informed him that it was nothing personal, but it was impossible for Colleen to respond to his repeated inquiries.

Nevertheless, Greenberg and the Howes had shared plenty of good times together.

He remembers Howe telling him about the time he challenged referee Bill Friday's decision to throw one of his sons out of a World Hockey Association game. Here is Greenberg's version of what Howe told him.

"Bill," asked Gordie, "Why did you throw my kid out of the game?"

"Because he called me a homer and a son of a bitch," Friday said.

"What if he hadn't said that, would you have tossed him?" Gordie asked.

"Well if he had just *thought* I was a son of bitch and a homer I would not have thrown him out," Friday said.

"Well then," Gordie said, "I *think* you are a son of a bitch and a homer."

Greenberg, himself a noted punster, loved Gordie's sense of humor, and enjoyed how Gordie used that sense of humor often to make a point, such as the time he told Friday, "I think you are the second best referee in the WHA."

"Thanks, Gord," Friday had said.

"All the others are tied for first," Howe had replied, grinning that he had gotten Friday with one of his oft-repeated jokes. Like any good comedian, Howe had material that he bent and twisted to fit every situation.

Greenberg owns a box full of letters that Colleen sent him over the years. He treasures his friendship with her.

"She was so competent that nothing fazed her," Greenberg said, "except sometimes unfortunate and undeserved remarks made by people out of jealousy and envy."

Even Colleen's reaction to criticism struck Greenberg as noble. "It really hurt her," he said. "It wasn't anger. I don't think she had the capacity to be vengeful. It hurt her that her good intentions were not viewed as such."

Greenberg was always struck by how willing Colleen was to listen to anyone who had troubles. Colleen was an only child, and an amateur psychologist might suggest that Colleen was always looking to make sure others didn't feel alone with their problems.

"She loved people," Greenberg said. "She made up for that lack of love in her early years in the way she treated others."

It was the Howe's thoughtfulness that always overwhelmed him. He remembers the time that Gordie Howe visited the White House and the evening's entertainment included opera. Mr. Hockey secured the featured soprano's autograph for Greenberg because he knew Greenberg loved opera.

In 1974, Greenberg was traveling with the WHA team that competed against the Soviets in Moscow and he met one of his first cousins for the first time. She had run into the team at the airport and showed the players Mort's picture.

At their first meeting, the first full sentence out of her mouth after the introductions was, "I would like very much to meet the man who plays with his two children."

Remember the Soviet Union was still a closed society back then and Russians didn't have every modern convenience. At the post-tournament party, Marty Howe told everyone that "Mort Greenberg has relatives over here" and anyone who has any items that they don't want to lug back home—they they should be given to Greenberg to give to them. Greenberg was touched by the gesture, particularly after Frank Mahovlich suggested that the spare rubles should also be left.

"The Howes always had a desire to be known as people rather than personalities," Greenberg said.

Greenberg won't ever forget Gordie Howe's 50th birthday celebration put on by the Hartford Whalers. It was quite an affair with numerous famous guests. Howard Cosell was the master of ceremonies. It was clearly the coronation of hockey's king.

The Howes had invited Greenberg to stay with them at their home. He was quite cozy in the den when he heard Howe descending the stairs at daybreak. He remembers reviewing the wonder of the night before in his head, and was curious about what Gordie had thought about the occasion. What would be the first words out of his mouth after such a star-studded gala?

"Well, I guess I will take the garbage out," Gordie said.

Greenberg laughs at the memory. "It was an incredible moment that indicated what a humble, wonderful man he was. I love that man so dearly; it's hard to express it."

Photo by Aaron Howard

Steve Graus, President of DC Sports with Mr. Hockey® and The Captain Steve Yzerman at a private signing.

Photo by Del Reddy

Mr. Hockey® drops the ceremonial puck at the Staples Center in Los Angeles, 2002. Taking the faceoff are two superstars themselves-- Hollywood's Jerry Bruckheimer and television's David E. Kelley.

Photo by Aaron Howard

Mr. Hockey® congratulates Brett Hull the day after he scored his 700th goal. During his career Gordie scored 1071 goals.

Photo by Aaron Howard

Mrs. Hockey® presents Steven Kirkpatrick with his own van-- compliments of the Howe Foundation.

Photo by Kevin McCrory

Mrs. Hockey® poses with Steven Kirkpatrick during the unveiling of the new sign on the Colleen J. Howe Arena in Sandusky, Michigan.

Card Compliments of Upper Deck®

Aaron Howard, Del Reddy, Mr. & Mrs. Hockey® and Kevin McCrory with Goalie Steven Kirkpatrick. He became the first person ever in a wheelchair to appear in a pro hockey game. Amazingly, while afflicted with muscular dystrophy and hooked to a ventilator, he starred as a goalie in a game for the Indianapolis Ice on April 1, 2001. Remarkably, he made a save on the game's opening shot.

Phil Pritchard of the Hockey Hall of Fame with Frozen Pond's CEO Hersh Borenstein, Power Play's Aaron Howard, and Mr. Hockey® pose with the most famous trophy in sports.

Photo by Helen Cottrell

Mr. Hockey® with Detroit Red Wing's executive Mike Bayoff.

Photo by Del Reddy

Mr. Hockey®, with WHA co-founder Dennis Murphy and the NHL Production's Executive Producer Ken Rosen.

Photo by Aaron Howard

"Fire In My Soul" author Delbert McCoy and his fiancé Renee Brandon at DC Sports with Mrs. Hockey®.

Colleen and Gordie helped commemorate the Disabled Athletes Hall of Fame in 1999. The Hall of Fame was the inspiration of Tony Filippis.

Photo by Helen Cottrell

Photo by Aaron Howard

Mr. Hockey® with talented hockey writer Paul Harris. Pictured to the right is the nation's most influential hockey journalist, Kevin Allen.

Mr. Hockey® appears at Tom's Collectibles in Taylor, Michigan. Gordie makes over 75 appearances a year.

Photo by Aaron Howard

Mr. & Mrs. Hockey® and Michigan's Entrepreneur of the year, Jack Krasula, discuss a charitable venture at Andiamos restaurant.

Photo by Del Reddy

Tracey and Larry Miller with Gordie at Power Play's office in Commerce Township.

Photo by Del Reddy

Kitty with her husband Joe Girard, the World's Greatest Salesman, and the world's greatest hockey player. The Girards purchased the painting of Mrs. Hockey® at a live auction to raise funds for autism and dementia.

The Power Play team of Rita & Felix Gatt, Mr. Hockey®, Aaron Howard and Del Reddy. They have assisted and travelled with Gordie to over 100 appearances during the last 3 years.

Mr. Hockey® with Paige and Walter Ray Williams, Jr. Gordie is the first celebrity ever to bowl a ceremonial ball on national television for the PBA tour. Walter Ray is the greatest bowler in the world today.(March 2003)

Photo by Del Reddy

NHL Alumni Association leaders Pat Flatley, Wendy McCreary and Brian Conacher with Mr. Hockey® at the all star festivities in Minnesota.

Photo by Aaron Howard

Photo by Aaron Howard

Mr. Hockey®, Ray Borque, and Patrick Roy at the All Star Game press conference in 2004. Each was selected as the greatest player ever at their position.

Mr. Hockey® with NHL Enterprises President Ed Horne, NHL's Andrew Judelson and Nextel Vice President Kevin Flynn before the 2004 All Star press conference.

Photo by Fekix Gatt

Ron Toigo and Scott Bonner of the Vancouver Giants meet with Del Reddy and Aaron Howard, the originators of the world's largest autographed bobblehead giveway. Gordie signed 4,000 Mr. Hockey® bobbleheads that were distributed complimentary at a Giant's game. The historic event celebrated Colleen's 70th birthday and raised money for dementia.

Colleen, her nurse Stacey Stanley, Gordie, Felix & Rita Gatt admire Mr. Hockey's® 75th birthday gift from Frameworth.

Photo by Aaron Howard

Photo by Lynn Gregg

Chuck Gaidica of WDIV Detroit interviews Grand Marshals, Mr. Hockey® and Bill Gadsby at America's Thanksgiving Day Parade.(2003)

Photo by David Story

Immortal Investments Mike Reddy, Gordie and David Story display the new limited edition collectible photo featuring Mr. Hockey® & the Golden Bear, Jack Nicklaus.

Photo by Del Reddy

George Wallace with Mr. Hockey® outside his Sports Collector's Haven store.

Photo by Paul Madder

The Houston Aeros retired Gordie's famous number nine at their last regular season game ever at the Compaq Center on April 5, 2003.

Photo by Aaron Howard

Mr. Hockey® and Red Wing's General Manager Ken Holland on the day of Ken's induction into the BC Sports Hall of Fame.

Photo by Rita Gatt

Director of Merchandising for the Red Wings, Karen Wenson, watches Mr. Hockey® sign books at Joe Louis Arena.

Photo by Del Reddy

Red Wing Executive Randy Lippe poses with Gordie inside Joe Louis Arena. Mr. & Mrs. Hockey® helped make Detroit "Hockeytown".

Photo by Del Reddy

Mr & Mrs. Hockey® with Red Wing's television broadcaster Ken Daniels outside the Red Wing's locker room.

Photo by Lynn Gregg

Scotty Bowman, Felix Gatt, Aaron Howard, Mr. Hockey®, Brian Ehrenworth, Budd Lynch, Gus Mollasis and Del Reddy at the opening night for the Red Wings on October 17, 2002.

Photo by John Sobczak

The greatest hockey player and the greatest fastpitch softball player— "The King", Eddie Feigner.

Photo by Del Reddy

Handplay founders Jay Barrymore and Marley Blood assist Mr. Hockey® with the first historic hand print project.

Photo by Del Reddy

The Power Play staff meeting with Sun Communities. Pictured are Felix Gatt, Veronica D`Hondt,Gary Jewell, Jim Hoekstra, Mr. Hockey®, and Brian Fannon.

Photo by Aaron Howard

Mr. Hockey®,"The Golden Jet" and "The Great One" enjoy the photo shoot that depicts the only players in history to score over 1000 goals.

Photo by Mr. Hockey®

John Stansik, Debbie Jewett, Craig O'Neill of Arctic Edge meet with the Power Play staff to preview the space for the new Mr. & Mrs. Hockey® Howe of Fame Museum. For over 3 decades, Colleen has dreamed of this museum to share their family's amazing archives to inspire future generations of fans.

Photo by Del Reddy

Mr. Hockey® is the spokesman for Ducks Unlimited Canada for 2004. Pictured are Jack Messer, Mike Thornton, Jerry Kwicinski, Bob Kindrachuk, Stephen Adamcryck, Ken Bailey, and Gord Edwards.

Photo by Mark Cunningham

Vern Howe,Gordie, Vic Howe, Don Howard and Bill Gadsby pose for a special picture at Creative Impressions.

Aaron Howard, Mr. Hockey®, Larry Gach of Ford Motor Company, and Del Reddy eating at Cheli's restaurant before the opening night game at Joe Louis Arena on October 9, 2003.

Photo by Aaron Howard

Mr. Hockey® jokes with executive producers Alan Kirschenbaum and Greg Garcia during a break at the filming of the CBS sitcom "YES, DEAR!" (March 2004)

Photo by Don Howard

The Howes await the arrival of their new van with service manager and friend Rick Burt.

Photo by Aaron Howard

Mike and Brenda Jaszcz, Angie and Al Marr with Gordie at a book signing appearance in Hockeytown Café.

Card produced by Upper Deck and photo taken by Lynn Gregg

Mr. & Mrs. Hockey®, the greatest hockey player of all-time and the most influential woman in the history of the sport. No other couple in the world has advanced the game of hockey more than Colleen and Gordie Howe®.

Photo by Aaron Howard

Mr. Hockey® pictured with Felix Gatt and Upper Deck® stars Adrianne Kieckhafer, Karvin Cheung, Mike Jackson, Bob Caruana, Dominick Magliaro, Josh Zusman, Joe Fallon, and Jeff Labovitch. Upper Deck® and its employees are the absolute best in the industry.

Photo by Lynn Gregg

Mr. & Mrs. Hockey® with Red Wing Owners Mike and Marian Ilitch. As Hall of Famers, each has contributed dramatically to the advancement of the greatest game in the world.

Mr. Hockey® poses on the Red Wing bench on the 40th anniversary of establishing the record as hockey's all-time scoring champ.

Photo by Del Reddy

Delbert McCoy

Co-Author of The Fire in My Soul, www.thefireinmysoul.com

Delbert McCoy's life is both a story of intense anguish and a profile in courage.

In 1969, McCoy was a 19-year old father of two working two jobs to support his family. He hadn't had a day off in two weeks, and he jumped at an invitation to join friends at a dance club called the The Soul Expression on Dexter and Rochester in Detroit.

McCoy was standing in a stairwell inside the Soul Expression waiting to pay his cover charge when a man threw a bottle of gasoline on the stairs. A match followed.

"The staircase became inflamed," McCoy said. "People were panicking and starting to run up the staircase. As I got four stairs up, there were people pushing and shoving and I slipped down and I fell right into the fire."

Initially McCoy believed he was dying, but he found the will to rise up and climb the stairs seconds before they collapsed. Someone covered him with a blanket to put out the flames.

When he arrived at Detroit General Hospital, he had burns over 85 percent of his body.

"I asked my dad, 'How do I look?'" McCoy said. "They were telling me I looked all right, but I could tell by the expression in his face that I was very bad."

He was in the hospital for three years and they changed his dressings twice daily and McCoy said the pain "was indescribable." He would watch the clock in intensive care and when it got close to the hour for the dressing change "I would go to pieces."

Infections threatened to kill him regularly during his recovery and he faced incredible odds to survive. But he did survive, although his body was terribly disfigured. Since then, McCoy has endured 108 surgeries. It took 30 years before surgeons could reconstruct his eyelids to allow him to blink again and close his eyes when he slept.

Kate Lawson of the *Detroit News* published a story about McCoy selling candy outside a Kroger store to help pay for his surgeries. The

Howe's representative Del Reddy read the article and shared the inspirational story with Mr. and Mrs. Hockey.

In the summer of 2000, Reddy encountered McCoy outside a Rite Aid store selling candy. They talked at length. Reddy told Delbert that he and the Howes had talked before about McCoy's amazing life. Del asked McCoy if he would like to meet Colleen and Gordie because they sure would like to meet him. Del called the Howes. They were on their way.

McCoy admits now that he wasn't sure that he really believed that the Howes were coming until he saw a van pull up and Colleen and Gordie got out.

"I called my fiancée Renee and she raced up to the store, too. Del took pictures of Renee and me with Colleen and Gordie. They both signed their book *and...HOWE!* and gave me the copy.

"For people this famous to take time out to give of themselves is really amazing," said McCoy. "In the world today, you don't see people who are willing to come and talk to someone who is really, in a sense, a nobody. They are known all over the world."

The Howes didn't view McCoy as a nobody. They saw him as a fighter, and a hero. At a few of their autograph appearances, proceeds were generated for McCoy to help defray the cost of his surgeries.

When McCoy began writing his life story, the Howes volunteered to author the book's foreword.

"That helped the book tremendously," McCoy says. "People saw that Mr. and Mrs. Hockey thought enough of me to help."

When the book, *The Fire in My Soul*, was finished, McCoy began doing book signings as well as candy sales.

"Gordie and Del even showed up at one of my book signings," McCoy said. "A lot of people saw Gordie there and quite naturally that pushed my book sales.

McCoy said a lot of people have stepped up to help him, "but Colleen and Gordie were the first sports celebrities."

Jim Haskins

NHL's Senior Director of Consumer Products

NHL executive Jim Haskins can provide eyewitness testimony to the truth that Mr. Hockey is even a celebrity to other celebrities.

Even Emmy-winning writer-producer David E. Kelley stood in line for Howe's autograph at Niketown in conjunction with the Los Angeles NHL All-Star game in 2002.

"He showed up as a fan and he waited in line like every one else." Haskins said. "We offered that he could come back to the VIP room, and he wouldn't do any of that. He was there for Gordie's whole two hour appearance. He stood behind the stanchions and asked Gordie questions."

Kelley's father, Jack, had been the general manager of the New England Whalers when Gordie played there in the late 1970's.

"Here was a guy who makes a living bringing personalities, characters, storylines and heroes to life," Haskins says. "And yet you could see the fan in David Kelley. He was talking to his ultimate hero."

At the 2004 All-Star game in St. Paul, Minnesota, Haskins saw it again as he watched Ray Bourque's "eyes get big as saucers" as he greeted Mr. Hockey during the on ice recognition.

"He goes over, chats with him, and helps him off the ice," Haskins said. "When they got underneath (the stands) he was asking him all of these questions. He was like a kid in a candy store."

What makes that so interesting is that both Howe and Bourque were being honored, along with Patrick Roy, Bobby Orr, Bobby Hull and Wayne Gretzky, as members of Nextel's all-time All-Star team.

At the Minnesota event, Howe was frequently mobbed by well wishers and autograph seekers.

He also had the best line at the Legendary All-Star press conference. When asked how he would increase scoring in the NHL, Howe joked, "They started already. They got rid of Patrick."

Haskins noted that Colleen was quite savvy in her ability to protect Howe's image rights. "At the time there weren't a lot of folks creating a marketing platform the way she was for Gordie," he said.

He noted that Colleen is known for a style of being assertive at the boardroom negotiating table. She frequently followed up deals with "notes, hugs and kisses."

"There was always some class with Colleen and a lot of respect," he said.

When Gary Bettman became NHL Commissioner in 1993, he was looking to soothe the wounds with older stars caused by a pension lawsuit. Gordie and Colleen Howe were among those called first.

"He was trying to create a much more welcome atmosphere for older players," Haskins said. "Gary thinks the world of Gordie and Colleen. They have had a number of conversations relating to hockey and the marketing of the game."

Dr. Paul Olson

Retired Physician and Long-Time Hockey Fan

Dr. Paul Olson recalls with great amusement that the first time he saw Gordie Howe in a NHL game, he mistakenly believed he was watching Syd Howe. Having been a devout fan since the 1930's, Olson lost track of the game for a few years while he was in the Air Force and then attending college in Montreal. "When people said here comes Howe, I thought he was too big for Syd Howe," Olson remembers. "I had never seen Syd Howe but I knew who he was and how big he was supposed to be."

The guy behind Olson said "that's not Syd Howe. That's Gordie Howe."

"Well," I said, "if he's half as good as Syd, he's going to be a helluva player." Olson laughs, "he turned out to be a helluva lot better than Syd."

Syd Howe was a Hall of Fame player from Ottawa, Ontario who played from 1929-1930 to 1945-1946, with his last 11 seasons with the Red Wings. He won three Stanley Cup Championships with the Red Wings. He was no relation to Gordie.

Olson was a goalie as a youngster,and actually played against Maurice "Rocket" Richard. "I had the experience of Rocket scoring 12 goals on me, and we lost 14-0," Olson said. "But I had 100 shots on goal."

He also was an assistant physician for the Toronto Maple Leafs and certainly knew his hockey. "Gordie is the greatest," said Olson who remembers listening to the Red Wings game when Mud Bruneteau scored the Stanley Cup game winner in the sixth overtime. "Gordie was better than anyone who has ever put on skates."

To Olson, a former youth coach and a student of the game, Howe separated himself from rivals by playing an unmatched all-around game. Olson said his stick handling, back checking and defensive prowess were all first rate, as was his physical dominance. "His backhand was treacherous," Olson commented. "My wife hated the guy because of the damage he did to their team," Olson added, laughing. "She was a Toronto Maple Leafs fan."

In summation, Olson said, "when Mr. Hockey was on the ice, it was like no one else was out there with him."

Olson began his medical career in Toronto, and then moved to Detroit where his children began playing hockey against the Howe's sons.

"When Ted Lindsay, then GM of the Red Wings, said the Detroit team wasn't interested in the Howes after they left the Houston Aeros in 1977, Olson was dismayed, even angered because Lindsay had been critical of Colleen. "To me it was an insult," Olson said. "Colleen had contributed more to hockey than any other woman and she got damn little credit for it."

Doc Olson has strong feelings about Mrs. Hockey as a person and her pioneering role in hockey history. "I have four children and three of my boys were always playing hockey. I saw Colleen so many times at different rinks when she was there with her sons," recalls Olson. "I had many conversations with her. One thing that really sticks out is that she was really kind and she was very knowledgeable about all aspects of the game. She knew her hockey and she always tried to assist whoever was in need of help. She was shot down in flames many times because so many people were jealous of her and Gordie," said Olson.

Olson presently lives as a retiree in Naples, Florida. In November of 2000, his son Len called and said he was flying his Mom and Dad to see the Howe Family enshrined into the U.S. Hockey Hall of Fame. Gordie, Colleen, Mark and Marty were all honored. Mrs. Hockey became the first woman in history ever enshrined into a major hockey hall of fame.

"Leonard called and said as a surprise he was bringing us to the event. We were delighted because I am such a fan, especially because Colleen would be enshrined. What an honor that is for her. I was brought into the event in a wheelchair because of my emphysema and also had my oxygen apparatus. Len pushed me up to our table about two rows behind the Howes. When the people at our table heard us talking about the Howes, my son looked worried. He thought I might look bad if the Howes didn't recognize me. He said, "Do you think they know you?" I replied, "Are you kidding?" At that moment, Colleen turned her head and saw me. She jumped out of her chair, hit Gordie on the arm, and said in an excited voice "Hey, there is Doc Olson." We shook hands, took pictures and had a great reunion."

Olson has a deep sentiment for the impact that both Colleen and Gordie have had on his life. In his professional career, he was considered a leader in his field. His life experiences provided him with keen insight on others. "Of all the hockey people I have known for over 50 years, there was never a more conscientious person or nicer woman in sports than Mrs. Colleen Howe. It took the best to be with the best. They complemented each other. Thank you Colleen! You have been like a sister I never had. Of course, I will always admire your husband Gordie, too."

John Littlejohn and Rick Murphy

Owners of D3 Artworks

As Mr. Hockey was reviewing photographs with artist John Littlejohn and Rich Murphy, he pointed out that he had scored a goal with the specific stick he was holding in a 50-year-old snapshot. Murphy was flabbergasted that Howe could be so sure that he had tallied a goal with that particular stick. "That's when he told me about the superstition, psyche or routine he had," Murphy said. "If he scored a goal with a stick, he would whittle off one of the chevrons. He found that if he didn't do that he wouldn't score with that stick any more." There was a chevron missing on the stick he was holding in the picture.

D3 artist's John Littlejohn and Rick Murphy were commissioned to create the "definitive" 14-foot Howe portrait for the refurbished Galt Arena Gardens. They studied scores of photos and interviewed people about how Mr. Hockey played. They found one odd photo that showed Howe playing with "something stuffed in his skate" and his ankle tightly wrapped. They discovered that Howe was playing with numerous stitches in his foot and he found some foam rubber to give him some more cushion. "It just showed how innovative he was to get out there and play at all costs," Littlejohn said.

The Mr. Hockey portrait was unveiled at Galt Arena along with a spectacular 24 foot *Fan's* scene. A few months before the official unveiling, Gordie, Colleen, and the Howe's associates Del Reddy, and Aaron Howard visited D3 Artworks studio in Cambridge, Ontario to get a preliminary look at the giant image of Gordie. As they walked into the studio, a large tarp covered the work in progress. Littlejohn and Murphy yanked on a cord and watched Gordie's response as the painting was revealed. "I will never ever forget his reaction, says Littlejohn. As soon as he saw it, he took a step back and had a lump in his throat. Rick and I knew we had done our job. It was very touching. Both Gordie and Colleen loved it."

As a sixteen year old, Howe played for the Galt Red Wings. On the day of the official unveiling, the Howe's agenda started before daybreak when they drove from Detroit to Cambridge. Events were planned all day. They dropped the puck at the junior game that night, and then watched some of the hockey before driving to Toronto. The next morning they had an early morning television appearance for the national show Canada AM. Littlejohn and Murphy had other obligations in Cambridge and they arrived at the Toronto hotel at 11:30 in the evening and camera flashes were popping as they approached the door.

"As a joke, my partner said 'wouldn't that be funny if the Howes were still out there meeting the fans?' We all laughed," Murphy said. "And sure enough, it was them making time for people—just the way they have done countless times over the years."

One of the highlights of their association with Mr. and Mrs. Hockey was eating breakfast with Gordie and Colleen in the Harbor Castle Hotel in Toronto and having Lanny McDonald, plus Tony and Phil Esposito and others drop by the table to say hello. "They simply wouldn't pass up an opportunity to pay their respects," said Littlejohn. "Our partner, Perry Carter, still talks about that day. He was like a kid again."

While at the Canada AM television studio, Murphy and Littlejohn came in contact with former Canadian Prime Minister Jean Chretien. Reddy arranged a photo with the artists, Mr. Hockey and the Prime Minister. Littlejohn and Murphy promised Chretien a signed lithograph.

They actually did get the artwork signed personally by Gordie for the Prime Minister, but because of a cultural artwork contract in Gander, Newfoundland, they were unable to deliver it. Eight months later his own member of parliament, Janco Peric, called Murphy to say the Prime Minister wanted his print. When the signed lithograph was delivered, Littlejohn and Murphy were brought to Chretian's office, which would be the equivalent of being invited to the Oval Office in the White House. Weeks later, Littlejohn and Murphy got a signed picture of Chretian delivered to them. "That's the power that Gordie had, from the common man, to the hierarcy of Canadian government," Murphy said.

Murphy points out that Colleen's involvement in the Galt project turned it from a single portrait into a project that benefited D3, the community and became a business opportunity.

"I still can't believe how these two incredible people have impacted our lives. In 1998, we had hoped to utilize hockey's greatest player in conjunction with Coca-Cola for the Cambridge project. When I first met Colleen, Gordie, and Del at the Royal York Hotel, little did I know that my association with them would help propel D3 Artworks into an international operation," Murphy said.

"My partner Rick and I have seen first hand the magic of Mr. and Mrs. Hockey, said Littlejohn. They are truly an amazing team."

Del Reddy

Agent, Business Manager, Promoter and Personal Friend For Mr. and Mrs. Hockey

---

For nearly a decade Del Reddy has had an extraordinary glimpse of what makes hockey's greatest couple so special. In a job description that has evolved over time, beginning in October 1995, Reddy has been their promoter, publicist, representative, agent, business manager and personal friend. "I love Colleen and Gordie dearly," Reddy imparts. "No two people, besides my Mom and Dad, have had a greater impact on my life than Mr. and Mrs. Hockey."

On a non-stop basis since late 1995, Reddy has spent nearly every day with Colleen and Gordie or been in contact with them. During that period, he has accompanied them to over 300 public appearances throughout North America.

"Some experiences are very humorous. Once we drove down Ragged Ass Road in Yellowknife, Canada, to eat at The Wild Cat Café. The people from the local hockey association took us there for dinner after the Howes signed *and...HOWE!* books for four hours for their group's fundraiser."

Reddy continues, "It's been an amazing odyssey. So much of the time spent was a lot of hard work, travel, preparation, negotiations, coordination, logistics, etc., and long hours—some weeks one hundred hours—but the experiences with them and how they impact people are priceless. So much was done out of love for them, too. You sacrifice most of your personal time because of the intense schedule. I did it because they are truly, genuinely, one of a kind people and friends."

On many trips, the Howes also traveled with fellow employee and friend Aaron Howard. "Our job was always to help in a variety of ways. I have negotiated hundreds of their appearances, and each one is unique with different variables. Helping others has always been at the forefront of their motivation." Reddy said.

"Moreover, we have spent a lot of free time with Colleen and Gordie in their daily lives. This includes trips to Meijers, the cleaners, the 100th birthday of Colleen's Grandma, staying overnight at the hospital while Gordie recovered from his double knee replacement surgery, always trying to help as many fans enjoy their encounter with Mr. and Mrs.

Hockey—wherever that may be. We have driven back and forth from Detroit to Traverse City over 50 times, attended church, moved the Howes, and also helped in a very difficult time when Colleen had the early signs of dementia."

"During the nine years I have been with Colleen and Gordie, they have moved three times. I've done the same in order to be as close to their home as possible," Del remarks. "Since we were working on a number of things everyday and their schedule was so non-stop, it was easier to help out." From his unique vantage point, Reddy has been able to keenly observe and witness the phenomenon of Mr. and Mrs. Hockey in everyday occurrences. "Whatever happened to them affected my daily life. Aaron and I are not just employees. Colleen and Gordie treat us like family."

When the *and...HOWE!* book, self-published by Colleen, was first released, Reddy rushed into high gear to help the Howes move out their new autobiography. Because the book was not available in stores, they had to be creative, hardworking, and dynamic in selling the books.

"I lived in a two-bedroom apartment in Westland, Michigan. Aaron Howard would come over during the day and set up the books. At times, there were 2,000 of them in my place. Books everywhere, stacked on tables in the living room, down the hall, in the kitchen, and even some boxes in the bathroom," said Reddy. "Colleen and Gordie would come over and sign them. Many times they were driving back and forth to Traverse City, Michigan, where their home was at in 1995."

Once an appearance was booked for the Howes to sign at, frequently the people hosting the event would stop by the apartment to pick up the books for their fundraiser. There were many funny reactions from people when they arrived. They had no idea Colleen and Gordie would be signing books in this little apartment. Once there though, the people always appreciated the Howe's down to earth demeanor.

One of the funniest stories that Del recalls was when an 18-wheeler delivery truck pulled over on the road near Reddy's apartment complex. Del heard the truck pull up so he walked outside to meet the driver. As he walked over to greet him, Reddy saw that the driver looked confused.

"When I walked up to him, 'I said are you here to deliver the pallet of books?'"

"He replied, 'Yeah, I am, but the address says it is at this apartment and there is no way. There are four big crates here and they must be going to a warehouse.'"

"As I was explaining that he did have the right destination, both Colleen and Gordie walked outside. When the driver saw them, he did a double take; he shook his head as if he was in disbelief. Both the Howes said hello, shook his hand, and assured the perplexed driver that he had the right location," Reddy said.

Ten minutes later, a group of people comprised of Howard, Reddy, Reddy's dad, Del's brothers, some friends, and Colleen and Gordie used a human rotation system (hand the box to the person behind you—one box at a time and finally into the apartment) just like a Ford Motor assembly line. Without the use of a hydraulic ramp or forklift, the improvised team unloaded the truck of over 200, 32-pound boxes—much to the relief of the driver.

"We did whatever we could to move out the books. There were many times when we would all work 100 hours a week," Reddy remembers. Ultimately, the *and...HOWE!* book would assist hundreds of groups and generate nearly a million dollars for charity.

Because it is so difficult to compact nine years of special experiences into a few pages, Del highlighted some of his unique observations of Colleen and Gordie. "You can argue that Gordie is the only athlete in the world where you could take just the second half of his career and he would still qualify for the Hall of Fame," Reddy noted.

Mr. Hockey played professionally for 32 years retiring at the inconceivable age of 52. If you took the last 16 years he played, his statistics are startling. Even after age 35, Gordie scored nearly 500 goals, was named an All-Star 15 out of 16 seasons. He registered 100 points in three different seasons after age 40, including accumulating 102 points for the Houston Aeros in 1975-1976 when he was 48. He helped the Aeros win two Avco Cups after the age of 40. He was MVP at the age of 45. Amazingly, after the age of 50, he scored 30 goals and he was still one of the toughest players in the game.

"If you look at the statistics of Babe Ruth, Joe Louis, Muhammad Ali, Michael Jordan or any of the other elite athletes in their 40's, they declined dramatically," Reddy said. "Gordie simply maintained an exceptionally high level of performance. Additionally, he is the only athlete in the world with a name that is synonymous with the entire sport. He did it on the ice and off the ice to earn this astounding accolade."

Reddy continued, "Gordie was also a scratch golfer, batted .393 in Semi-Pro baseball in Canada, and was a gifted fisherman. When God created Mr. Hockey, he created the world's most perfect athlete."

As the world's foremost Mr. and Mrs. Hockey historian, Del has read hundreds of books and thousands of articles spotlighting Colleen and Gordie. He has spoken with the players who spanned the history of the game and heard first hand why Gordie was so incomparable. "Gordie was also a genius on the ice," offers Reddy. "(Look at) how he described the equipment, the subtle elements of the games, the contour of the boards, the speed, the sticks…he would analyze the blades, and the rocker on the skate with engineering precision."

Howe was known for analyzing echoes, or the sound the puck made hitting the boards, to determine where a carom would go. He often used the reflection in the plexi-glass to determine where his opponents were. He practiced a form of psychological warfare, by patiently waiting for the right opportunity to even a score.

Reddy also believes that Howe's aura and reputation puts him in class by himself in the athletic world.

"No athlete has endeared himself to the public greater than Gordie," Reddy insists. "Richard Petty certainly has been an icon and a prolific signer, but Gordie was doing the innumerable banquets, church events, fundraisers, hockey camps, youth games, charity functions for all of those years. People sometimes forget Gordie signed autographs before hockey games, sometimes during the intermission and after every game. It is incalculable how much time he has spent with fans. No one in the history of sports spent more quality time with admirers than Mr. Hockey. He is unquestionably the game's finest ambassador and possibly for all sports."

Reddy is still amazed at the reverence that fans have for Howe in his every day activities. "I've seen grown men, very successful, cry when they meet Gordie," Reddy said. "I have watched people shake, nearly faint, lose their ability to speak, and absolutely break out into a cold sweat when they first meet him. His appeal and magnetism is astonishing."

One of Reddy's favorite illustrations of the Howe aura came on the streets of Greektown when a man walking down the street suddenly recognized Howe coming the other way. "Dammitt, it's Gordie Howe," he screamed. "Man, can you believe it?" Reddy chuckles at the memory. "Colleen, Gordie and I were all amused because he was jumping up and down and slapping his legs and screaming extremely loud. Gordie and Colleen both signed his shirt; but he just couldn't believe he met *THE* Gordie Howe."

Once while traveling with Mr. and Mrs. Hockey to Vancouver by plane, Reddy encountered former Canadian Prime Minister Pierre Trudeau and struck up a conversation with him. Del told him he was honored to meet him and asked for his autograph. Reddy explained that he was traveling with Colleen and Gordie who were behind Trudeau a few seats back.

Trudeau replied to Reddy, "I will gladly sign your autograph if you get me Gordie and Colleen's autograph."

Despite Howe's worldwide appeal, Reddy said he is always amazed at how humble Gordie has remained.

In 2004, Howe attended a benefit for former Detroit Red Wings defenseman Vladimir Konstantinov and team masseur Sergei Mnatsakonov who were injured in an automobile accident. Howe, along with Reddy, friend Felix Gatt, and associate Aaron Howard were in a private room with 18 current Red Wings. Reddy remembers that Howe said he felt "a little out of place" because he was a retired player among current stars.

"I said, 'Gordie these guys want to talk to you, and they feel out of place approaching you.'"

"When Don Mattingly and Wade Boggs got to sit down and talk baseball with Ted Williams it was the greatest highlight of their careers. They still talk about that. For these guys to sit down and talk to you is like talking to Babe Ruth."

About a minute later, Howe was sitting down with Red Wings Kris Draper and Kirk Maltby and having a good time.

According to Reddy, Howe still sees himself as a common man, and he theorizes that's why fans have always appreciated Colleen and Gordie.

While Howe was playing in Detroit, they lived in Southfield Lathrup Village, kids would stop by the house, and Colleen would invite them in. That's the way they are. Howe liked crossword puzzles and Colleen liked doing crafts. Gordie liked putzing around the house and Colleen liked sewing.

People relate to Gordie's sense of humor. Once in crowded elevator, Howe moved all the way to the back of the elevator and a woman remarked that she hated to see Gordie getting shoved to the rear.

"Oh, I always liked the corners," Howe said, cracking up the folks inside.

"It's phenomenal how much time the Howes have spent with people through the years," Reddy said. "They had Gordie Howe Hockeyland, the 65-city tour that raised over $1 million for charity and these events were not an hour, they were entire day functions in small towns where they never had someone as famous as the Howes there."

Reddy summarizes his thoughts on Mr. Hockey. Gordie is truly the most level person I have ever met. His demeanor is always the same—very even. He has exceptional patience with people—probably meeting more fans personally than any sports figure in history. He is also smart. He has a keen insight on how things really work and he provides many ideas that are truly helpful. Overall, his life has been a gift to the world and his presence has provided inestimable joy to an astonishing number of people.

Before accepting a job with the Howes, Reddy was crafting a book, featuring interviews with the top pioneers in a wide range of vocations from the scientific, to the business, to the athletic and beyond.

"I was fortunate to interview people from all fields," Reddy says, "from the top inventors in the world, business leaders, scientific pioneers, aviation, automotive—a veritable who's who. I would say that of all the people I've interviewed, the person who impressed me with having the most balanced life, maximizing all areas of her life, is Colleen."

With Gordie on the road for 32 seasons, Colleen "was in many ways superhuman," Reddy points out. She succeeded, in raising all four of her children to be well rounded, successful adults. She still managed time for friends, hobbies, business ventures, political ambition, civic responsibility and charitable endeavors.

"The (player salaries) weren't what they are today," Reddy said. "To do the things they liked and live comfortably, she had to find new income. She became the first female sports agent/manager in the world." She was the power maker, always creating, coordinating and managing a multitude of business endeavors. Her enterprises ranged from travel, cattle, multi-level marketing, management, insurance, consulting and fund raising. Her forays also included politics and serving others."

Colleen only had the benefit of a high school education, and a few community college classes. She was self-taught. She had no mentors. She learned by doing, and analyzing her own performance. She watched motivational tapes, read positive thinking books, and she also worked out of her home long before that became an accepted practice. And she did it all while making sure her children were having a normal social life, complete with sleepovers and playtime.

"She used her own wits and intelligence and she did phenomenally well," Reddy said. "She was a pioneer and a visionary. She is not only a role model for women but for all people. Her passion was always to help people. She always included others in opportunities. Her stewardship of her family and her work ethic are legendary."

According to Del, it was Colleen who helped nurture Howe's relationship with his fans, making sure about 500,000 letters were answered through the years. She always stressed how important the fans were—how much she and Gordie appreciated their support. Their number was always listed. Mr. and Mrs. Hockey were accessible by phone and in person.

"In all areas, Colleen had balance," said Reddy. "She knew what was right. Her motivation wasn't just to make more money. Her motivation was to make sure her family and others would feel good about themselves. She enjoyed accomplishing things and the challenge of creating and innovating. Also, she was always there to help deal with the adversities."

Reddy believes her contributions as a female in hockey is overlooked. "Can you think of any other woman in sports—basketball, football or baseball—except maybe as an athlete, coach or ownership capacity—who did as much as Colleen?" Reddy said.

It was Colleen who encouraged Gordie to mortgage their house to build Gordie Howe Hockeyland. It was Colleen who initiated the start-up of the Detroit Junior Red Wings. Reddy points out that Colleen was a founder of the International Professional Hockey Alumni Association to assist former players. She produced award winning instructional tapes; she was an author, publisher, writer and international speaker on sports and motivation.

"In one day, Colleen could generate more sound ideas than some marketing companies could in a week, comments Reddy. "On many levels, she was brilliant."

"She engineered the first family, multi-player, multi-year contract in sports,' Reddy says, "just to bring Mark, Marty and Gordie to Houston."

Colleen was always masterful at finding appropriate settings for Gordie. It's been forgotten that Gordie did the first commercial for ESPN when that cable network debuted. In fact, Colleen and Gordie, both helped the original founder's Bill and Scott Rassmussen launch ESPN. Colleen put together a deal for 10 players and their wives to have their stories told in a book, called *After the Applause.* She even co-founded a bank.

One of her crowning achievements was the self-published biography of the Howe family called *and...HOWE!* in 1995. While many predicted failure, she turned that into the top selling self-published sports book of all-time. Just in the first year, the Howes made about 175 appearances to sign the book. Hundreds of charities also benefited.

"At some of these appearances, we watched time and time again as Colleen would get involved in people's lives just by meeting them at an event. Her philanthropic endeavors have rarely been publicized because that's the way Colleen wanted it," said Reddy. At one point, Colleen met a blind athlete named Craig McFarlane and was so inspired she invited him to live with the Howes for a couple of years. She helped promote Craig and expended an exceptional amount of time to help further his career and assist him daily.

"Colleen also had a tremendous passion for children," Reddy said. A few years ago Mr. and Mrs. Hockey were invited to the Minnesota Wilds press conference to announce the team had sold their 12,000th season ticket. It was a great start for a new franchise. While there, Colleen and Gordie congratulated the club and the fans for their success. When she was concluding her talk, Colleen remarked, "Gordie and I are overwhelmed at your efforts to bring hockey to this market. We are going to purchase four premium season tickets to every game and donate them to children. We want kids who never get the opportunity or who can't afford to go to a game, to now be able to do so." There was a hush in the room after the touching offer.

"I've always thought there was a magic circle around Gordie," Reddy said. "There was this awe, charisma. But now I realize, there is a magic circle around Colleen as well. As much as Gordie casts a vast shadow, Colleen also casts a vast shadow of her own."

Del and Gordie talked about Colleen going "two days in a row without sleep" to work on a particular project. "Her energy level, her drive, her passion to make things happen and effect positive change was so powerful," Reddy said.

In essence, Del looked to Colleen as a mentor. Her approach was always that contracts had to be looked upon as "symbiotic relationships." To Colleen, it wasn't about just getting the best deal for the Howes. It was asking what the Howes could do to help the relationship grow long-term. She was "win-win" when the term wasn't in vogue.

"Colleen always gave me positive feedback. She was a tremendous friend who opened many doors for so many people. I know that Aaron and I try everyday to perpetuate her and Gordie's philosophy of respecting people, running a business with integrity, and perpetuating good will and philanthropy," Reddy explains.

But Colleen also taught him that it's not easy to navigate in the business world without some precautions. "The business is much tougher than anybody realizes. Many people assume that just because the Howes are world famous that everything goes smoothly. That simply is not the case," remarked Reddy.

In working with Mrs. Hockey, Reddy has learned, first hand, how people can be misjudged simply because they are working to accomplish something—trying to improve a situation or pioneer a new direction.

"Colleen was often a positive force operating in a negative atmosphere," Reddy said. "So many people were negative towards Colleen who didn't even know her."

Del believes Colleen was unjustly criticized through the years because she was willing to defend her family without worrying about the consequences to her image. "She would also defend a friend to the end," Reddy said. What is so ironic is that she truly is one of the most compassionate and heartwarming people you could ever meet."

The Howes have always had a soft spot in their hearts to assist people who were less fortunate. That's why Del is so saddened by the kind of illness that Colleen is enduring. If it were some physical ailment that didn't impair her mind, Reddy says, "Colleen would be championing the cause to find a cure."

To provide insight to Colleen's true nature as a humanitarian and her passion for helping children, Reddy cites a note Colleen enclosed along with her donation in 1994 to Covenant House—an organization in New York that helps indigent youth.

To the Children at Covenant House:

The challenges ahead of you are never as big as the power behind you!

That power may be your friends, your family and those who love you. But most certainly it is God and you! The perfect team!

Lovingly, Colleen Howe.

"In my mind, God designed the perfect athlete when he made Mr. Hockey, but when he designed Colleen Howe he created an individual who was giving, brilliant, passionate, and remarkably productive who has earned the title Mrs. Hockey," said Reddy.

Al and Claire Arbour

Hall of Famer and Wife

When 6-foot 2-inch 180-pound defenseman, Al Arbour, joined the Detroit Red Wings as a rookie in 1953-1954, he learned the enormity of Mr. Hockey's strength and the depth of his humor in a single act.

Arbour was just trying to weigh himself when Howe came up behind him. "With his hand, he grabbed me by the back of the neck and lifted me right off the scale," Arbour remembered. "He put me down on the side."

A stunned Arbour was speechless. "It was like I weighed ten pounds," Arbour recalled, chuckling. "He just about strangled me."

Arbour, who won Stanley Cup Championships as both a player and coach, believes Howe is one of the most incredible athletes the world has witnessed in any sport.

The wonder of Howe's dominance, according to Arbour, was how he made every brilliant play look routine.

"It's like a great golfer, they swing so nice and easy and they make it seem so simple," Arbour said. "You go and try to duplicate that swing and it's impossible."

Arbour recalls that Howe had such a fluid style that people would say, "He wasn't working."

"No one could do it like Mr. Hockey," Arbour said. "No matter what it was, he could do it well, whether it was killing penalties, power playing or making passes."

Opponents often misjudged Gordie's skating prowess. "If someone was getting close to catching Howe, he would put it into the next gear," Arbour said.

The first game Arbour ever saw Howe play against Montreal, Mr. Hockey came down the wing with the puck and shifted the stick from his right to his left hand. Then Montreal goalie Bill Durnan shifted the goal stick into his other hand.

"I thought 'oh my God I'm never going to play in this league,'" Arbour said, laughing. "I thought everyone could do that."

Arbour noted that general manager Jack Adams made Howe quit using both hands and "I don't know why."

The more that Arbour got to know Mr. Hockey, the more he realized that Howe's gifts were extraordinary. He watched Howe take batting practice with the Detroit Tigers and look like a major league player. "He hardly played golf and he was a scratch golfer," Arbour said. " He was just a natural."

Arbour arrived in Detroit during a golden era, with players such as Howe, Ted Lindsay, Red Kelly, Marty Pavelich and many premium players on the roster. Nevertheless, on a team brimming with talent, Howe's dominance seemed almost unbelievable.

"He could be mild and meek or tougher than nails," Arbour said. "The next minute you could be picking yourself off the ice wondering what had happened there."

Arbour and his wife, Claire, also have fond memories of being befriended by Colleen in their early days with the Red Wings. As Claire says, "Colleen rescued me from the motel," when Al was just promoted to the Red Wings. It was near Christmas and Colleen invited her and her seven-month old daughter Joanne to a Howe Christmas gathering when Al was on the road.

She was very gracious and very comforting to the young wives arriving," Claire remembered. "She was a Detroit girl and she made us comfortable."

Claire says NHL wives in that era were considered a "necessity" but were not to be "seen and not to make too much noise."

"But Colleen forged ahead," Claire said. "I admire her bravery. We were in no-man's land."

Whenever Claire encountered Colleen through the years at NHL events, "it was like we were long-lost friends."

"Gordie was bigger than life in hockey and she was this incredible force behind him," Claire said. "She is absolutely a pioneer."

Christina Lovio-George

Founder and President Lovio-George Inc.

As a communication's specialist for more than 25 years, Christina Lovio-George admired that Mrs. Hockey gave a voice to a group that seemed to have none of its own.

"I remember her talking well before it became an issue about all the (Original Six era NHL players) who were abused and used by their franchise," said Lovio-George. "They didn't have a pension, and they couldn't take care of their families, and they couldn't do anything else. She was very strident about the rights of players."

Lovio-George says Colleen "became the voice of the conscience for the National Hockey League."

With Lovio-George's background, she can appreciate that it took gumption for Colleen to be vocal in a profession that was 100 percent male. Colleen took a limited number of college courses. Her ability was primarily self-taught. But her experience in the business world was commensurate with some of the men who worked for major companies.

Colleen knew that Gordie was receiving $1,400 per month as a pension after playing 25 years in the NHL, and those other players were earning far less. She wasn't timid about talking about that injustice.

"If someone had a raised eyebrow, she was not one to relent," Lovio-George said. "If it was right to do, it was right to do, no matter who the audience was, or what the obstacle was."

Lovio-George became acquainted with the Howes while working with them when Mr. Hockey was a spokesperson for a company she represented.

She recalls Gordie's humility at appearances. "There was an innocence about him that I believe he would have played for nothing," Lovio-George said.

At one signing, she recalls Gordie having a private conversation with a child while he signed his hockey stick. "The little boy said I want to be just like Gordie and Gordie said, 'No you don't. You want to be just like you.' It was moving to see."

But Colleen had an admiration for Lovio-George who will be working on the Detroit Super Bowl and 35th Ryder Cup campaigns. As women, they understood the other's challenges.

It impressed Lovio-George that Colleen had learned to be a business manager "on the run."

"She was very much ahead of her time," Lovio-George said. "She was inspiring. She was a wonderful wife. They were in love for a long time. To balance the business and home side is a tribute to her. Very few woman could do that in her generation."

Al Sinclair

President of Sports Card Expo

When Toronto card show promoter Al Sinclair prepared for his first meeting with Colleen Howe he recalls he was "quaking in his boots because I figured I was meeting this horrible woman who was going to chew my head off and spit me out for breakfast."

He laughs now that Mrs. Hockey had been presented to him in such a negative light.

"I met with her and found out she that she was a nice, sweet lady who was trying to be a pioneer in an industry. Players had been taken advantage of over the years," Sinclair said. "All she was doing is trying to protect Gordie from people who wanted to take advantage of him."

Sinclair said he found her to be more of "an elder stateswoman."

"I came away from the meeting with a new understanding of the industry from her standpoint," Sinclair said. "The one thing that became very apparent in dealing with Colleen the first time is that her fight wasn't just about Gordie, it was about all the players."

According to Sinclair, many of the safeguards that Mrs. Hockey built into contracts for Gordie now appear in all player's deals. She was a visionary in the memorabilia world.

"They are now getting their rewards for being good players (in the past)," Sinclair said. "The fact a lot of them have a second career now, more or less, is a direct result of how Colleen structured things 15 years ago."

Sinclair said no one was looking after the interests of older players in the early days of the collectibles boom. Sinclair said he remembers trying to sign some of the Toronto Maple Leafs heroes of his youth and he was flabbergasted to learn how poorly they were living. "With some of them you wondered how their cars made it to the engagement even when they lived in Toronto," he said.

According to Sinclair, Colleen worked hard to make sure that all players received fair wages for attending shows and for the use of their images. Arrangements she instituted years ago for athletes are now standard operating procedures.

Sinclair has a great respect for the Howes and certainly appreciates Mr. Hockey's place in the collectibles market.

"An appearance by Gordie is money in the bank for a promoter," said Sinclair. "He is always a gentleman with the crowd. He has no ego about it at all."

Sinclair theorizes that the difference between Howe and a modern athlete is that "Gordie understands that the autograph isn't really why the people are there."

"It's the experience of meeting the player," Sinclair said. "Why would people stand five hours in line to get an autograph from Gordie when realistically they can buy one on-line? Where did you get the Howe autograph? Did you buy it on-line? No, I just watched Gordie Howe as he signed '"To Billy' on my picture and I shook his hand."

At Sinclair's shows, he remembers fans bringing hockey artifacts they had owned since they were kids to have Howe sign them. "And their hands are shaking from finally getting a chance to meet him," Sinclair says.

Bill Swanson

Retired Photo Finisher

Mr. Hockey once had a moment with a cancer-stricken child similar in impact to the famed moment of Babe Ruth calling his home run shot.

Bill Swanson, from Alanson, Michigan, said he was a 13-year old fan who was brought to a game at Olympia Stadium in October 1967 because he was suffering from bone cancer in his knee joint. At the time, he was only given a one in a hundred chance of surviving. A few weeks later doctors amputated his leg below the knee.

"I wasn't expected to live more than six months," Swanson recalled. "My parents were trying to get me to places and experience things before I died."

Swanson's dad was acquainted with Detroit police officer James Bannon, and he helped arrange for Bill to attend the game. Originally, the idea had been for Swanson to sit on the bench. "But they thought I might be too fragile for that," Swanson recalled.

They settled on seats behind the bench, and Swanson, now 49, said Howe leaned over at one point during a break in the action and "rubbed his stick on my bad leg and said "I will score a goal for you.'"

Swanson, originally from Livonia, said Gordie didn't tell him the goal would come on the next shift. Dramatically, that's when it occurred.

"After he scored, he gave me a nod," Swanson said. "We were shuttled out of the game before it was over. I was pretty sick and they got me out of there."

Swanson has shared his story with family and friends, but hasn't been public with it until he sent an email to the Howes. "I don't tell it to a lot of people, because I don't even know if they would believe me," he said.

Glenn Davis

Television Producer

Writer/Producers Glenn Davis and Bill Laurin had started brainstorming name ideas for the lead female character for a television show about a fictitious woman hockey executive navigating in an all-male environment. Then they came up with a name that is well known in the real hockey world.

They decided to call their character "Colleen."

"I can't remember whether it was me or Bill who said "Colleen"," Davis said. "But we just jumped on it because we knew it was perfect. It reflected the kind of background that we wanted to give that woman, and it's a woman operating in hockey. It was nice tip of the cap to Colleen Howe."

The show, "Power Play," was about the struggles of the Hamilton (Ontario) Steelheads, a professional hockey team, told from the behind-the-scene perspective. Colleen Blessed, played by Kari Matchett, was the strong willed team president.

"She was standing up to these men and using her brains and using her wits and getting by," Davis recalled. "We wanted to do a show about the real heroes of hockey, the people behind the scenes who pioneered and built the game into what it is. Obviously it includes Gordie Howe, but it also includes Colleen."

Matchett played the role brilliantly, and the show depicted people saying disparaging thing about the character. It was similar to some of the real treatment that Colleen experienced operating in the man's world of the National Hockey League.

"But the character soldiered on and we came to know that there was real heart and warmth under that fighting service," Davis said.

The prime time show ran for 26 episodes from 1998 to 2000, and was seen in Canada nationally and in the United States on UPN. Fans remember also that a Mr. Hockey poster and the *and...HOWE!* book was also on display in the team president's office, which was another salute to the Howes.

Before the show was cancelled, the Howe's agent Del Reddy was negotiating with producer Wendy Grean about having the real Colleen and Gordie appear on the show. Davis said the script idea for the Howes had already been hatched, and it was going to center on the fictional Steelheads owner Duff McArdle (Gordon Pinsent) and his memory of playing against Gordie in junior hockey.

In the show, the owner hadn't played in the NHL, but had played junior hockey in Hamilton and often talked about playing against Howe when he was in Galt.

"And Gordie had hit him and knocked him out and that was the proudest moment of his hockey career," Davis recalled.

Dorothy Ringler

Colleen's Long-Time Secretary

Colleen Howe probably generated more creative business ideas than Gordie Howe scored goals during his long professional hockey career.

"Her brain never rested," said Dorothy Ringler who was Colleen's secretary in Detroit, Houston and Hartford

Although Colleen was her employer, Ringler was truthfully a friend as well as an employee. They often worked out of the Howe household, and Colleen would sometimes ask Ringler to spend the night rather than make a long drive home, particularly if Gordie was on a road trip.

Ringler recalls that Colleen would often develop elaborate plans before she even wiped the sleep out of her eyes.

"We would get up in the morning and she would say, 'I've been thinking,'" Ringler said, clearly nostalgic about her thoughts. "I would say, 'Don't you ever sleep?'"

"She was always just filled with good ideas that would just come to her," Ringler recalled.

In the 1960's, Dorothy Ringler and her husband Rocky, a Detroit police officer, were devoted Red Wings fans when they became acquainted with the Howes. The Ringlers knew a number of players from every NHL team, and visiting players would often stop by the Ringlers while they were in town for a drink. "We had a draft beer machine that the guys liked and they would stop by," Ringler said.

As was Colleen's nature, she saw something in Dorothy that drew her to ask if she would consider coming to work for the Howes.

Ringler's efficiency was perfect for someone like Colleen who wasn't content unless she was juggling 15 business projects, raising her children and maintaining dozens of close friendships. Ringler would testify that Colleen always worked and planned as if every day contained 36 hours. She was tireless in her involvement in life.

"I have always described her as the first hockey agent," said Ringler.

In the 1960's, NHL players certainly didn't have agents as we know them today. They didn't have business experts working behind the scenes to help an athlete maximize his earning potential and keeping his profile strong in the community. That's what Colleen was doing for Gordie.

In 1958, she had negotiated her first contract, crafting a 12-year deal worth $20,000 annually from Eatons Department Store in Canada. Colleen has said many times that Gordie was mortified when she initially rejected Eaton's first offer, "and was kicking me under the table." (This amount exceeded Gordie's annual salary from hockey).

The deal she negotiated came 25 to 30 years before agents were making a significant impact in the hockey world.

"She was so intelligent, so talented in so many fields," Ringler said.

Colleen always was loyal to her friends, and appreciated those who were loyal to her. When the Howes left Detroit to go to Houston, Ringler's husband had just retired from the police force and Colleen convinced them to move to Houston.

When Colleen engineered the deal to bring the family from Houston to Hartford, Ringler thought she was going to retire.

Coincidently when the Howes had been settled into Connecticut for a short while, the Ringlers were taking a driving vacation to Maine. Colleen asked to stop by en route.

After an hour of visiting, Colleen surprised her when she asked, "How would you like to come back to work?"

Over the course of the evening, the two families discussed the details and finally Dorothy Ringler said she would rejoin the Howes. She said she would probably need a couple of months to organize the move from Houston.

"Oh, no," Colleen said. "Two weeks…I need you in two weeks."

Colleen explained that she had already gone through three different secretaries.

"I can understand why someone couldn't handle that job," said Ringler, laughing. "I knew how Colleen worked. I knew where everything went. It would have been overwhelming for a new person to come in."

Ringler put her life in storage in Houston and went to Connecticut, mostly because Colleen was a dear friend who needed her.

"If you were Colleen's friend, she would die for you," Ringler says.

Ringler recalled that when she had undergone major surgery, Colleen had insisted she move into the Howe home because, she said, "if you go home, you will never stay off your feet."

Ringler's home is filled with personal Howe mementos, such as cards that the Howe children, Cathy and Murray wrote, pictures of the Howe family and her cherished possessions, notes from Colleen.

Often times Ringler would arrive at work to find a note of appreciation from Colleen on her desk, especially after a major project.

In one such note, Colleen penned, "Now that you have typed everyone else's thank you note, it's time that you received yours. Just couldn't have managed without all of your skill and coordination to make the show a real success. It's so great to have an extra right arm like yours. You know how much I appreciate what you do for me. Love Colleen."

Ringler got an insider's view of the Howe marriage, and loved the sense of humor that the family had. She recalls that Gordie always liked to tease her about how she was older than he was, no matter whom they were with.

She recalls that Gordie, as busy as he was, always enjoyed helping out around the house.

"Colleen was a great cook and it would seem like it was no effort," Dorothy recalled. "But Gordie would get up every morning and make porridge for the kids. They pitched in together."

Ringler knew the Howe's children so well that she says, "they were like my own."

She also knew Colleen's Aunt Elsie and Uncle Hughie and Gordie's parents as well. No one can say why Gordie played the way he did on the ice, but Dorothy Ringler is convinced she knows why Gordie Howe is such a considerate human being.

"He's the way he is because of the way his mother was," Ringler said. "She was the sweetest person you would ever meet."

Bob Trimble

Broadcaster for Empire Sports in Buffalo

Broadcaster Bob Trimble insists that Mr. Hockey even set higher standards as a human being than he did as a National Hockey League and World Hockey Association player.

"Since I have been into my career I've based everything I know about an athlete against Gordie Howe and it's hard for the rest of these guys to live up to that," he says. "And it goes well beyond what he did on the ice."

In more than two decades of media work, Trimble says he has not met anyone quite like Colleen and Gordie in terms of their loyalty and willingness to be helpful.

In 1998, the night of the Detroit Red Wings Stanley Cup celebration parade, Trimble was in the midst of a short break from a four-hour shift as a talk show host at WJR radio when his producer said "there is a woman on the phone and she says she has Gordie Howe with her."

"Is it Colleen Howe?" Trimble asked.

Informed that it was, Trimble took the call and Mrs. Hockey told him that Gordie was having both of his knees replaced the next day in Toledo. They were en route to Ohio when the Howe's associate Del Reddy heard Trimble on the radio. The trio wanted to call and share with Trimble the excitement of the celebration. Trimble was overwhelmed by the sentiment.

"I got goose bumps," he said. "The reporter is only the messenger. We have a take but we aren't the story. To think that with all the Howes had on their mind that they took the time to call me. It was amazing. Here is Gordie on the phone talking about the Wings winning the championship and comparing it to when he won the Stanley Cup. You talk about the perfect guest. And it was completely out of the blue. He was probably on the air 10 minutes."

Trimble had grown up in the Pittsburgh area, but he had been a Howe fan. After becoming acquainted with the Howes, he became a bigger fan and a friend.

"If every athlete could take a page out of the way Gordie acts, we would never have any problems," Trimble said.

Trimble recalls with great excitement that Colleen called him in 1997 to give him a tip that there would be a press conference announcing Gordie's one-game contract with the Detroit Vipers. When she was done providing him with the details, she asked him whether "that would be a good time" for his station.

Having been in the business since the 1980's, Trimble wasn't accustomed to a star asking the media whether a press conference was being held at a convenient time.

"But she said she wanted me to be there," Trimble said.

Trimble wanted to be present to see Howe, then 69, become the first player to play professionally in six different decades, even if Mr. Hockey was going to play just one shift.

"I never got to see Gordie play in person (before his retirement) and to see him in his Vipers jersey and to interview him after was really special," said Trimble who treasures the photo he had taken with Mr. and Mrs. Hockey that memorable evening.

Like many others that attended the historic game, Trimble said, "I had this weird feeling that someone on that other team would like to make a name for himself by giving him a shot. But there was reverence there when he got on the ice. The Kansas City Blades wanted to beat the Vipers, but you could feel the respect from both teams."

He recalls that Howe was slower than the other players on the ice, but his skating was effortless. "He did not look out of place," Trimble insists. "He seemed like the grand old man of hockey making his final stand."

Jerry Green

Detroit News Sportswriter

When Jerry Green was interviewed for this book, he offered that Gordie Howe "was the best athlete" he had ever witnessed.

That's a weighty statement, considering that Green has been with the *Detroit News* since 1963 and has been chronicling sports feats for about half of a century. He is a member of the Michigan Sports Hall of Fame, and is clearly one of the most respected wordsmiths ever to grace the pages of Detroit newspapers.

There has always been a mutual respect between Howe and Green. Before Colleen's illness was publicly announced Gordie conferred with Del Reddy, the Howe's agent, about who should make the sensitive issue public. After careful consideration, Gordie granted Green the first interview. For nearly 50 years, Green had consistently and credibly covered the Howe's public lives.

Green talked eloquently about the Howes in his interview for the book, but Green is a writer, a gifted writer and a revered writer. It would be more appropriate to excerpt some of his words about Howe from a story he wrote for the *Detroit News* about Mr. Hockey on the occasion of Gordie Howe Day on March 12, 1972.

"Gordon Howe is the greatest athlete these eyes ever beheld," Green wrote. "That is stated categorically, and Howe is without challenger. I haven't the vaguest notion who is second best."

"The most impressive thing about Howe is that he is so much a human being," Green continued. "He dominated a sport for 25 years, yet is as unpretentious today as he was when he was an impoverished rookie in 1946. He jury-rigged his own sleeping quarters in a vacant Olympia storeroom to attend his first training camp with the Red Wings."

He added, "After his first year of minor league hockey he had saved $1,800. He spent every penny of it to have plumbing installed in his parent's home in Floral, Saskatchewan.

"The word is humility, then and now, always."

Green concluded his well-crafted prose in 1972 by detailing his four favorite Howe moments:

On the night that Howe broke Rocket Richard's record, Green recalled that gentlemanly Jean Beliveau skated away from his "miffed" Montreal Canadiens teammates to shake Howe's hand.

Green recalled a Howe encounter with hard-hitting defenseman Bobby Baun that started with Baun cutting Howe in the first period and ended with Howe exacting revenge in the third period. Green wrote that Howe "leaned and applied pressure with his elbow against Baun's head while they moved along the partitioned glass. Then Howe skated to the bench, with Baun's head dripping blood."

The expression on a "loudmouth" Boston fan's face when Howe stuck his stick over the boards and "gave him a nudge."

The 600 balloons that were strung to the rafters in Olympia Stadium in anticipation of Howe's 600th NHL goal.

"It was all set up," Gordie told Green. "But they had to wait so long the air went out of them."

Andre Lacroix

World Hockey Association's All-Time Leading Scorer

Andre Lacroix, billed as "The Magician" for his puck-handling wizardry during his WHA days, believes Colleen worked magic when she made all the pressure disappear for Mark Howe.

"She took all the pressure of Mark being Gordie's son," Lacroix said. "If he would have gone to the NHL first, all of his career he would have been compared to Gordie and Mark never would have been good enough. He would not have been able to be who he really was."

Lacroix believes that Colleen thought about that issue when she contacted the Houston Aeros about the possibility of bringing the whole family to Houston.

Marty was a defenseman and he was going to be insulated somewhat from comparisons to Gordie, but Mark was a winger then and he had played at age 16 for the United States Olympic Team at Sapporo, Japan, in 1972. He was the one who would face comparisons to Gordie, much like Howe's brother Vic faced when he arrived in the NHL in 1950-51.

"Colleen took the pressure off Mark and put it on the family," said Lacroix. "She was saying we can all make a decent living and have a great time if we stay together as a family."

Lacroix, currently the director for junior hockey in Oakland, California, calls Colleen "a mastermind" for her ability to secure opportunities for her family.

He compares Colleen to Hillary Clinton because she was a strong, forceful presence standing next to a powerful male figure.

"Colleen was tough in the right way," Lacroix said. "A lot of people who didn't like Colleen were jealous of Colleen. She had something that others did not because she could market very well."

According to Lacroix, those who believed that Colleen was convincing Gordie to do things he didn't want to do simply didn't know Gordie very well.

"Colleen was the brain and she would make things happen," Lacroix said. "Colleen had Gordie going all over the place because that's what he wanted to do and to this day Gordie wouldn't want it any other way. He loves to be busy."

Lacroix played with Howe on the New England Whalers and against him throughout the Howe's WHA experience. Clearly, he was impressed with the way Mr. and Mrs. Hockey conducted themselves.

"Colleen was always very busy but she found time for the other wives," Lacroix remembered. "And when she was around them, she just wanted to be another wife. She never treated the other wives like she was the mother of all wives. If you were looking for advice, she would give you advice. But she wasn't one to tell someone what to do."

Lacroix was very impressed with Gordie as a role model, and a parent. "He was not like a babysitter for his kids," Lacroix said, "He let his boys learn the ropes on their own away from the rink. He had enough respect for their kids that he let them do what they needed to do."

Howe's ability to handle his fame and deal with autograph seekers always fascinated Lacroix.

"If people sat down with him, Gordie would always start out by telling them a joke," Lacroix said. "He wanted people to feel comfortable."

Lacroix noted that Howe would size up the age of the fans that came up to him and tell stories involving players from their era. Older fans got stories about Terry Sawchuk and Sid Abel, while a middle-aged fan might get a Frank Mahovlich story and a young fan would get stories about current players.

"He just didn't want people coming to talk to him and being scared to death," Lacroix said.

When young fans would ask for an autograph, Lacroix recalls, Howe would attempt to educate them on manners and courteous behavior.

"He would say, 'What's the magic word?''' Lacroix said. "And if they said, 'Please,' he would give them an autograph. If he was eating or busy, he would say 'You are missing something.' He was a teacher and he believed that maybe the next time they would say 'excuse me or please.'"

In Gordie, Lacroix saw a man who enjoys the trappings of being an athlete as much as he enjoyed competing in the sport. He believes Colleen knew immediately that Gordie had retired too early from the Red Wings.

"He loves to be with the guys," Lacroix said. "He didn't want to retire because he would miss the guys and I think Colleen saw that in him."

Lacroix was a superstar in the WHA, finishing his career as the WHA's all-time leading scorer with 798 points. That was 160 points more than Bobby Hull registered in his WHA career, even though they both played seven seasons in the WHA. With his 32-game point scoring streak during his WHA career, plus NHL experience, Lacroix is certainly qualified to make a talent comparison.

He is convinced that Howe faced much tougher competition on a nightly basis than his modern counterparts faced. His argument: all of the world's best talent was concentrated in six teams in those days. In Howe's early years, NHL teams only played three lines and four defensemen. He points out that Howe faced a Hall of Famer checking him every night along with a Hall of Fame goaltender. Today, the world's best talent is spread over 30 NHL teams and those teams are using four lines and six defenseman.

"If Gordie played today, it would be a circus," Lacroix said. "He would be unbelievable."

Tom Lennox

Vancouver Business Entrepreneur

When the late NBA legend Wilt Chamberlain authored a book in which he stated he had sex with 20,000 women a bemused Colleen Howe sent him a silver balloon shaped like a condom with the inscription "good for 20,000 uses, Love Colleen."

Not many people realized that Colleen had a good friendship with the seven-foot man who revolutionized basketball.

"They were a lot alike because they were very inquisitive," said Tom Lennox, a businessman who introduced Chamberlain to the Howes at the Rendezvous 1987 All-Star Hockey weekend in Quebec City, Quebec. "Whenever they met people, they were never telling their stories, they were always listening and getting more information about people."

Lennox met Chamberlain in Toronto when Chamberlain became interested in a line of big men's clothing that Lennox had introduced. They became such good friends that Chamberlain would often invite Lennox to big events. "I was his date at Rendezvous," jokes Lennox.

Chamberlain was late in arriving and Lennox met Mr. Hockey by chance when Gordie asked him if he could share his table at breakfast. Gordie introduced Colleen to Lennox and the next day Lennox introduced Colleen to Chamberlain. Gordie and Wilt had some fun together because they signed autographs at the same event, and Gordie was amused that Wilt's line for autographs was longer than his line and Wayne Gretzky's lines combined, even though Quebec City was a hockey town.

But Colleen and Chamberlain were fascinated by each other, because they were both so intrigued by what the other was doing. Wilt had traveled the world, and Colleen had a million stories about people from all walks of life. They were both well read. Chamberlain was a Renaissance man and Colleen was a Renaissance woman.

With the balloon, Mrs. Hockey had sent the *and...HOWE!* book personally inscribed to Chamberlin.

"They got a kick out of each other," Lennox said. "They were so divergent, so different, but their passion for learning and studying people were parallel. They were similar in many ways."

Perhaps the bond between Colleen and Wilt also came from the fact that they were often misunderstood.

"Colleen and Wilt did a lot of things for people that no one ever knew about," said Lennox.

Lennox considers the Howes among the kindest people he has ever met, telling the story of how when the Howes and their associate Del Reddy visited him after an alumni game in Vancouver. Colleen had climbed into the back of a Suburban and pulled out a hockey stick that Gordie had used. She gave it to his son, Shane. "What I didn't know is that Gordie rarely gave out his sticks," Lennox said.

He enjoyed Wilt and Colleen because of their caring nature. "You rarely meet celebrities like Wilt and Colleen who are more interested in you than you are in them," Lennox said. "They were always concerned about what was happening with everyone else."

Howard Baldwin

Former Owner, New England and Hartford Whalers

Howard Baldwin jokingly insists that it was Colleen Howe's goat and not Colleen Howe's negotiations that swayed him when he was trying to sign the Howe family for the WHA's New England Whalers in 1977.

In the final stages of negotiations, Whalers owner Baldwin flew to Michigan to close the deal. He arrived at what the Howes called their "ranch" and he found Colleen feeding her llamas.

"I am worried about the llamas, because I don't know llamas, and all of a sudden this little goat comes charging out and bites me in the ankle," says Baldwin, laughing.

When the deal was completed, and the Howes were introduced at a press conference, Colleen presented Baldwin with a stuffed goat as a memento of his negotiations with the Howes.

"I would have to say that the deal was huge in my career, and it might be at the top of the list," Baldwin said. I love Gordie and Colleen. Imagine being able to say you had a relationship with the 'Babe Ruth of hockey.'"

The Howes were free agents because their contract had expired in Houston, and Baldwin eventually ended up paying $450,000 for the family. (Gordie, Marty, Mark and Colleen). Initially, Gordie was just going to join the team in management, but Baldwin said as soon as he spent some time in Hartford it was clear he wanted to continue playing. "We bumped the contract up fifty thousand and he played," Baldwin recalled.

The team's general manager Jack Kelly started negotiations, and they had gone on for months because the Howes had options. The Boston Bruins were serious contenders, and it seemed at one point that the Howes were destined for Boston. Baldwin was only supposed to be called if they were close to getting something done.

"Here I came in thinking it would take an hour or two and it went until two or three in the morning," Baldwin said, laughing. "When my eyes were glazed over, I think Gordie and Colleen realized it was time to get the deal done.

Mrs. Hockey handled the entire negotiations, said Baldwin, “and she did a beautiful job.”

“I can say nothing but good things about her style of negotiating and her knowledge of what was equitable,” Baldwin said.

The deal was announced the next morning, much to the dismay of the Bruins who badly wanted the Howes. “I believe the Bruins had called a press conference to announce they had them. It was that dramatic,” Baldwin said.

The deal was somewhat complicated. “Two years later I think we got a deal inked,” Baldwin said, laughing. “It took a long time to get it into writing. However, we had no issues at all about what we shook hands on. They are honorable people.”

Baldwin is now president and CEO of Crusader Entertainment, a movie production company. He’s actively involved in putting together a movie about the Howe family’s exploits in the World Hockey Association.

He has a great fondness for the Howes, and a passel of great memories about his experiences with the family. Among his favorite moments was when he was flying to Birmingham to see Howe score his 1000th goal. There was no television coverage or even a photograph, but Baldwin recalls it was a clean shot, no deflection.

“They had to do a drawing of it in the newspaper in the Hartford Courant,” Baldwin said, laughing. “It was like a sighting of a UFO.”

He remembers a Whaler’s exhibition game in Detroit and Howe receiving an ovation that wouldn’t stop. He headed down to the dressing room after the game, and “by the time I got down there the fans were still going; they wouldn’t leave the building.”

When the WHA was annexed by the NHL and the Hartford Whalers became an NHL franchise in 1979-1980, he recalls going into Toronto and owner Harold Ballard huffing and puffing about Baldwin’s team having Dave Keon, Bobby Hull and Gordie.

“In the newspaper (the day before) he said they were too old and they couldn’t play and we beat them,” Baldwin said. “I believe Gordie had two goals and Dave Keon one. I remember looking for Ballard and they said he’s down in that bunker, which was the most unpleasant looking thing I’ve ever seen.”

One of Baldwin’s prized possessions was a photograph of Keon, Howe and Hull going through the post-playoff handshake line after the playoff loss to Montreal. “They played together at one point and I think that line averaged about 50 years of age.”

Actually, Howe was 52, Hull was 41 and Keon was 41. That makes their average age about 44.

In addition to what Howe did on the ice, Baldwin said Mr. and Mrs. Hockey became the team's best public relations agents. "They immersed themselves in the community," Baldwin said. "Colleen even ran for Congress. It's too bad she lost because she would have been a great Congresswoman."

Baldwin still kicks himself over allowing the Whalers to trade Mark Howe for Ken Linseman and Greg Adams in 1982.

"It was the wrong decision," said Baldwin. "Ultimately, it's my fault because I let it happen. But the truth is that even after that, we all stayed very close."

Ralph Backstrom

Former NHL and WHA Standout

Ralph Backstrom didn't even have to see Gordie Howe's hit against a Soviet player at the 1974 Summit Series to know that it was one of the most memorable and devastating bodychecks in hockey history.

"I was skating up ice and I heard a noise behind me and I turned to the left a little bit and I saw this red Russian helmet rolling across the ice," Backstrom said.

A few minutes before, Backstrom remembers being on the bench and listening to Gordie and Mark Howe discussing Mark Howe's bloody nose.

"All Gordie said was, 'What number?' and Mark gave him the number," Backstrom said.

It was the very next shift that Howe flattened Mark's assailant. "The guy was down and we went back to the bench, and Gordie said, "Was that the guy? And Mark said it was."

In hindsight, Backstrom said, it was a small incident in a game, "but knowing what happened without having to look back makes that incident indelible in my mind."

Backstrom, who played on a line with Mark and Gordie, says without reservation that Howe was the "best player in that series."

"When you play with a guy, you see his contributions on and off the ice," Backstrom said. "There are a lot of intangibles that go with him. With Gordie there he was certainly the leader. For a guy at the age of 46 playing against the world class athletes of Russia, he was remarkable. I really thought he was the best player on the ice."

The Soviet squad included Valery Kharlamov, Boris Mikailov, Alexander Maltsev and Alexander Yakushev among others. They are considered some of the best soviet players of all-time.

Backstrom had eight points in that eight-game series, won by the Soviets. But he says playing on a line with Mr. Hockey "was a big thrill for me."

"There is no question Gordie was the greatest player of all time, and I played with some great players in Montreal with "Rocket" Richard, Jean

Beliveau, Doug Harvey and Jacques Plante," Backstrom said. "He could shoot left-handed and right-handed. He played every position including defense. He took face-offs. He is the man."

Even in Montreal, says Backstrom, Howe was respected, even though the city had a long list of French Canadian heroes.

"Most players in the Original Six era would tell you that he was the greatest of all time," Backstrom says.

Backstrom became acquainted with Colleen during that Summit Series and came away very impressed, as did the Russians apparently.

Gordie has often said the Russians liked Colleen better than they liked him in 1974.

"One of the KGB guys assigned to the team seemed to be fascinated with Colleen," Gordie said. "He gave her candy when we were out, and he jokingly said to me one day, "You go home, but she stays."

Adds Backstrom, "Colleen was a driving force, very energetic, very personable. And I respected how wonderful she was with Gordie, and not just as a wife, but as a true partner."

Sometimes random, seemingly innocuous moments help define an athlete's greatness. Backstrom says he had a better understanding of Howe's overwhelming talent when he watched Howe choose a hockey stick.

"He just grabbed one, and said, 'This will do' and it was someone else's stick," Backstrom recalled. "We were all so finicky and fussy about our sticks and here is Gordie Howe picking up a stick and saying 'this will do.' I don't think he sweated the small stuff. He just played the game. He just enjoyed playing the game. If you looked at how long he played, no one played with more of a love for the game or with more passion than he did.

The funny thing about Gordie Howe in that Summit Series is that everyone remembers that he played tough, gritty, forceful and rough and yet he only ended up with two penalty minutes. Backstrom totaled 10 penalty minutes in that series

Backstrom just remembers Howe being dominant, especially in Moscow. Says Backstrom, "Gordie lived up to his reputation as Mr. Elbows."

Editors note: Mr. Hockey, Marty and Mark all appeared in the series together. It was another historic first. This marked the only time a father and sons played professional sports together in international competition.

Glenn Hall (Mr. Goalie)

Hall of Fame Goaltender

Once in the Detroit Red Wings dressing room a reporter was asking Glenn Hall "what player gives you the most trouble?'

"The one with the puck," interjected a grinning Gordie Howe who was seated nearby.

Everyone laughed, but wrapped in Mr. Hockey's humor, according to Hall, was another reason why Howe was the best in the game. He could boil down the game in his mind, and prioritize the potential danger of any situation. "Gordie was right, if a guy doesn't have the puck, it's not a huge problem," Hall said.

According to Hall, Howe didn't even screen a goalie the same way other forwards would attempt to do it.

"Everyone would interfere with you a little bit, but he was so smart about it," Hall said. "Most guys would be whacking and slamming at you or the puck. I remember him just hooking his stick on the handle of my stick."

When Howe pulled down on his stick, the toe or the blade of Hall's stick would come off the ice.

"It was not something an official would be looking at," Hall said. "It was just a smart move and that's what he did so well."

Even when the puck would carom into the air around the net Howe's approach was different.

"If any player touches the puck with his stick above your head, it's an automatic whistle," Hall said. "So instead of going for the puck Gordie would hook his stick around your hand and pull it down. He would come down on your back. I remember having to recover from a situation that would have been quite simple had I been able to catch it."

Essentially Howe would subtly create enough havoc to interfere with the goalie's ability to catch the puck. When the puck would hit the ice, Howe was ready to get his whacks at it.

"He would just move your hand enough so the puck would hit the back of your hand," Hall said. "It was really good thinking."

Hall recalls that Mr. Hockey had a "good, heavy shot" but his real strength was the quick release.

"He didn't have a big slap shot," Hall remembered. "He would take a two foot slap shot; but he would have as much on it as guys who took a full slap shot."

According to Hall, there is no question in his mind that Howe was the best player of all time. He was also the toughest.

"Because of the way he played, he seemed so big," Hall said. "When I see him today I expect to look up at someone being six-foot-five, and now I think, really, I was as tall as he was."

Truthfully, Mr. Hockey and Mr. Goalie were both six-feet tall.

"Gordie also protected the puck so well," Hall said. "He and Rocket Richard were the big names and they would cut in with the defenseman beat. They would put the knee out and cut in real sharp. Howe was strong and he could get that shot up with one hand if he needed to."

Hall said Howe always got "a lot of room" to play because of his reputation. "People talk about the elbows but I think it was everything," he says.

Chuckling, Hall says, "He was just easier to play with than against. We are all a bunch of old guys now who enjoyed playing the game, and nobody played it like Gordie."

Hall certainly knew Colleen as well, and he credits her for some of the extra income former stars have earned through the years on memorabilia signings. He believes she helped create the marketplace.

"She did a lot for all hockey players because once she would do something for Gordie, we derived the benefits," said Hall, elected to the Hall of Fame in 1975. "We would look at Gordie with his card signings and think, if you are making money off of these, why can't we? It snowballed to the point that the rest of the players reaped the benefits from what she has done."

Marty Howe

Son of Gordie and Colleen

As much as others remember how Gordie Howe protected his sons in the World Hockey Association, Marty Howe fondly remembers the moment he rose in defense of his mother.

In 1977, after the Howes had played four seasons in Houston, the franchise was experiencing financial difficulty and was trying to renege on a no-trade clause that Colleen had shrewdly included into the Howe contracts.

"The conversation got pretty heated," Marty recalled. "It had nothing to do with hockey, and my mom was blasting back."

Marty says his temper usually has a long fuse. "I'm pretty calm, pretty calm, and then all the sudden I just go," he says. That's what happened in this meeting.

In Marty's mind, his mother was taking "undeserved" abuse "for being a female" in this sit-down with the Aeros' brass.

"I just stood up and gave them a few verbal blasts back and told them where they could put their contract," Marty said. "That's when we walked out and started looking at other places."

That moment certainly symbolized the strong family bond that the Howes enjoyed. If you attacked one Howe, you were attacking them all.

"It was always about sticking together as a family," said Marty, now an assistant coach for the American League's Chicago Wolves. "If I didn't say it, someone else would have."

Shortly thereafter, the Howes became free agents, thanks to Colleen's foresight regarding the no-trade clause. It had also been Mrs. Hockey's discovery of the draft loophole that allowed Mark and Marty to play pro hockey two years before Mark was eligible for the NHL draft and one year before Marty was eligible. Moreover, it was Colleen who had astutely structured the contract so they would be free to consider options if the Aeros' deal fell apart.

"When your agent is your family, you get looked after," Marty said. "Going into Hartford we had a guaranteed contract, and that didn't usually go on in those days. She was ahead of her time. She was stubborn and she liked to run things, and that helped us. We had a chance to earn some good money playing in the WHA."

Colleen was like Gordie in that she was a different person in the game than she was away from the game.

"Off the ice Dad was the nicest man you will ever meet, but put skates on him and you don't know who he is," Marty said. "And my mom was the same (in terms of toughness) when she negotiated. But as soon as you are done negotiating, then it's okay, let's go to lunch."

Marty pauses. "It was like someone flicked a switch for them to become different people."

It's sometimes forgotten that Marty enjoyed a good career in the WHA, averaging 12 goals a season from his defensive position over his final five seasons in that league. He netted 17 goals, had 103 penalty minutes, and made the WHA All-Star team in his final campaign in Houston. He played 449 games in the WHA and 179 in the NHL.

Clearly, Marty appreciated his parents for helping him launch his career. He remembers the early days in the WHA with fondness. Early on the boys started calling their father "Gordie" during the games. "He never asked us to call him Gordie, but we learned he wouldn't answer us if we didn't," Marty said. "We would go back to 'Dad' if he got hurt."

Certainly, Gordie tried to guide his teen-agers as pros. "We always had a rule, everything in moderation. We ignored it completely and continued to do what we were doing," joked Marty who has his parent's sense of humor.

Gordie hung around his kids at home, but never at night, unless it was a team function. "We were at the disco and bar and all that other stuff, and we probably embarrassed him," Marty said, chuckling at the memory.

He listened when Gordie gave hockey advice, although he never had his father's ability to inflict punishment. Marty could stand up for himself, but he couldn't intimidate like his father.

Marty said his father always knew how much he was hurting an opponent. He had a knack for knowing how much damage he was causing. "He could nick someone and give them three or four stitches, depending on the doctor," Marty said. "That's the feel he had with his stick."

He always marveled at how his mother could strike some balance between her family and business endeavors. "She was one of those people who can survive on three hours of sleep whether she needed it not," Marty said.

During the hockey season growing up, Marty said they didn't see their dad much. However, in the summer he would make up for it with fishing trips and outings that were clearly devised for strengthening the family bond. This is a close family.

"We picked on Murray but he seemed to turn out okay," said Marty, noting that his brother is a now a doctor. "He knew how to hide from us when he needed to."

Maybe that's why the Howes enjoyed the early days with the Aeros because there was a family atmosphere on the team.

"What we had in Houston was a close knit bunch of guys," Marty recalled.

Fun was a staple for the group. At Christmas, he remembers the single players getting together in two vans for a rousing night of caroling. "This was before designated drivers," Marty said, laughing. "But we had some."

The idea was that the carolers would go to each married player's house and sing "as best we could" until they were invited in for beers. After beers, they would leave.

When they arrived at defenseman Poul Popiel's house one year he was just getting ready for a Christmas feast. Guests were dressed in suits and ties. The turkey had just exited the oven. The tabled was trimmed with Christmas decorations.

It wasn't as if Popiel wasn't expecting the boys. He had a keg cooling on ice.

"The mistake was they set a barrel of beer right in front of the counter where the turkey was," Marty said, laughing. "Of course everyone dips in, grabs a beer and a leg, grabs a beer, and a wing. There are 12 or 13 of us and by the time we got through there was no turkey left."

Marty continues to laugh, "They ended up having a fancy dinner with pizza."

Mark Howe

Son of Gordie and Colleen

When Gordie and Colleen Howe talked to their son about jumping directly from junior hockey to the World Hockey Association in 1973-74, he wasn't initially convinced that it was his best option.

"I thought I could use one more year of junior hockey to be prepared," Mark said. "My dad talked to me, and said the way you improve is to play against guys who are better than you."

Mark still wasn't persuaded, "I still thought I needed another year."

Then Colleen began the negotiations with the Houston Aeros and Mark received his first peek at what the Aeros were willing to pay him to be an 18-year old rookie in pro hockey.

Just the signing bonus was $125,000, and Mark was starting to warm to the idea but still had a hesitation. Then he was reminded that his dad only made $100,000 in the final two seasons of his contract with the Red Wings.

"That was 25 percent more than he ever made, and he looked at me and said, 'if you don't sign that contract, I'm going to break your arm and I'm going to sign it for you.'" Mark said laughing.

Having played in the NHL for 25 years, Mr. Hockey knew his sons were ready and his faith wasn't misplaced because Mark scored 36 goals that season, two more than Gordie, to win the Lou Kaplan Trophy as the WHA's Rookie of the Year. Mark played 929 NHL games and 426 WHA games.

When training camp started, Mark recalls that he and Marty were worried that it was their dad, then 46, who may not have been ready. Mark remembers going to his mom and expressing some concern about Gordie's ability to handle the rigors of the game. Then, within a day or two of the meeting with their mother, Gordie began to look like he had never retired.

Playing with his dad was certainly a joy for Mark, but he laughingly admits that it also required some adjustments early in the season when Gordie was probably being overly protective of his teenagers.

Although the Aeros preferred to carry the puck into the zone, they would occasionally dump it in and Mark could utilize his speed to be the first one to retrieve it. An opposing defenseman would bang him along the boards, "then a second later there would be a big thud," and Mark would have the wind knocked out of him.

It was Gordie smacking the player who had checked his son. When Gordie's weight was being added to the defender's weight, Mark always felt as if he had been run into by a cement mixer.

Mark didn't say anything for the first month of the season but then he had to pull his dad aside and explained the problem.

"I can take a hit from anybody," Mark said. "But you are killing me by hitting the guy who is hitting me."

Mark laughs at the memory. "I don't know how many guys have had to tell Gordie how to play," he says laughing.

He had to make another request later. "Sometimes when he would pass the puck to me he would pass it slow to make it easier to handle," Mark recalled. "The problem was the defender was getting there at the same time as the puck."

Mark was getting walloped because of the soft passes. Another adjustment was made.

Nevertheless, mostly what Mark received from his father were valuable lessons about how hockey should be played, and about how athletes should conduct themselves. Mark recalls that the Aeros were beating a team 5-1 late in the third period. He tried to beat a defender wide and a "guy came over and got a good piece of me."

When Mark got to the bench, his father asked him whether he had learned anything from that experience.

Mark said he was learning what players he needed to be aware of, but his father said that was the wrong answer.

"We are up 5-1 with three minutes to go and you are trying to embarrass that guy," Gordie said. "You should be dumping that puck in and taking your win. You don't want to tick off that guy. Down the road it will be easier on your body."

Mark understood the lesson. Gordie didn't believe in piling up goals or points for the sake of having gaudy numbers. When the victory was assured, Mr. Hockey put his gun in his holster.

Without question, insists Mark, his father was still intimidating the opposition physically even in his late 40's.

"He was the meanest, nastiest man on a pair of skates I've ever seen. Off the ice he was the most gentlemanly man I ever met," Mark said.

His physique was sculpted by manual labor, rather than by exercise apparatus. Mark recalls hearing how Gordie, like many of the boys in Saskatchewan, got work in the paving industry. Gordie's dad would make extra income by making bets on how many cement bags Gordie could carry. Gordie ended up with a double hernia and his dad made a few extra bucks.

"Everyone was carrying one and he was carrying three," Mark said. "It's not the same as being in a gym, but you are doing a lot of heavy lifting."

He also remembers his father laboring at the family cottage on Bear Lake every summer to repair the beach from the harshness of the previous winter. "When you are shoveling wet sand for two or three days, you're building up your muscles," Mark said.

No one knew how to use his muscle more effectively than Gordie. Stories of Gordie defending his boys are not exaggerated, even though his sons believed they could fight their own battles. "But really he would stand up for anyone on his team," Mark said

Gordie seemed to have even more passion for retribution and protection when it came to Mark and Marty. Mark recalls a conversation that occurred after Marty had received a scratched cornea and he and Gordie were visiting him in the hospital.

"Hey Dad, can I ask you a favor?" Marty said.

"You don't even need to ask this one," Gordie had said.

The message was clear. This Howe family had a tight bond. Colleen and Gordie stressed that to the boys at an early age. There was a need to look after each other. Friends come and go, but your family is with you for a lifetime.

According to Mark, it was a "family-first" commitment that really prompted his mother Colleen to become involved in taking care of Gordie's business interests.

"Dad's temperament was that you put your trust in people because you are doing the right thing for them and they should be doing the right thing for you," Mark said.

However, Gordie discovered the Red Wings hadn't been square with him through the years.

"Bobby Baun said to him, 'We have to have lunch because I'm getting twice as much as you and you are the best player in the world,'" Mark said. "I remember how much that hurt Dad, and that's when Mom started to get more involved. She gets a bad rap, but she only did what she did because Dad wouldn't speak up for himself. And mom would battle her heart out for anyone, and especially her family."

According to Mark, at the time Baun enlightened Gordie about the NHL's pay structure. Baun was making $60,000 and Gordie was making $30,000.

Colleen's involvement clearly corrected an injustice. It can be said without contradiction that after Colleen took charge of negotiations that Gordie received a fairer wage by industry standards.

"Colleen was very goal oriented, very determined," Mark said. "If there was something she wanted, she would not take no for an answer. She would battle for it and everything she did was for the good of the family; her family ties were so strong. We weren't just a client."

To Mark, what made her performance in the business ring more amazing is that it was accomplished while she was also playing the role of super mom. Remember, Gordie was a traveling hockey player for 32 NHL seasons and all but eight of them occurring after Gordie and Colleen were married on April 15, 1953, at the Calvary Presbyterian Church near Olympia Stadium

"Dad was always gone," Mark said. "And I remember at one point all three of the boys were on three different teams and we were practicing two or three days a week, playing 90 to 100 games. And we had kids staying at our house and she started the junior team. She was always busy."

When Colleen's kids were grown and had children of their own, she shifted from being a super mom to being a super grandmother. When Colleen's illness was diagnosed, Mark went to his parent's home to help sort through his mother's files. He discovered every piece of artwork, greeting card, report card, poem and school report ever sent to her by her grandkids. They had all been kept, along with all of those keepsakes from her own children.

"With all that she had going, there was nothing more important to her than her grandchildren," Mark said. "She never had the upbringing she wanted, and I think she wanted to make sure her family did."

Mark said his daughter, Azia, always seemed to have a special bond with her grandmother and recently some never-before-seen photos of Colleen as a youngster were sent to him. The family was stunned to see how much Azia looked like her grandmother.

"If you had a hockey question you always called Dad," Mark said. "But if you had a problem in life, that's when you called Mom. She was so strong, so supportive."

If you were a Howe, you simply understood how important family was. It was really an extension of Gordie's philosophy about being part of a team.

After playing six seasons in the WHA, Mark made the difficult conversion from forward to defense. Maybe genetics played a significant role in that process because his father was always comfortable on the blue line as well. Most high-scoring forwards might have rebelled against that change, but not a Howe.

"I was born and raised to be a team player," Mark says. "The important thing was to win. So you did what was asked of you to do that."

Bill Dineen had utilized Mark on defense for a few weeks when injuries hit the Aeros at one point in Houston. But it was New England coach Don Blackburn who had permanently moved Mark to defense.

Mark remembers coming into the dressing room and seeing his name listed at defense. He assumed teammates were playing a prank so he erased his name and wrote himself into a left wing spot. "Then Blackburn came in and said, "Who the hell is screwing around with my board?" said Mark.

However, Mark remembers clearly that it wasn't a professional coach or even his father who first planted the seed that someday he might play defense. It was his former youth coach Carl Lindstrom who used him at forward, not defense. "He was the best amateur coach I ever had," Mark said. "One day we had done some wind sprints and he said to me, 'Someday you are going to be a great defenseman in the NHL. I was 14 at the time and I looked at him and thought he was crazy."

Mark was eight when Gordie broke Rocket Richard's goal scoring record, and that may be the moment that he realized that his father's sphere of influence extended well beyond the confines of the Howe's Lathrup Village household. People stood and applauded with a passion and enthusiasm that Mark had never witnessed before. "Everyone was clapping, cheering and screaming," Mark recalled. "The decibel level would drop and then it would go way up again, and drop and then rise again."

It was a moment of enlightenment, and perhaps it was the launch point of a family pride that he would know for many, many, many years. "I remember saying," recalled Mark, "Wow, that's my dad out there and I was the only one in the whole building who could say that."

Vern and Amelia Howe

Gordie's Older Brother and Sister in Law

If Adolph Hitler had not had visions of world domination, the National Hockey League might have had to contend with a third Howe brother in the 1940's and 1950's.

At the time that the Detroit Red Wings were taking notice of Gordie Howe, his brothers Vern and Norm were serving their country in World War II. Norm, now deceased, was in the Navy and Vern was initially in the tank corps in the European theater. He was then transferred to the infantry.

With two sons in harm's way, Gordie's father, Albert, wasn't overly excited about the NHL courting another son.

Red Wings Scout Fred Pinckney, credited with discovering Gordie, received an earful one day from Albert Howe before he actually signed Gordie. Pinckney had made the mistake of continually calling the Howe home. "Listen, I got two boys over in the war and every time I hear the phone I expect bad news," Albert Howe told Pinckney. "Either sign the kid or forget it."

Vern Howe was a rugged, spirited defenseman, and it was wildly held that he would have advanced to the NHL if not for World War II. He was seven years older than Gordie and was in the army for the duration of the conflict.

"The five years in the Army killed his career," said brother Vic who did make the NHL with the New York Rangers. "He would have been more like Gordie because he didn't mind a mean streak once in a while."

Gordie has been quoted as saying that his older brother Vern was one of the most competitive defenseman he ever saw. Vern actually played while he was in the Army. However, when he was ordered overseas he sent his equipment home for Gordie.

"It was yellow and orange and ugly," said Amelia Howe, Vern's wife; who was living at the Howe household while her husband was overseas. "But Gordie wouldn't go to bed without those sweaters. Even his mother couldn't get him to take those off."

Gordie carried a picture of Vern's military team. "He had it all tattered because he idolized his brother," Amelia remembered. "That's how bad he wanted to play hockey."

Vern remembers getting mail about Gordie's career, such as when the Red Wings sent him to Galt. "I got the note and I thought 'Who are the Galt Red Wings?''' Vern said, laughing. "And when he went to the Omaha Knights, I didn't know that team either."

When Vern had left home he remembers that Gord hadn't even mastered skating yet. "In my opinion Vic was a smoother skater than Gord was," Vern says. "I was scratching when he got up to the NHL because when he left he couldn't skate."

What Vern didn't know, says his wife, was that Gordie was going "out every day" to play hockey while he was overseas.

Even when he signed in the NHL, Vern jokes that he wasn't thrilled. "Red Wings? What about the Maple Leafs? That's what I thought," Vern said.

Vern had more to worry about than hockey. He was a tank mechanic and occasionally drove them. "They turned two over on me, and burned one," Vern said. Figuring he was running out of good luck, Vern asked to be transferred to the infantry.

Norm, Gordie's other brother, had joined the Navy even though he couldn't swim a stroke. "If I'm out in the middle of the ocean, it won't make a difference," he had told his family.

Back home in Floral, Saskatchewan, Amelia recalls when Gordie went off to the New York Rangers tryout camp in Winnipeg the Rangers weren't sure what to make of the 15 year old. However, the family believed Gordie would play because "he just loved the game so much. It fit his personality," Amelia said

Vern and Amelia both recall that Gord, as a young child, would relentlessly search the area for discarded Beehive syrup bottles because the labels could be mailed to the company and exchanged for pictures of NHL players.

Gordie's toughness was established at a tender age when he literally walked on hot coals. The Howes had a coal stove, and the father would dump the hot ashes outside the back porch until they could be transported elsewhere at a later time. One time Gordie was getting chased through the house when he grabbed some galoshes, slapped his feet in them, and ran out the door.

"He jumped off the porch and right into the hot ashes," Vern said. "They were scared that he would never be able to walk. He was really blistered up by the time they got those galoshes off."

Gordie's respect for Vern's talent didn't end when he turned professional. He has said that Vern taught him the value of using your elbows effectively in a game. "I remember him asking Vern, 'How do you do that thing with your elbows and never get caught?'" Amelia said.

Vern was best man at Gordie and Colleen's wedding and he actually worked at Olympia Stadium as a maintenance manager. At the point Gordie started to have some difficulty with Red Wings management, Vern was having difficulty with a new boss who essentially wanted him to be on call 24 hours a day.

"I said to the guy, 'I will pull you over the top of the desk, strap you overhead and throw you out the window,'" Vern recalled.

The bosses immediately called Gordie and Gordie stood beside his brother. He said, "Tell Vern to take off and leave some for me," Vern said, laughing. It was the Howe way to stand up for each other; something Gordie always demonstrated when he played with his sons.

"You couldn't say anything bad about Gordie with my Dad around or you would get slapped right in the nose," Vern said, laughing.

Vern was there when Colleen founded the Junior Red Wings and remembers how hard she worked to get that moving forward. He remembers they played a fundraising exhibition game and Vern played on defense with Gordie's son Murray, while Mark, Marty and Gordie played up front. "The only Howe we didn't have was a goaltender," Vern recalled.

No one appreciated Gordie's athleticism more than Vern who seemed to have similar hockey genes. He had played hockey in Britain for the Wembley Lions when he could get away from his military duties. He thought Gordie had enough talent that he could have picked his sport. "He could have gone to pro baseball," Vern insists

What Amelia recalls is that it was also Gordie's attitude that separated him from others. "He was always so positive about everything," she says.

Amelia remembers when Gordie was a young teen-ager sitting at the table filling up two notebooks with his signature. Gordie asked her to help him pick out his best autograph. Amelia remembers Gordie's mom laughing in the background.

"Gord said, 'I should practice my signature because I will need a good signature when I play hockey in the NHL,'" Amelia recalled.

Vic Howe

Gordie's Younger Brother
Former New York Ranger

Mr. Hockey came close to not becoming hockey's greatest player because of an event that happened hundreds of miles away from the nearest National Hockey League arena.

"I pretty near blew his head off with a shot gun," his brother Vic Howe recalls.

The near tragic accident happened in 1947 after Gordie had come home from his first NHL season. Gordie and Vic were driving a spanking-new Dodge in the countryside on a Saturday morning, essentially hunting for prairie chickens or partridges because, as Vic says, "they made a pretty good dinner."

Vic was sitting in the backseat, with a 12-gauge shotgun, which he had never before fired.

They spotted a hawk sitting defiantly on a fence post along the road.

"See if you can get a shot at it," Gordie said to his younger brother.

Vic popped a shell into the chamber of the shotgun, swiveled the barrel out the window and fired just as the bird took flight. He pulled the gun back into the car, but Gordie was hollering. "Shoot again. I think you hit him."

About 57 years after the fact, Vic can only theorize what happened next. He knows he loaded the shell into the chamber. "And I must have had my finger still on the trigger because the ol' shotgun went off and it blew a hole in the roof of the car about three inches above the rear door," Vic remembers.

Vic said the blast was about 10 to 12 inches behind Gordie's head.

"I'm not sure what Gordie said because the shot made so much noise I couldn't hear for about five minutes," Vic said. "But it scared the hell out of us."

About 20 months younger than Gordie, Vic Howe followed in his brothers' footsteps and carved out his own professional career. He had a seven-year professional career, highlighted by three short tours of duty with the New York Rangers.

In 1950-1951, he was playing for the New York Rovers in the Eastern League when the Rangers called him up for the first time to play against his brother's Detroit Red Wings. Pictures were taken to commemorate the two brothers being in the game together, but he didn't receive too many shifts on the ice.

During the brief photo session, Gordie had only four words of advice for his younger brother, "Keep your head up."

They weren't on the ice together until 1954-1955 when Vic played 29 games for the Rangers. One of his two goals that season was a third period tying goal against the Red Wings at Olympia.

In those days fraternization with opposing players was forbidden, but Vic had gotten permission to go to Gordie's house and Gordie served him steak.

After Vic's tying goal, Gordie quipped, "Next time you buy your own steak."

Vic said it was obvious when Gordie was young that he was going to be a dominant player. When Gordie was in eighth grade and Vic was in seventh at King George, they had the same teacher, Mr. Trickey, and he would allow the Howe boys to leave school to go play on what was a makeshift school team.

He remembers once Gordie coming back to school and reporting, "Vic beat 'em 9-0, and Vic got the winner and I got the rest of them."

In Mr. Hockey's fourth season in the NHL, Vic had earned a place on the Windsor Spitfires, a Ontario Hockey Association team. He would often cross the river to watch his brother play. He was at the first playoff game against Toronto the night, March 28, 1950, Gordie almost lost his life because of a brain injury suffered as a result of a collision involving Toronto player Teeder Kennedy.

"Near as I could tell Kennedy had come from behind the Toronto net and started up through center and Gord was coming from his right to cut him off," Vic recalled about the start of the play. "Kennedy was swinging over toward the left boards."

According to Vic, Howie Meeker was over on right wing.

"Just before Gord got there I know what Kennedy was thinking," Vic said. "Jack Stewart was coming at him from one direction and Howe was coming at him from another direction. Get rid of the puck. So he threw the backhand pass across the ice to Meeker. When he did, the stick came up."

The point of Kennedy's stick caught Howe just below the eye, opening up a deep gash.

"If it would have been a half inch higher he would have lost the eye," Vic says.

Howe and Kennedy both tumbled to the ice, and Stewart ended up piled on top of them.

When Gordie had to be carried from the ice, Vic hustled downstairs to the first aid room just as Detroit trainer Lefty Wilson was exiting the room.

"He's OK," Wilson told Vic. "He just has a cut above his left. There is no problem."

Vic went back up to watch the third period. When he went down after the game, Wilson had a different expression on his face.

"You had better wait around because they have called an ambulance," Wilson told him.

When the unconscious Howe was transported to the hospital, with his equipment still on, Vic was in the ambulance with him.

At the hospital, two x-ray technicians couldn't get Howe's bulky body properly aligned near the x-ray machine and Vic was called in to help.

After the x-rays were done, Vic was left alone and he said Gordie woke up and asked where he was. Vic told him he was at the hospital and Gordie said his stomach hurt. Then he slipped to unconsciousness yet again.

That night surgeons had to drill a hole in Gordie's skull to relieve the pressure caused by brain swelling.

Gordie's mother and family members were flown in the next day and it was painfully evident that Gordie had almost lost his life.

Vic remembers that his mother was always worried about Gordie playing hockey and this incident didn't ease her worries.

Gordie's encounter with Kennedy wasn't the most gruesome encounter Vic would see during his career. He was playing his first game in Maple Leaf Gardens the night that Bill Gadsby, who is now one of Gordie's dearest friends, hit Tim Horton with what could be called the most famous bodycheck in NHL history.

"I was chasing Horton down the right wing," Vic recalled. "I was just poking at him, but I couldn't keep up with him. As soon as he got down to our blue line he cut to the center ice, and Gadsby came out and geez did he hit him."

Gadsby has said he thought he might have killed Horton at first.

"He didn't bounce or do anything, he just dropped like a sack of oats," Vic recalled. "His foot was at an odd angle and he was going to say something, but he couldn't even talk because he had a broken jaw too."

Many folks don't realize that the Howe children, including Gordie, were technically American citizens at birth. Gordie's father, Albert, was born in Wisconsin and lived there until he was 12 years old. That's when Howe's grandfather, James, decided to move the family to Saskatchewan to take advantage of a Canadian land grab.

Vic points out that his brother Norm was working for an oil company in Houston and was having immigration problems until he got the paperwork to prove that he was technically an American.

"Basically we are all dual citizens," Vic says.

After Gordie's first season in the NHL in 1946-47, Vic Howe remembers that another Saskatoon NHL player, Vic Lynn, got back to town before Gordie arrived back. Lynn had played three games for the Detroit Red Wings as an 18-year-old player.

"How'd Gordie make out in his first season," Vic asked Lynn.

"Man," said Lynn. "Gordie is the meanest son of a bitch in the NHL."

Playing right wing and bearing the Howe name, Vic faced a near impossible task of trying to chisel out his own career. He didn't have Gordie's penchant for roughness, but he was a solid performer who scored 27 goals for the Troy Uncle Sam Trojans in the defunct Eastern Hockey League in 1952-53. After playing 33 games over three different seasons with the Rangers, Vic even spent a season playing in Britain. He retired from pro hockey in 1962.

It certainly helped him that he had a good sense of humor about being the brother of a NHL superstar. The trash talkers of his era would say, "You aren't as good as your brother."

"Well, who the hell is?" he would reply.

Thanks

Our Superstars --- Special thanks to our friends and associates:

Upper Deck ♦ Creative Impressions ♦ Paddock Pools ♦ Vancouver Giants D3 Artworks ♦ DC Sports ♦ Frameworth ♦ Frozen Pond ♦ Motor City Sports Detroit Red Wings ♦ CCM ♦ WG Authentic ♦ Hand Play ♦ Sun Communities Ducks Unlimitied ♦ Author Jon A. Jackson ♦ White Spot Restaurants ♦ Colleen & Gordie Howe® Middle School ♦ Mitchell & Ness ♦ Tom's Collectibles Author Robert J. Thomas ♦ Melton World Vehicles ♦ Bell Canada ♦ Nike Town Cadillac News Center ♦ NHL Cool Shots ♦ Junior & College Hockey News Mike Brown ♦ Hope Fridal ♦ Author Steve Hamilton ♦ Karen Wenson Randy Lippe ♦ Jay Barrymore ♦ Marley Blood ♦ Vince Maisano ♦ Gary Bettman Steve Graus ♦ "Zac" Zaccardelli ♦ Hersh Borenstein ♦ Ron Toigo ♦ Roger Lemire Felix & Rita Gatt ♦ Jeff & Claire Gatt ♦ Joe & Sue Gatt ♦ Mike Bayoff Joe Stevens ♦ Paul W. Smith ♦ Richard McWilliams ♦ Chris Stuart ♦ Reid Middleton Adrianne Kieckhafer ♦ Mike Jackson ♦ Josh Zusman ♦ Joe Fallon ♦ Jeff Labovitch Steve Buchanan ♦ Stan Peterson ♦ Ross McCracken ♦ Dan Blamer ♦ Sue Eddy Steven Hubley ♦ Dennis Fassett ♦ Mike Holyeross ♦ Donald Scott ♦ Lynn Gregg Chuck & Jean Robertson ♦ Brian Fannon ♦ Gary Shifman ♦ Veronica D'Hondt Robertson Family ♦ Steve Tanzilli ♦ Terry Walker ♦ Mike Reddy Jr. Rick Murhpy ♦ John Littlejohn ♦ Mike Trudell ♦ Jerry Millen ♦ Lou Toarmina Dan Stahl ♦ Rick Burt ♦ Jack Krasula ♦ George Wallace ♦ Anita Pefley Rick Dodson ♦ Kelly Eggers♦ Bernd Eisner ♦Karen Currie ♦ Tanya Nicely Keith Famie ♦ James Bawol ♦ Dr. Joe Molfetto ♦Angelo Plakas Matt Howard ♦ Art Regner ♦ Mike Illitch, Jr.♦ Howard & Karen Baldwin Lynnette Shady ♦ John McCollouch ♦ Dave Monak ♦ Lorrie Reddy Nick Selimi ♦ Steve Downs ♦ Frank Sopovitz ♦ Gary Waxman ♦ Dennis Schrader Jill Cook ♦ Ray Kawa Bruce Mugerian ♦ Craig O'Neil ♦ Deb Jewett Vince Law ♦ Mike & Michelle Lynch ♦ Chris Amoroso ♦ Brandon Steiner Jared Weiss ♦ Mark Neal ♦ Mark Diehl Patrick Derrig ♦ Gia-DC SPORTS Gary Ference ♦ Mayor Sandra Cicirelli ♦ Dr. Gary Evans ♦ Fred Heuman Jill Thomas ♦ Don Nelligan ♦ Mike Nelligan ♦ Barb Gunia ♦ Kathy King Jean Schroeder ♦ Mark Mitchell ♦ Bob Brandt ♦ Jim Godbout ♦ Bill Wild Gayle Young ♦ George Riley ♦ Stan Ference ♦ Kevin Reikman ♦ Rob Simpson Ross Forman ♦ Dan Legrow ♦ Rob Miller ♦ Cleon Daskalauis ♦ Raymond Schulte David Levy ♦ Susan Rosenfeld ♦ Bob Scott ♦ Anne & Ted Henning Glenn Shaw Jr. ♦ Gregory Bajorek ♦ Bill McGraw ♦ Troy Wallace Penny Pynkala ♦ Phil Cooper ♦ Ross Niskar ♦ Jim McCory ♦ Darrell Kesteloot Lee Cochenour ♦ Dian Wilkins ♦ Dan Wheeler ♦ Ricky & Jimmy Crawford Tom Riopelle ♦ Bob Bianconi ♦ Dr. Tom Kazmierczak ♦ Matt Fiorito Martin McQuaig ♦ Dean Hjelden ♦ Johhny V ♦ Joe Castelli ♦ Emerson B. Ohl Wayne Wilson ♦ Larry Paladino ♦ Aleah Scheick ♦ Dr. Arnie Zuroff Tom Kapinowski ♦ Dr. Steinmen ♦ Dr. Patel ♦ Paul Madder ♦ Don Shane ♦ Bob Duff ♦ Tom Clark ♦ Cathy Sexton ♦ Mike Reid ♦ Penny Circle ♦ Judy Risk Ken Schweitzer ♦ Danny Elias ♦ Senator Bruce Patterson ♦ Lillie Guyer Alan Ives ♦ Kathy Levine ♦ Andy Bathgate ♦ Jason Kay ♦ Fred Heuman ♦ Faz Margaret & Jim Russo ♦ Greg Causley ♦ Doug Bechler ♦ Elliott Trumbull Bonnie Lindros ♦ Eli-The Pilot ♦ Howard Cornfield ♦ Paul Runkle ♦ Ken Getzinger Dan Fredendall

A MESSAGE FROM THE PUBLISHER

Michael J. Reddy
Publisher

Mr. & Mrs. Hockey® are not only the sport's greatest couple they are also two of the finest people I have ever met. As immortals, their lives have enhanced the world. They exemplify the qualities of greatness: integrity, excellence, dedication, humanitarianism, family values, improvement of the lives of children and an unsurpassed work ethic. We are honored to publish this incredible tribute to a couple unmatched in history for their popularization of the sport of hockey.

At Immortal Investments Publishing, we only produce books that move, inspire, and spotlight the best of human achievement and the human spirit. To order our other outstanding titles please log onto www.immortalinvestments.com or call 1-800-475-2066. Please let us know if you have suggestions for other exceptional books. Also, you may order Hockey Hall of Famer Bill Gadsby's The Grateful Gadsby, or Eddie Feigner's (of the "King and His Court"), From an Orphan to a King. If you have a story to share regarding this book or the other listed titles, please contact us at the website or address below.

*This publishing venture is also unique because this book is not distributed to bookstores. It is available exclusively through Immortal Investments Publishing. To personally bring Mr. Hockey to your fundraising event or corporate function please contact www.mrandmrshockey.com or www.immortalinvestments.com.

Order your signed copy by Mr. Hockey® today!
1-800-475-2066.

NOT SOLD IN BOOKSTORES

Immortal Investmants Publishing
35122 W. Michigan Ave. Wayne, MI 48184

The Immortal Investments Book Team!

Editor Lynn Gregg, Publisher Mike Reddy, Felix Gatt, Mr. Hockey®, Aaron Howard, and Del Reddy (Not pictured author Kevin Allen)

Photo & Formatting

Photos: James Zech, Steve Waetjen, David Story, with Book Formatter Jill Thomas.

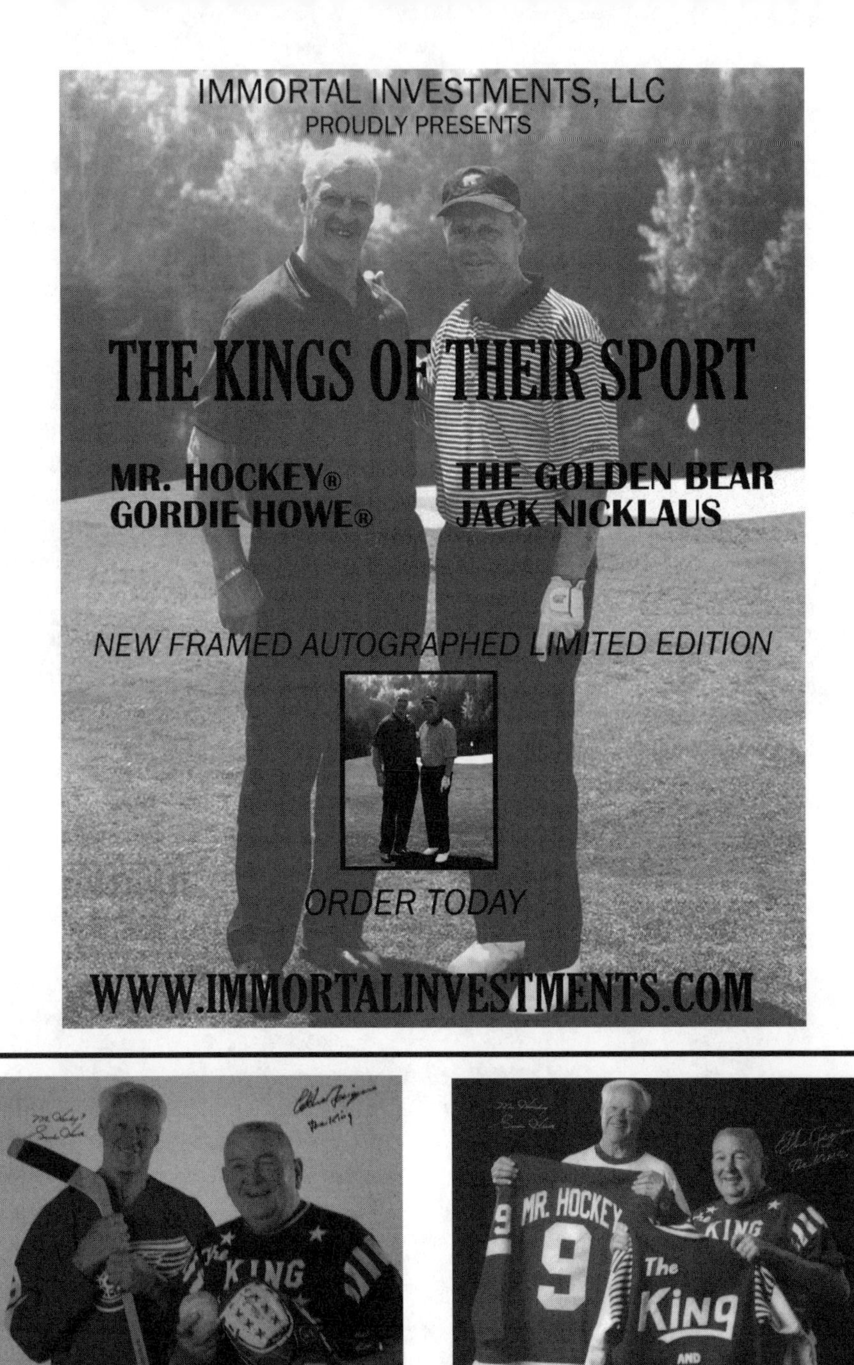
IMMORTAL INVESTMENTS, LLC
PROUDLY PRESENTS
THE KINGS OF THEIR SPORT
MR. HOCKEY®
GORDIE HOWE®
THE GOLDEN BEAR
JACK NICKLAUS
NEW FRAMED AUTOGRAPHED LIMITED EDITION
ORDER TODAY
WWW.IMMORTALINVESTMENTS.COM
MR. HOCKEY
9
The
King

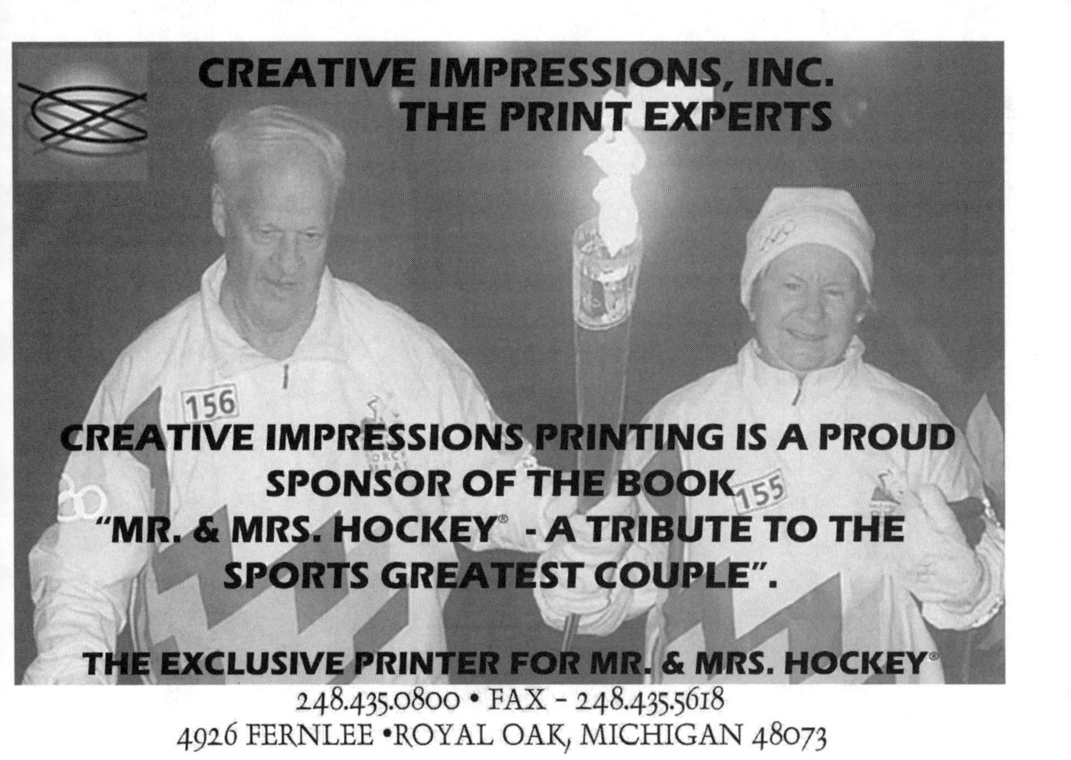

248.435.0800 • FAX - 248.435.5618
4926 FERNLEE •ROYAL OAK, MICHIGAN 48073

We are proud to be associated with the game's greatest couple -

MR. & MRS. HOCKEY®

Thank you for all you have done for the sport. We are honored to call you "friends"!

For the world's largest quality selection of autographed hockey memorabilia - please visit www.frozenpond.com

FROZEN POND 3232 Steeles Ave. W. #12, Concord, Ontario, Canada, L4K 4C8
905-760-8404 - info@frozenpond.com